MW00450687

THE AGE OF AUDEN

PRINCETON UNIVERSITY PRESS   Princeton and Oxford

AIDAN WASLEY

THE AGE OF AUDEN

POSTWAR POETRY AND THE AMERICAN SCENE

Copyright © 2011 by Princeton University Press

Published by Princeton University Press, 41 William Street, Princeton,
New Jersey 08540

In the United Kingdom: Princeton University Press, 6 Oxford Street,
Woodstock, Oxfordshire OX20 1TW

press.princeton.edu

All Rights Reserved

Library of Congress Cataloging-in-Publication Data
Wasley, Aidan, 1968–
   The age of Auden : postwar poetry and the American scene / Aidan Wasley.
      p.   cm.
   Includes bibliographical references and index.
   ISBN 978-0-691-13679-0 (alk. paper)
      1. American poetry—20th century—History and criticism.   2. Auden, W. H.
(Wystan Hugh), 1907–1973—Influence.   3. Influence (Literary, artistic, etc.)—
History—20th century.   I. Title.
   PS323.5.W37 2011
   813'.5409—dc22   2010025252

British Library Cataloging-in-Publication Data is available

This book has been composed in Garamond Premier Pro

Printed on acid-free paper. ∞

Printed in the United States of America

10 9 8 7 6 5 4 3 2 1

To Jan and Vernagh Wasley

CONTENTS

ABBREVIATIONS

ACW   Adrienne Rich, *A Change of World* (New Haven, CT:
             Yale University Press 1951).

ADW   Adrienne Rich, *An Atlas of a Difficult World: Poems
             1988–1991* (New York: W. W. Norton, 1991).

AWK   John Ashbery, *As We Know* (New York: Penguin,
             1979).

BBP   Adrienne Rich, *Blood, Bread, and Poetry: Selected Prose*
             (New York: W. W. Norton, 1986).

CLS   James Merrill, *The Changing Light at Sandover* (New
             York: Knopf, 1992).

CN   James Merrill, *Collected Novels and Plays* (New York:
             Knopf, 2002).

[Auden] CP   W. H. Auden, *Collected Poems* (New York: Vintage,
             1991).

[Merrill] CP James Merrill, *Collected Poems* (New York: Alfred A.
             Knopf, 2002)

CPM	James Merrill, *Collected Prose* (New York: Knopf, 2004).
DCL	Adrienne Rich, *Dream of a Common Language: Poems 1974–1977* (New York: W. W. Norton, 1993).
DF	Adrienne Rich, *Dark Fields of the Republic* (New York: W. W. Norton, 1995).
DM	W. H. Auden, *Double Man* (New York: Random House, 1941).
DH	W. H. Auden, *The Dyer's Hand* (New York: Vintage, 1989).
EA	W. H. Auden, *The English Auden: Poems, Essays and Dramatic Writings 1927–1939*, Edward Mendelson, ed. (London: Faber and Faber, 1986).
FD	Adrienne Rich, *The Fact of a Doorframe: Poems Selected and New 1950–1984* (New York: W. W. Norton, 1984).
HL	John Ashbery, *Hotel Lautréamont* (New York: Knopf, 1992).
Libretti	W. H. Auden, *The Complete Works of W. H. Auden: Libretti 1939–1973*, Edward Mendelson, ed. (Princeton, NJ: Princeton University Press: 1993).
LSS	Adrienne Rich, *On Lies, Secrets, and Silence: Selected Prose 1966–1978* (New York: W. W. Norton, 1979).
MS	Adrienne Rich, *Midnight Salvage* (New York: W. W. Norton, 1999).
Prose	W. H. Auden, *The Complete Works of Auden: Prose Volume II 1939–1948*, Edward Mendelson, ed. (Princeton, NJ: Princeton University Press, 2002).
RS	John Ashbery, *Reported Sightings: Art Chronicles 1957–1987* (Cambridge, MA: Harvard University Press, 1989).
S	Adrienne Rich, *Sources* (Woodside, CA: Heyeck Press, 1983).
[Ashbery] *SP*	John Ashbery, *Selected Poems* (New York: Viking, 1985).

[Auden] *SP*   W. H. Auden, *Selected Poems* (New York: Vintage, 1979).

ST   John Ashbery, *Some Trees* (New Haven, CT: Yale University Press, 1956).

TP   John Ashbery, *Three Poems* (New York: Ecco, 1989).

TPlays   John Ashbery, *Three Plays* (Manchester, UK: Carcanet, 1988).

VN   John Ashbery, *The Vermont Notebook* (Los Angeles: Black Sparrow Press, 1975).

WFT   Adrienne Rich, *What Is Found There* (New York: W. W. Norton, 1993).

PREFACE

When W. H. Auden died in 1973, Elizabeth Bishop offered this tribute in a special memorial issue of *The Harvard Advocate*:

> When I was in college, and all through the thirties and for-
> ties, I and all my friends who were interested in poetry, read
> him constantly. We hurried to see his latest poem or book, and
> either wrote as much like him as possible, or tried hard not to.
> His then leftist politics, his ominous landscape, his intimations
> of betrayed loves, war on its way, disasters and death, matched
> exactly the mood of our late-depression and post-depression
> youth. We admired his apparent toughness, his sexual cour-
> age—actually more honest than Ginsberg's, say, is now, while
> still giving expression to technically dazzling poetry. Even the
> most hermetic early poems gave us the feeling that here was
> someone who *knew*—about psychology, geology, birds, love, the
> evils of capitalism—what have you? They colored our air and
> made us feel tough, ready, and in the know, too.[1]

As Bishop recalls, for American poets of her generation, including Randall Jarrell and Robert Lowell, Auden's poetry exerted a glamorous and influential appeal. His honesty, his boldness, his engagement with science and politics, and his facility with form all seemed to suggest for these poets a promising path out of the Waste Land, and a number of them—particularly Jarrell—early on began to import characteristically Audenesque diction, imagery, and attitudes into their own work. But for these poets it was the English Auden—the Auden of the 1930s—that mattered, and by the time he arrived in New York in 1939, their careers were already underway, their poetic identities formed, and Auden's importance to their writing was on the wane. Indeed, by the early 1940s, Jarrell had begun to turn on his mentor, harshly attacking Auden in reviews and inaugurating a critical assault on Auden's perceived American decline that Jarrell would forcefully pursue for the rest of his career.

But the poets of the generation after Bishop and Jarrell had a very different relation to Auden. For them, it was the American Auden who had the greatest impact on their careers. This generation began writing poetry during an extended historical period—from the early 1940s to the late 1950s—when Auden reigned as his adopted nation's chief arbiter of poetic fashion and form. From his famously cluttered apartment on St. Mark's Place in Greenwich Village and his summer home on Ischia off the coast of Naples, Auden presided over the American poetic landscape, turning his legendary industriousness not only toward remaking his own poetic project, but toward shaping, fostering, and guiding the generation of American poets who would follow him. These poets not only read Auden, many of them actually got to know him personally during crucial early moments in their poetic growth. He was, for countless younger writers, a defining figure for post–World War II American poetry and a major influence on their own poetic art.

The Age of Auden explores the scope and depth of that influence. When introducing American poetry to British readers in 1956, Auden observed, "The first thing that strikes a reader about the best American poets is how utterly unlike each other they are" [*DH*, 366]. If American poetry has always been defined by its diversity, one of the aims of this book is to show how the expatriate Auden himself helped point an enormous range of American poets on their own different paths, and to argue that it is impossible to talk about American poetry in the second half of the twentieth century—in all its diversity—without talking about Auden. An important frame for that argument is the tension posed by the apparent paradox in the first poem Auden wrote after moving to America, in which he claims that "Poetry makes nothing happen" and yet can still be "A way of happening." American poets after Auden arrange themselves in relation to his influence often in terms of how they read those two competing lines, and the obsessive recurrence of this tension in the poems of Auden's inheritors—and necessarily in this book—is one more way of gauging what Auden makes happen in American poetry.

This is a book about poetry and people, since the story of Auden's American influence is one of human connections almost as much as it is about links across texts. It proposes a new literary history that sees Auden as a central figure in postwar American poetic culture while also suggesting new readings, not just of Auden's American project, but of those of a number of his major American successors. And while readers of American poetry and readers of Auden—especially academic readers—have at times occupied opposing critical turf, I hope this book can put these two readerships in fruitful and friendly conversation, since Auden and American poets were themselves most certainly talking to, and occasionally getting drunk with, each other.

The book's title itself opens a conversation: "The Age of Auden" is a phrase with many previous lives, all of them relevant to this book's interest in considering connections across countries, generations, and genres of poetry. The phrase was already a cliché before Auden left England as an expression of his dominance of the British literary generation of the 1930s, and it has been used countless times since—as a critical commonplace or, for some, as a label of scorn—to describe Auden's American postwar cultural authority. The rich and sometimes contentious history of the idea of an "Age of Auden" is part of the title's meaning, admitting both enthusiastic and ironic readings, including a new one that Don Bachardy's haunting and beautiful portrait on the book's cover makes poignantly visible. As we look at Auden's legendarily furrowed, leonine face, with that strangely sad, faraway gaze, we're reminded simultaneously of the humble human physicality of the iconic abstracted figure who gets an "Age" named after him, and also, literally, of the significance of Auden's *age* to his cultural meaning. Auden was both celebrated as an emblem of staggeringly precocious youth and also seen to have become, not long after his arrival in America, somehow prematurely ancient, such that he was regarded as a venerable literary monument long before his relatively early death at sixty-six. The aging of Auden, and its relation to his work and to that of his younger American interlocutors, is another story this book is interested in telling.

The structure of the book also enacts its dual concern—what Auden would call its "double-focus"—with both Auden's broader cultural presence and his specific relations with individual younger poets. A prologue provides historical, thematic, and interpretive context for Auden's American career, while the first chapter offers an overview of Auden's American reception and a survey of the various roles—teacher, itinerant lecturer, book reviewer, editor, contest judge, public intellectual, gay celebrity, unwelcome literary invader, mentor, lover, party-host, and poet—that he performed for younger poets and American literary culture generally during the years of his greatest influence. The second part of the book includes three chapters on three different major American inheritors of Auden—James Merrill, John Ashbery, and Adrienne Rich—and examines each poet's self-defining engagements with Auden's example. The book concludes with a leave-taking epilogue that sketches Auden's legacy by reading poems about him written by American poets after his death.

If "poetry makes nothing happen," then books *about* poetry would seem to do even less. But like many of Auden's American inheritors, I choose to hear that line as a hopeful provocation rather than as a despairing resignation to futility. When I read a poem like "Musée des Beaux Arts" with students in class, I'm always amazed at their response. As we read the poem—composed in Brussels in 1938 in the looming shadow of war and less than a month before Auden left permanently for America—we are confronted with the clear, melancholy moral lesson of the poem. Describing the fall of Icarus as depicted in a Renaissance painting by Brueghel, the poem points to the sober wisdom of the painting, which shows both a farmer and an "expensive delicate ship" apparently oblivious, or indifferent, to the astonishing sight of a boy falling from the sky into the sea. What Brueghel understands, the poem tells us, is that there is very little we as individuals can do to make anything happen to stem the inescapable tide of human suffering that always surrounds us. The best we can do is keep our shoulders to the plow, along with the farmer in the painting, because if we tried to attend to all the infinite occasions of suffering in the world we would collapse in para- lyzed despair and madness. This reading of Auden's much-anthologized poem—enshrined now in the museum of school textbooks just as Brue- ghel's masterpiece hangs augustly on the wall of the museum in Brussels that gives the poem its title—is a depressingly realist one, and certainly makes sense in the light of Auden's own feelings of artistic failure in 1938, having spent a decade making art that aspired, Icarus-like, to heal a sick world and help prevent an oncoming war. With war seemingly inevitable (Brussels, home of Brueghel and his painting, would fall to the Nazis less than 18 months later), Auden's idealizing ambitions had come to grief and his art revealed as useless or, worse, irrelevant ("not an important failure," as the poem describes Icarus's plunge). The poem offers a pow- erful and personal articulation of his resigned conviction that, indeed, "poetry makes nothing happen"—words he would write a few months later after his emigration to New York. This reading of the poem also offers us, its readers, a strange kind of existential relief, since seeing the world as so overpoweringly bleak excuses us from any effort to change it, as we—like Icarus and Auden—would be doomed inevitably to fail. But when talking about this poem with students, it also exerts a remarkable counter-tug that almost unfailingly someone in the class responds to: It asks us to rebel against this apparently clear-eyed and unsentimental di- agnosis of the unalterable "human position" of suffering. Further stirred by the imperious lecturing tone the poem affects ("About suffering they were never wrong, the Old Masters . . ."), one or more students are pro- voked into talking back to the poem, saying things like: "No! I wouldn't be like that ship or that farmer! If I were on that ship I would at least try to save that boy. I might not be able to stop a war or wipe out human pain, but at least I can do *something* to help someone who is suffering right in front of me!" As the students feel it, the poem forces us to make an interpretive choice that is also a kind of moral choice. Our reading of the poem brings with it a moral choice in the real world. We can keep our heads down in the interests of our own sanity, or we can go out into the world and do *something*, however small. The poem gives us options, but the choice, the hard intellectual and moral work, is ours alone. The students, reliably and inspiringly, leave the classroom a little wrought up, their private moral compasses engaged and humming, provoked into grappling with the biggest and most pressing of all ethical questions by an old poem about a painting in a textbook. If that's not an example of poetry being "a way of happening," I don't know what is. And it is precisely that *way* that Auden was looking for when he moved to America, and which this book, in its own way, hopes to honor.

◆ ◆ ◆

In one of his very last poems, Auden thanks by name his poetic influences for the guidance and support he'd found in them throughout his life: "Fondly I ponder You all: / without You I couldn't have managed / even my weakest of lines." In a book about the intersection between literary and human influence, it gives me huge pleasure to name and fondly ponder the many people without whose help this book would never have been written. The book had its distant beginnings in three college classrooms with teachers whose influence I would feel delighted to reflect: Samuel Hynes, whose book on Auden is still the one I love best; John Shoptaw, who showed me how to read a poem; and J. D. McClatchy, whose encouragement at the very start of this project is now matched by his cheerful impatience to see it finished. That this book even exists, and if it has any merits at all, I entirely owe to two other teachers to whom I am, and will always remain, especially indebted: I'd be honored to think that this book's tutelary genius is John Hollander's, and that Lanny Hammer's insight, enthusiasm, patience, and friendship are written on every page. Both in their different ways have ideally modeled for me what it means to teach, think, and write with intellectual passion and humane concern, and I could not be more grateful to be their student.

Along its winding way, this book has had the good fortune of many astute and generous readers and responders, including Mark Bauer, Stephen Burt, Bonnie Costello, Susannah Young-ah Gottlieb, Piotr Gwiazda, Peter Howarth, Nicholas Jenkins, Pericles Lewis, Lucy McDiarmid, Steven Monte, Meghan O'Rourke, Willard Spiegelman, Michael Thurston, and Rachel Wetzsteon. John Ashbery, Anthony Hecht, and Richard Howard offered me their time and their memories, along with their remarkable poetry, and I deeply appreciate their kind willingness to answer my rambling questions. I'm thrilled to have Don Bachardy's stunning portrait of Auden on the cover of my book and I'm immensely grateful both to him for allowing me permission to use it, and to David

Koslow for helping make it happen. I've benefited from practical and institutional support from the Willson Center for the Arts and Humanities and the University of Georgia Research Foundation, from the Mellon and Whiting Foundations, and, for a happy summer immersed in the Isherwood archives, from the Huntington Library. The Stonington Village Improvement Association gave me the priceless gift of a year's residency at the James Merrill House where much of this book took shape, inspired by the changing light and the company of friendly spirits. I'm indebted to the Berg Collection of the New York Public Library, the Department of Special Collections at Stanford, and Harvard's Houghton Library for allowing me access to their manuscript archives. My editor at Princeton, Hanne Winarsky, has combined advocacy, intelligence, and patience in ways that make me marvel, and Heath Renfroe, Christopher Chung, and Michael McGee at the Press have all helped make this book its best. I am very thankful for my friends and colleagues at the University of Georgia, in particular Andrew Cole, Hubert McAlexander, Adam Parkes, Ed Pavlic, Chris Pizzino, Jed Rasula, Channette Romero, Susan Rosenbaum, Sarah Spence, and Andrew Zawacki, for their various and individual contributions to this project and for giving Georgia's Athens an intellectual community worthy of its ancient, less funky namesake. With special gratitude and endless affection, I am pleased to put the names of Chuck Baraw, Andrew Dimock, Hannah Eigerman, Ticky Kennedy, Karla Oeler, Sean O'Sullivan, Sharon Palmer, David Rosen, and Alex Woloch at the beginning of my book, since they have done so much to see it to its completion. Without Kim Kersey this book would never have been finished, and she knows how happy we both are that it is. And finally, to my family and especially my parents, Jan and Vernagh: This book, with all my love, is dedicated to you.

Portions of the Prologue appeared in *Symbiosis* 7.1 (April 2003), and versions of chapter 3 and the Epilogue were published in *Contemporary Literature* 43.4 (Winter 2002) and *Raritan* 19.2 (Fall 1999), respectively. I am grateful to the editors of these journals for permission to reprint these materials.

THE AGE OF AUDEN

Auden in "Atlantis"

When W. H. Auden sailed out of Southampton on January 19, 1939 he was doing more than simply leaving behind friends, family, and a record of poetic achievement that had made him already, at the age of 32, England's most prominent and influential public poet. When he arrived in a wintry New York harbor a week later, he was embarking on a quest of poetic and self-reinvention that would change the course of American poetry. Auden's emigration from England, and his arrival in America, marked a crucial moment in twentieth-century literary history, when the heir apparent to T. S. Eliot as the dominant presence in British poetry abandoned his English career and retraced Eliot's own path back across the Atlantic to start anew. The impact of that moment, and Auden's subsequent American career, are still being felt in American poetry seven decades later.

But in New York, in 1939, Auden faced two daunting tasks. First, as a poet who had spent much of the previous decade diagnosing the cultural and moral malaise of "England, this country of ours where nobody is well" [*EA*, 62], and gaining fame as the leader of a group of young leftist artists and intellectuals in the literary fight against fascism, Auden was confronted with the question of what kind of poet he was now to be. In

I

this new country to which he had no cultural, historical, or familial connection, and in a world where—despite his poems—fascism had already triumphed across much of Europe, Auden needed to discover what kind of poetry could meet the demands of his altered circumstances and perspective, if indeed any poetry could—or should—be written at all. His first American poem, "In Memory of W. B. Yeats," begun in a Manhattan hotel room, acutely reflects this private vocational crisis in memorably public terms. His elegy for Yeats, whose death "on a dark cold day" coincided with Auden's American arrival, depicts a world bleakly indifferent to the earthly departure of the most celebrated of poets, not to mention the debarking of an ambitious younger one in snowy New York. And in the face of the horror unfolding back across the Atlantic, where "In the nightmare of the dark / All the dogs of Europe bark, / And the living nations wait, / Each sequestered in its hate" [*CP*, 248]. Auden's requiem for Yeats and for his earlier idealistic self sounds its famous cry of poetry's impotence in the world of politics, wars, and injustice: "Poetry makes nothing happen."

His second task, related to the first, was to understand, and imaginatively define, America itself. Before deciding to move there permanently, he had spent only two weeks in the United States during the summer of 1938, on the tail-end of a trip to China with Christopher Isherwood that produced their soberly voyeuristic travelogue, *Journey to a War*. In anticipation of a return visit to the United States, he and Isherwood had contracted with their British publisher to write another travel book, to be titled *Address Not Known*, but by the time they landed in Manhattan the book had been abandoned and Auden's outlook had shifted from adventuring tourist to long-term émigré. While the new life and career that he began in 1939 would profoundly shape the course of the next half-century of American poetry, in those earliest months and years of Auden's American life, the question of what America *was*, and what it meant to his poetic future, was a central unanswered question.

As a new immigrant, Auden's knowledge of the United States came almost entirely from books as well as films, with which he had some experience himself as a member of the British Post Office's documentary film unit of the mid-1930s. In fact, rather than writing their book when they got to America, he and Isherwood initially proposed making a film about it instead. Drafted around the same time as his Yeats elegy, and among Auden's first artistic engagements with America, the film was to be called *The Life of an American,* which they described as follows:

> An interesting and cheap four-reeler could be made in which the part of the central character was taken by the camera. The hero sees life through the lens of the camera, so that the audience identifies itself with him. To make this possible, the story must be as ordinary and universal as possible. We suggest the life of an average American. [*Libretti,* 419]

Literalizing the narrative metaphor of Isherwood's *Good-Bye to Berlin,* published the same year and whose passive protagonist famously declares to the reader, "I am a camera," Auden and Isherwood planned to tell the story of "an average American" through a series of vignettes in the life of their specific but "ordinary and universal" hero who, we learn, is to be "born in a small Middle-West town about 1887." From childhood, to first love, to experience in war, to mid-life adulterous affair, to financial ruin in the stock market crash, to deathbed, with the camera vantage point rising vertically as the character grows taller with age, we follow the representative events of the unremarkable hero's life, looking out at the world and people around him through the eye of the camera lens until the final fatal fade to black. The choice of a fictional film as one of his first American projects is suggestive perhaps of both Auden's uncertainty as to his literary path in his new home, and a view of that home as a vast blank screen onto which he could cinematically project his "ordinary and universal" concerns.[1] The unseen protagonist, whose outward gaze aims to comprehend the experience of the "average American" viewer, further reflects Auden's complex task of constructing a narrative of a self in relation to his new American audience and circumstance. The protagonist-viewer finds out *who* he is only through the reflection of the world's responses to his unarticulated self. We are inside the character's head, seeing only what he sees, allowing the universal viewer to "identify with him," but his situation is particularly American, imposing an imagined Americanness back upon that viewer. Even amid the riot of experience and the impact of others on his life, his—and our—existential solitude is painfully clarified by the unvarying unshared subjectivity of the singular camera eye. He is at once universal and unique, average and alone, everyman and American.

For Auden, like the generic hero of his unmade film, the job of constructing his post-immigration self rested on the paradox, and dialectic, of solitude and communal identification. And in the work he wrote after leaving England, especially during the 1940s as he set about conquering the transatlantic literary establishment, he found in America itself both the private site, and a universal emblem, of that dialectic. In another of his earliest American efforts, the operetta *Paul Bunyan*, composed largely in late 1939, he put to the music of his fellow English émigré Benjamin Britten words that can be seen as defining both Auden's universalizing vision of America, and its reflection of his own particular personal situation and ambitions. Throughout the operetta, for reasons of both theatrical practicality and theme, the mythical title character, a giant lumberjack, is never seen onstage, embodied only as a booming, oracular, offstage voice. As Bunyan prepares to leave his camp and crew at the opera's end, having accomplished his epic task of clearing the land for the new America, he is asked by one of his men, "What's to become of America now?" Bunyan responds in verse: "Every day America's destroyed and re-created / America is what you do, / America is I and you, / America is what we choose to make it" [*Libretti*, 46].

On the occasion of the opera's first production in New York, Auden acknowledged his act of private appropriation of an icon of American national identity, while insisting, as in the *Life of an American* film, on its transcendence beyond the personal or merely literary: "At first sight it may seem presumptuous for a foreigner to take an American folk-tale as his subject, but in fact the implications of the Bunyan legend are not only American but universal" [*Libretti*, 572]. That universality, he says, stems from the dilemma of technological modernity he sees manifested most clearly and representatively in America: "Now that, in a material sense, we can do anything almost that we like, how are we to know what is the right thing to do, and what is the wrong thing to avoid."

Auden repeatedly affirmed the connection between his vision of America and the broader problem of moral choice in the modern world, as illustrated in a lecture entitled "America Is Where You Find It," which he delivered in January 1940 at Johns Hopkins, almost exactly a year after his American arrival. As summarized in a contemporary student newspaper account, Auden's lecture argued that "in Europe today the real effect of the machine age is hidden while America, because of its swift develop-

ment, sees the effect and can cope with it. America clearly shows this . . .
by the loneliness of the characters in our literature; and, therefore, since
America alone realizes the necessity of individual isolation, America will
take the lead in art and literature."[2] In a syllabus for a fifteen-week poetry
course he taught at the New School that Spring, he devoted his last class
to this same argument, further asserting that the task of the citizen is the
same as that of the poet: "May 15. America is where you find it. The task
of the poet today" [*Prose*, 465]. And the next month he reiterated this
theme during a commencement address he was invited to give at Smith
College, taking as his subject the question of how an "open society" is in
general to be defined and achieved. Once again, he found the universal
answer in his own personal immigrant experience:

> If coming to the United States has been for me one of the
> most significant experiences of my life, it is because owing to
> America's historical discontinuity, its mixed population, and the
> arrival of the industrial revolution while the geographical fron-
> tier was still open, I think I have learned here what I could have
> learned nowhere else: what the special demands and dangers of
> an open society are. Let me try, then, to paint America not, alas,
> as it is, but as it might or ought to be.
>
> Physically, economically, and culturally it knows no fron-
> tier. Conscious both of what it possesses and what it lacks, it
> exchanges freely with all other countries. Economically special-
> ized, it has a range of occupations for all to choose from so wide
> that there is no one, however exceptional his nature, who can-
> not find a genuine vocation. As a society it is tolerant because it
> finds every person useful, and its individuals are socially respon-
> sible because they are conscious of being needed. Mechanized, it
> has conquered nature, but this conquest is recognized by all for
> what it is: not the abolition of necessity, but the transformation
> of much of the external, causal necessity of matter into the inner
> logical necessity of moral choice. [*Prose*, 66–67]

While Auden's American vista is an idealizing one, it isn't a purely
intellectual abstraction. America's specific landscape, history, and culture
are, he suggests, universally illuminating and pedagogical, and America
as it is is not the same "as it might or ought to be." What it teaches, and

where it points, is the inescapability of moral choice and the existential paradox of democracy: "There can be no democracy unless each of us accepts the fact that in the last analysis we live our lives alone. Alone we choose, alone we are responsible" [*Prose*, 70]. Like his camera-eye film hero, to be American is to be fundamentally alone, and, he suggests, with that solitude comes a special burden of moral self-consciousness.[3]

Importantly, Auden connects America's idealized capacity to instruct its citizens in their own private moral necessities to, as he sees it, the similar promise of art, telling his audience of graduating students, "Never forget that by nature we are all bad. It is only by art that we become good. It will be hard enough to remain as sensitive and intelligent as you are now; to become better will require unceasing effort" [*Prose*, 69–70]. The tension here between the notion of art making its audience "good" and the sense of poetry's practical futility expressed in the Yeats elegy is the fundamental crux of Auden's post-immigration work, and it is, for the poet, America itself that allows both of these ideas to dialectically coexist. Auden's America is the place where poetry both "makes nothing happen" and yet can be, crucially, as he says a few lines later in the same elegy, a "way of happening."

♦ ♦ ♦

In a poem called "Atlantis," written a few months after his Smith address, he invokes another myth, that of the lost utopia, to illustrate what he calls "a poetic vision" of art's capacity for moral instruction, even as it recognizes its limitations. Derived in form and spirit from Cavafy's "Ithaka," an Odyssean parable of self-discovery, Auden's poem offers a narrative of a voyaging quester seeking the "Atlantis" of individual truth on a journey that takes him through a sequence of allegorical islands in pursuit of the mythical place where the needs of self and society meet in idealized harmony. The hero must confront and grapple with the many "counterfeit Atlantises" of competing ideologies, aesthetics, and temptations—among them soulless intellectual rationalism and empty sensual lust—if he is to achieve "salvation" and "recognize the true." Each island of tempting ideological certitude or hedonistic abandon and apathy is a stop on a *via negativa*—"Thus they shall teach you the ways / To doubt that you may believe"—leading to the hero's epiphanic recognition and embrace of his fate to be always "Travelling and tormented, / Dialectic and bizarre" [*CP*, 315–16].[4]

Soon after arriving in America, Auden began a Kierkegaardian reassessment of his longstanding religious skepticism that would lead him to the devout Christianity of his later years, but the salvation he speaks of in "Atlantis" is not to be understood in simply theological terms. Rather, in this existentialist fable, the quester's salvation is his discovery that his solitary dialectical journey itself *is* Atlantis, experienced—if never actually fully inhabitable—through the negotiation between, and choice among, the multiple alternative available truths of his, and our, traveling and tormented existences. The "unceasing effort" to "remain . . . sensitive and intelligent" that he required of the Smith graduates is here translated into the hero's poetic quest to understand, and productively contain, his "dialectic and bizarre" self. "Atlantis" is also a love poem, reflecting another of the significant beginnings in Auden's American life: that of his relationship with Chester Kallman, a Brooklyn college student he met at one of his earliest American public poetry readings in April of 1939, and to whom he would remain devoted—through considerable romantic tempests—for the rest of his life. The questing hero, called a "dear friend" in the poem, is both Kallman, whose education was enforcing a temporary farewell between the poet and his lover, and Auden himself, navigating his own search for identity. In "Atlantis," the poetic hero himself enacts the dialectical relation of lover and beloved, self and other, just as the "ordinary and universal" hero of *The Life of an American* embodies existential solitude and collective American experience, and Paul Bunyan is both individual epic striver and America itself. The name "Atlantis" also marks the mythical object of the hero's quest as a distinctively trans-Atlantic locale (the Mediterranean origins of the myth notwithstanding). Indeed, the association of America with Atlantis has a long history, including Francis Bacon's seventeenth-century identification of the New World with Plato's lost city, and William Blake's imagining, in *America: A Prophecy*, of a sunken Atlantis that once bridged "America & Albion's shore, / Now barr'd out by the Atlantic sea." And Auden also knew (though did not particularly admire) the more recent work of Hart Crane, whose ecstatic 1930 epic *The Bridge*, in a kaleidoscopically Whitmanian vision of America filtered through the prism of an Eliotic high modernism, figures the emblem of the nation itself as a vast Roebling-inspired span across regions and history, and ends with a soaring hymn, entitled "Atlantis," in praise of America's prophetic promise.[5]

What is notable here is that Auden is defining America itself in explicitly poetic terms: The conditions he sees governing the American experience are precisely the same ones he aims to represent and enact in his art. His America, a community of isolated souls, each condemned to choose their own truth, finds its reflection in poems like "Atlantis" and the contemporary sonnet sequence "The Quest," where solitary heroes pursue their dialectical quests for salvation. Indeed, one could say that newly arrived Auden sees America itself *as* a poem, and it is here that he manages to solve both of the difficult tasks facing his post-immigration life—defining his new poetics and defining America—at the same time. His newly adopted country, or at least the "poetic vision" he has of it, offers Auden a model for the kind of poem he now needs to write in a world where "poetry makes nothing happen." If America is a poem, his poems will be an America, an Atlantis, through which the questing reader/citizen must voyage, but the path they take—the meaning, the truth they negotiate—will be their own. His new American poetry would eschew the specific cultural criticisms and polemics of the poetry he left behind in England. Rather, it would aim to be undogmatically didactic, forcing the reader to engage, within the imaginative bounds of the poem, with the same kind of dizzying interpretive demands—"dialectic and bizarre"—found in the world outside the poem. His poems would "teach [the reader] the ways / To doubt that [they] may believe." In this way, the United States becomes not just his personal and political refuge in a world shadowed by violence and despair; it also provides Auden a path to poetic salvation. Facing a crisis of poetic purpose, Auden found in his new nation a living emblem for the solution to his impasse.

◆ ◆ ◆

The clearest place to see Auden's struggle to articulate a new American self through his poetry is in "New Year Letter," his first American long poem. Begun in January 1940 (coincident with his various public lectures on American loneliness) and finished that spring (as he is concluding his class at the New School on "the task of the poet today" and talking to the Smith students about the meaning of America), "New Year Letter" is a 1,700-line verse epistle, divided into three parts, with each part addressing one of the crucial questions facing the poet in his new life.[6] First, how to write poetry now? Second, how might that poetry ideally define itself? And third, what function would it have in the world, if any? The poem is conversational, meditative, and philosophically and structurally complex, encompassing in its considerable length and in the extensive notes that accompany the poem a vast sweep of personal, intellectual, and political concerns. It is a debate Auden is having with himself, a stock-taking on the occasion of his first American New Year, and in it he offers provisional answers to each of the three questions he poses for himself.

To the question of how he is to find his American voice, he answers: With help. In particular, with the help of influential voices from the literary past. To the question of how that poetry would work, he proposes that it should be open, undoctrinaire, and dialectical. And to the question of poetry's place and purpose in a world where "poetry makes nothing happen," he asserts that through the power of its dialectical vision and engagement, it can actually be a force for individual, if not social, change. It is a poem that aspires explicitly to be a new kind of project for Auden, a self-consciously *American* poem, with its questions and problems framed in a manifestly American context. And each of these questions, and Auden's answers to them, will be explored in subsequent chapters of this book in dialogue with the work of a number of Auden's American poetic inheritors, for whom Auden's example in wrestling with these questions proves highly influential in the development of their own work.

Early in the poem, Auden enumerates in specific detail the "influential ghosts" whose assistance he is seeking in his effort to construct his new poetic identity. Auden assembles his own personal "summary tribunal," each member of which offers something to the poem's content, form, and execution:

> The court is full; I catch the eyes
> Of several I recognize,
> For as I look up from the dock
> Embarrassed glances interlock.
> There Dryden sits with modest smile,

The master of the middle style,
Conscious Catullus who made all
His gutter-language musical,
Black Tennyson whose talents were
For an articulate despair,
Trim, dualistic Baudelaire,
Poet of cities, harbors, whores,
Acedia, gaslight and remorse,
Hardy whose Dorset gave much joy
To one unsocial English boy,
And Rilke whom *die Dinge* bless,
The Santa Claus of loneliness. [*CP*, 204]

Anticipating a poem written a few months before his death in 1973 and entitled "A Thanksgiving," in which he celebrates the poets and thinkers without whom, he says "I couldn't have managed / even my weakest of lines" [*CP*, 892], Auden here credits the various presences whose help enables him to write his epically ruminative poem, composed in essayistic couplets like Dryden, employing a "musical" Catullan vernacular, and addressing characteristic themes of Tennyson, Baudelaire, Hardy, and Rilke, including "despair," "dualism," "remorse," "human unsuccess," and "loneliness." He acknowledges and invokes these disparate presences to unite in him to form a poem, and a poetic identity, that is collective, diverse, and dialectical, and yet is distinctively and individually his own.

Chief among the questioners in Auden's ghostly tribunal in the poem are Dante, Blake, and Rimbaud. It is an odd collection of muses for a poet who wants to write a self-consciously American poem, but each one provides Auden with a crucial ingredient of his desired new American poetic identity.[7] From his chief inquisitor, Dante, "That lean hard-bitten pioneer / Who spoiled a temporal career," Auden derives the confidence to spurn his own career as a political poet, and Dante's vision of "a juster nucleus than Rome" and his faith in the power of poetry to help make that vision a reality, offer support to Auden's own vision of what he calls (following Plato) the "Just City" and his belief in poetry's ability to help build it. And further, Dante's relation to his own poetic precursor Virgil serves Auden as a great originary example of one poet acknowledging and relying on an earlier one to help chart his own path. The "choleric enthusiast, / Self-educated William Blake" is also especially important to the writing of this particular poem, as attested by another text he began writing in the summer of 1939 called "The Prolific and the Devourer," taking its title from Blake's anatomization of human identity in *The Marriage of Heaven and Hell* into warring halves, the creator and the consumer. Never finished nor published in Auden's lifetime, it was a collection of *pensées* that ended up serving as a prose draft of "New Year Letter," with many of its philosophical passages appearing in repurposed form in the extensive system of notes that accompanied the published poem. Just as Blake saw man as a unity consisting of infinite "emanations" of his being, Auden sees man, as he puts it in "The Prolific and the Devourer" (and in the poem's notes), as "divided beings composed of a number of selves, each with its false conception of self-interest," yet each contributing, in their dialectical relation to one another, to a unified identity.[8] "New Year Letter" was published in America in the volume *The Double Man*, and Blake's notion of a divided self whose identity is defined by oppositional yet complementary aspects also closely reflects the acute sense of self-division Auden's choice of book title expresses. The triumvirate of poetic inquisitors then concludes with Rimbaud who, despite Auden's disdain for France and its writers, is present, the poem tells us, because "guilt demands" him. As a paragon of poetic repudiation, Rimbaud is useful for Auden's own ambition to leave behind his earlier poetic identity, which is slyly caricatured in his description of the "adolescent" Rimbaud who, like the precociously famous Auden of the 1930s, was celebrated as a "skilful, intolerant and quick" iconoclast who "strangled an old rhetoric." But, in this self-portrait Rimbaud becomes, paradoxically, a figure for inclusion, since it suggests that Auden's earlier poetic self, though a subject of guilt, is not so much renounced as incorporated into his later, more mature identity. It becomes one of the many dialectical selves that make up his ever-evolving unity.

For Auden, the relation between what Eliot called "tradition and the individual talent" is one of personal and professional utility. As he explains in an essay from 1962, "The Poet & The City," a poet's authority and achievement are determined by the self-conscious choice and deployment of useful influences:

[Tradition] no longer means a way of working handed down
from one generation to the next; a sense of tradition now means
a consciousness of the whole of the past as well as the present,
yet at the same time as a structured whole the parts of which
are related in terms of before and after. Originality no longer
means a slight modification in the style of one's immediate
predecessors; it means a capacity to find in any work of any date
or place a clue to finding one's own authentic voice. The burden
of choice is put squarely upon the shoulders of each individual
poet and it is a heavy one. [*DH*, 80]

Auden argues that a poet's originality stems from his ability to
synthesize a voice—his own true voice—from the different voices of
the past, each of which can fill a need for the different aspects of his
poetic identity. The burden on the poet is the overwhelming number
of examples from which to choose, and the anxiety is whether or not
his choice of poetic model is the right one for his own poetic necessity.
Pointing to the importance of imitation in the development of a young
poet's own distinctive voice, Auden termed this model of poetic identity
construction "a literary transference" in an essay on Hardy's powerful
influence on his own early work, written at the same time as "New Year
Letter." "I cannot write objectively on Thomas Hardy because I was once
in love with him," he observes, framing the connection between individual talent and influence in terms of erotic desire, and also suggesting the relationship between a patient and the wise analyst who assists
in his quest for self-understanding, onto whom the patient projects his
own needs [*Prose*, 42]. The poet's difficult task is to identify the different aspects of his artistic self, and bring them into productive relation,
through a process of imitation and experimentation with different aspects of the tradition. Over time, the poet will gradually recognize, and
assimilate, those models that offer him what he needs. At the end of this
process, he will have reached poetic maturity and found his own true
voice. That voice may change over time to face the demands of different
circumstances, but—as in this pivotal moment in Auden's career—the
poet may call upon different voices and mentors—like Dante, Blake, or
Rimbaud—to help him revise and refine his current project, purpose,
and poetic persona.[9] In Auden's notion of how poetic identity is formed,

the contemporary poet acknowledges the extent to which his language is unoriginal—that he is speaking with borrowed voices and forms—and yet retains his own authority with a voice and identity that remain uniquely his own. In fact, it is precisely in his distinctive choice of voices that his poetic identity is defined.[10] Many of Auden's American poetic inheritors will follow in these theoretical footsteps, defining their diverse selves through their purposeful appropriation of the voices of the poetic past, Auden's own voice itself often echoing forcefully in their work as a chosen model.

In "New Year Letter," Auden also explicitly addresses the pressing question of the Yeats elegy of how, or if, a poet can actually make anything happen. After debating poetry's manifest inadequacies, asserting "Art is not life and cannot be / A midwife to society" [CP, 201], he yet concludes with a cautious optimism:

So, hidden in his hocus-pocus,
There lies the gift of double focus,
That magic lamp which looks so dull
And utterly impractical
Yet, if Aladdin use it right,
Can be a sesame to light. [CP, 220]

Auden suggests that poetry, which seems—especially at this moment—so useless, can instead—if used skillfully and correctly—be a powerful force in the world. It is a sophisticated instrument that, in the hands of one who knows its secrets, "can be a sesame to light." Auden assumes the role of Aladdin, using his magic lamp to disenchant the world, illuminating its delusions, unexamined assumptions, and what he calls in "September 1, 1939," "the folded lie, / the romantic lie in the brain" [SP, 88]. This is his ambition for his new American poetry, to "challenge, warn, and witness" [CP, 202], as he says the great poets of the past have done, and in doing so, "show an affirming flame" leading out of the darkness. And the "sesame" to this light, the "hocus-pocus" that gives poetry its power, is its singular capacity to reveal, enact, and suggest resolution to conflict, contradiction, and disharmony. It is in poetry's capacity to contain oppositions, and in its ability to force its reader to negotiate between those oppositions in an effort to resolve them, that poetry really could serve a constructive social purpose. The exercise of reading and interpreting a complex poem becomes, for the American Auden, an exercise in moral and civic virtue, in which the difficult process of trying to make sense of apparently contradictory perspectives contained within a single poem can serve as instruction for the reader in negotiating the personal, political, and moral complexities and contradictions in the world beyond the poem. Auden's new poetry was to be didactic yet rigorously non-dogmatic; the poem presents interpretive, and by implication, moral, options, but the lesson, the choice of which one to follow, is up to the reader. By forcing upon its reader what Auden terms "an awareness of the dialectic" [*DM*, 115], and making the reader attempt to engage and resolve that dialectic within the poem, he learns how to engage and act upon the conflicts both within himself and in the wider political world. For Auden, this is poetry's greatest gift, and its greatest claim: Its "double focus" allows us to see the world in all its complexity, and to see our moral obligation within it. This is how, for the immigrant Auden, poetry becomes a "way of happening."

But "awareness of the dialectic" also brings with it a kind of pathos. The recognition of one's relation to others necessarily also entails a recognition of one's separateness from them. "Aloneness is man's real condition," he observes in "New Year Letter," echoing his frequent diagnosis of American solitude and loneliness, and the sense of our own singularity in a disparate world provokes in us a concomitant sense of anxiety and longing. Just as the separation of language from life, representation from reality, one element of the dialectic from the other, inspires in us the longing for resolution, so too does the knowledge of our isolation as individuals prompt in us a longing for union with others. To be alive and aware is to be in a state of desire for connection with something outside oneself and, for Auden, poetry is a manifestation of that desire. Anxious about its artificiality, its detachment from life, poetry aspires to true representation and expression, to bridge the gap between writer and reader. But, as with the human desire for true connection and community, which is continually defeated by the exigencies of existence, poetry's lofty aspirations often also run afoul of actual practice. Poetry expresses, and shares in, the human pathos of never truly being able to achieve one's desire. We long for perfect communion and the poet longs for perfect communication, but, in an imperfect reality of conflict, misunderstanding, ignorance, inattention, and selfishness, rarely, if ever, is either fulfilled. The poet, like us, acknowledges the unlikeliness of his success in realizing true understanding, yet he, like us, must keep trying. Rather than despair of poetry's impotence, the poet presses on, undeceived but optimistic. The force that compels him—and us—is not intellect, says Auden, but *love*:

O when will men show common sense
And throw away intelligence,
That killjoy which discriminates,
Recover what appreciates,
The deep unsnobbish instinct which
Alone can make relation rich,
Upon the *Beischlaf* of the blood
Establish a real neighbourhood
Where art and industry and *moeurs*
Are governed by an *ordre du coeur*? [*CP*, 212]

The act of poetry, for Auden, is an act of love. It is a gesture of pure longing, of desire despite the odds, of hope in the face of despair. It recognizes the difficulty of reconciling difference and bridging division, but it keeps reaching for that ideal order of the heart where true relation is possible. It responds to disharmony and conflict not by resigning itself to the impossibility of resolution, but with a passionate, humane embrace—a "*Beischlaf* of the blood"—that asserts interdependence and mutual responsibility, not alienated disengagement. Auden construes his poetry as the site of hopeful exchange between himself and his reader, a "real neighbourhood" where "art and industry and *moeurs*" can productively cohabit. It answers the evils of passivity and denial of relation with an insistence on active reciprocity. As love always is for Auden, it is tempered by doubt and faithlessness, aware of its own contingency and ephemerality, but like the lover reclining "human on my faithless arm" in Auden's famously equivocal "Lullaby," it retains its ideality despite its frailty: "Mortal, guilty, but to me / Entirely beautiful" [*CP*, 157]. Auden's poems, from his earliest to his most explicitly political, had always placed love and its exultations and discontents at their center, though after his move to America and his discovery of a romantic partner that he felt finally answered his ideal, the erotic register of his work takes on a new character. The possibility of a true, loving, reciprocal relation no longer seemed so remote in his life, and that hopefulness—tempered by a wary realism—finds analogous expression in his American poetry's aspiration toward ideal readerly engagement and understanding.

Three months into the nine-month composition of "New Year Letter," Auden returns to the idea of "double focus" at length in a book review for the journal *Common Sense*. In it, he proposes that it is "the gift of double focus" that distinguishes the great men of history from their lesser peers—what he calls "the half-men and the half-women, the little either-or people"—who lack their dialectical vision:

> The one infallible symptom of greatness is the capacity for double focus. [Great men] know that all absolutes are heretical but that one can only act in a given circumstance by assuming one. Knowing themselves, they are skeptical about human nature but not despairing; they know that they are weak but not helpless; perfection is impossible but one can be or do better or worse. They are unconventional but not bohemian; it never occurs to think in terms of convention. Conscious of achievement and vocation they are conscious of how little depends on their free will and how much they are vehicles for powers which they can never fully understand but to which they can listen. Objective about themselves with the objectivity of the truly humble, they often shock the conceited out of their wits: e.g. Goethe's remark, "What do the Germans want? Have they not me?" Knowing that the only suffering that can be avoided is the attempt to escape from suffering, they are funny and enjoy life. [*Prose*, 56–57]

In what amounts to an idealized self-portrait, Auden outlines the qualities and characteristics of those with true "awareness of the dialectic." They reject absolutes and embrace the necessity of choice. Possessing genuine self-knowledge, they recognize their own imperfections and those of the world around them, but remain hopeful and constructive, working to "be or do better." Like the rumpled, carpet-slipper-wearing Auden, they are "unconventional but not bohemian," and maintain the same feelings of healthy self-esteem that prompted Auden to cheerfully proclaim to friends in 1945, "I'm the first major poet to fly the Atlantic."[11] These men also, like himself, have a strong sense of vocation while acknowledging their achievements are never simply theirs alone, that they are mere "vehicles for powers which they can never fully understand." Clearly, Auden is projecting his own vision of his better self upon those figures of the past whose example and achievement he would emulate, and in doing so stakes a claim that, if his ambitious poetic project of dialectical self-recreation is successful, he should be counted among their distinguished company. Auden is asserting both the significance and seriousness of his new artistic and cultural ambition, and arguing—in a simultaneously subtle yet grandiose way—that through the exercise of his art he can affect the world as those he admires have done. But the occasion of this discussion, the subject of Auden's review, is not a great artist like Dante or his beloved Goethe. Nor is it any of the famed thinkers, philosophers, and intellectuals like Rousseau, Marx, or Kierkegaard, whose ideas and insights Auden details at length in his poem's extensive survey of the dialectical permutations of Western thought. Rather, the "great man" of Auden's analysis is an American president: Abraham Lincoln.

Auden's choice of Lincoln as his example of "the gift of double focus" suggests two important things about Auden's conception of his double-focused poetic undertaking. First, it identifies Auden's project explicitly with America, personified in that most iconic of American leaders, who liberated a people in bondage and reunited a divided nation. And second, it associates its artistic aspirations with the realm of politics and the real world. The lengthy third and final part of "New Year Letter" asserts Auden's ambition to be an American poet—as specifically opposed to an English or European one—and situates his dialectical vision within a particularly American context. The double focus with which his new poetics aims to endow his readers is, he suggests, also a characteristically American quality and, as such, can take its place in, and make a contribution to, the national cultural discourse. In its practice, as well as in its progressive ambitions, it also shares a relation with the exercise, as Auden sees it, of American politics. Just as a poem holds meanings in opposition, encouraging an interpretive effort toward resolution, so too does the diversity in unity of democracy demand a constructive choice between contending perspectives: "[N]ow as then the voter hears / The battle cries of two ideas" [*CP*, 237]. The ideal function of American democracy is, for Auden, an analogue to the dialectical process of poetry.

Like poetry, democratic politics makes nothing happen in and of itself, but, through dissent, debate, and dialogue, becomes a way of happening. Unlike European politics, hobbled by class, history, and a legacy of authoritarianism, and whose catastrophic failure was being played out with blood and bombs, what Auden saw as the American tradition of "Only the Many make the One" [*CP*, 229] matches his model of how poetry could work constructively in the world.[12]

For Auden the enthusiastic immigrant, America is the place that most accurately reflects his poetic program of achieving collective betterment through individual self-knowledge and action:

> More even than in Europe, here
> The choice of patterns is made clear
> Which the machine imposes, what
> Is possible and what is not,
> To what conditions we must bow
> In building the Just City now. [*CP*, 238]

Mourning a Europe destroying itself in madness and ancient animosities, Auden sees America's open, democratic, idealistic vision of itself as an inspiration, and an opportunity, for his own poetic aspirations. Auden projects his own hopes for "building the Just City" onto the American dream of itself as the shining city on a hill, and proposes his own poetry as a vital element in its realization. In a union of his poetic and civic ideals, Auden applied for American citizenship—and registered for the draft—during the composition of "New Year Letter."[13]

Auden's identification with the promise of America also amounts to a justification of his own emigration from England. Grappling with the question of loyalty in the face of accusations that his departure for America on the eve of war had constituted a cowardly abandonment of his responsibilities and connections to his homeland, Auden asks himself, "But where to serve and when and how? / O none escape these questions now" [*CP*, 225]. His answer to this question is to suggest that his move from England to America was not the replacement of one nationality with another, but rather a move beyond the antiquated and dangerously parochial notion of nationality itself. The true task facing all men, he asserts, is not to pledge fealty to any particular locality or ideology, but to be "patriots of the Now" [*CP*, 229]. Loyalty becomes for Auden a question of moral choice, not historical obligation. "England to me is my own tongue, / And what I did when I was young," he declares, recognizing a certain sentimentality for its landscape of "limestone moors" and "derelict lead-smelting mills" [*CP*, 227–28] but disavowing any contemporary political obligation to it. The land and language of his birth are construed in similar terms as the assembly of literary masters, influences whose contributions to his identity are fondly recalled and acknowledged, but the choice as to how to apply or engage that influence remains his. His experience and memories of England helped make him who he is, but who he is "Now" depends on what he chooses to do with that inheritance, not on the fact of that inheritance itself. The poet is in control of his past, not the other way around.

Toward the end of "New Year Letter," Auden describes this new vision of the relation between self and nation, and the conditions that created it:

> However we decide to act,
> Decision must accept the fact
> That the machine has now destroyed
> The local customs we enjoyed,
> Replaced the bonds of blood and nation
> By personal confederation. [*CP*, 238]

Auden defines both America and American poetry not in terms of a collection of specific cultural inheritances, ideals, prejudices, and ambitions, but as a site of permanent, ongoing dialectical negotiation that offers the opportunity for escape from any imposed inheritance whatsoever. By turning himself into what he saw as an American poet, he paradoxically liberates himself from history, from fixed notions of identity, from nationality itself. Auden's American poetry asserts the possibility of a poetic (and private) identity determined by a *choice* of inheritance, a choice derived through negotiation with myriad possible options, and can encompass any form, any influence, any source from any time or place. Auden defines America as the *absence* of nationality. As he would recall in a 1963 lecture on "Influences," "America is the anti-country; that was why I had to join it."[14]

♦ ♦ ♦

Auden's project of defining himself as an American poet would itself have a defining impact on the future of American poetry. Yet in his grappling with the tensions inherent in that ambition, Auden also looks back specifically to the American literary past for guidance and instruction. As a student poet, Dickinson and Frost had played significant roles in his pantheon of early influences, with Dickinson's gnomic concision and Frost's plain-spoken ironies offering essential elements to the development of Auden's distinctive demotic yet elusive early poetic style. Auden also read and wrote with enthusiasm about Melville's allegorical imagination and found Laura Riding and Marianne Moore especially valuable rhetorical resources throughout his career. But upon arriving in America, two American writers in particular came to seem especially useful to his efforts at constructing his American poetic identity: Walt Whitman and, even more crucially, Henry James. Both Whitman and James make appearances in the literary gallery of "New Year Letter," Whitman (via the poem's Notes) as a diagnostician of the varieties of American souls and faces, and James as arbiter of fine distinctions among the moral options made uniquely visible by the American experience.

One of Auden's first American book reviews, of a biography of Matthew Arnold in April 1939, proposes the American Whitman, "with his endless lists and formless originality," as an expansive imaginative alternative to the English Arnold's "disciplined and fastidious abstractions" [*Prose*, 12]. And the scope, structure, and spirit of "New Year Letter," an earthbound song of Auden's new American self with its multitude-containing catalog of influences and ideas and composed within view of Whitman's Brooklyn tugboats and ferries,[15] reflects a Whitmanic ideal Auden would later approvingly quote in a 1956 essay on American poetry: "The Old World has had the poems of myths, fictions, feudalism, conquest, caste, dynastic wars, and splendid characters, which have been great; but the New World needs the poems of realities and science and of the democratic average and basic equality" [*DH*, 365]. Calling Whitman "the first clearly to recognize what the conditions were with which any future American poet would have to come to terms," Auden credits him with defining that "democratic average" not in terms of populist mediocrity but as the artistic creation of "the individual whose 'exceptional character' is not derived by birth, education, or occupation." Whitman's vision of America's democratic vistas, of a commonality grounded in equality amid difference, and of the United States itself as "essentially the greatest poem,"[16] would serve Auden as a useful inherited frame through which to see his own desire to place his immigrant distinctiveness into productive relation with a broader American narrative.

James plays an even bigger role in Auden's American imagination. Auden had begun reading James devotedly soon after arriving in New York, finding in the "Novelist, citizen of two countries, interpreter of his generation on both sides of the sea," as his gravestone describes him, a master to help him navigate his own journey—reversing James's path— from Englishman to American. Jamesian images, ideas, and phrases, like the notion of an idealized "Great Good Place" where the sensitive soul finds true contentment and self-knowledge, sprinkle themselves through Auden's early American poems, most notably in "At the Grave of Henry James," the grand elegy commemorating a pilgrimage to that same Boston gravestone in 1941. The original twenty-eight stanzas (later shortened to ten) situate Auden's engagement with James explicitly in the context of a "doubtful hour" of war and personal displacement:

> Now more than ever, when torches and snare-drum
> Excite the squat women of the saurian brain
>   Till a milling mob of fears
> Breaks in insultingly on anywhere, when in our dreams
> Pigs play on the organs and the blue sky runs shrieking
>   As the Crack of Dooms appears,
>
> Are good ghosts needed with the white magic
> Of their subtle loves. War has no ambiguities
>   Like a marriage; the result
> Required of its *affaire fatale* is simple and sad,
> The physical removal of all human objects
>   That conceal the Difficult.
>
> Then remember me that I may remember
> The test we have to learn to shudder for is not
>   An historical event,
> That neither the low democracy of a nightmare nor
> An army's primitive tidiness may deceive me
>   About our predicament.

> That catastrophic situation which neither
> Victory nor defeat can annul; to be
>   Deaf yet determined to sing,
> To be lame and blind yet burning for the Great Good Place,
> To be radically corrupt yet mournfully attracted
>   By the Real Distinguished Thing. [*SP*, 121]

Echoing the urgent question of the "Now" of "New Year Letter," which had appeared in *The Atlantic Monthly* (a frequent publisher of James in his day) just as Auden was contemplating James's tombstone, the poem invokes James and his language as moral exemplars of "subtle love" in a world increasingly tuned to war-drums, screams, and apocalyptic thunder. In this prayer to James as literary saint, the international disaster doubles as a private crisis, the predicament of global war reflecting the inner conflicts besetting the immigrant poet: to be silent or to sing, to surrender to despair or work to hope, to yield to the impossibility of making something happen with his art or strive for a new way of happening. James, the fundamental transatlantic man, points the way to wisdom: the necessary recognition of the "catastrophic situation" of existence, the inescapable human fate to be "dialectic and bizarre," as Auden put it in "Atlantis," written a few months earlier.[17]

The example and influence of James would continue to be central to Auden's American career, including the crucial Caliban chapter of 1944's "The Sea and the Mirror," which rewrites *The Tempest* as a drama between the warring aspects of an artist's creative imagination and puts the refined and refining voice of James's "subtle love" into Caliban's monstrous mouth. He was a proselytizing enthusiast for James's impressionistic native travelogue, *The American Scene*, pressing it upon British friends as the best book about the United States and scolding his American ones, ignorant of the book, "As an American, you must look into James's *American Scene*."[18] In 1946, he lobbied Scribner's to republish James's book (which had been out of print since its original 1907 edition), and edited and introduced it himself. In that introduction, later reprinted in *The Dyer's Hand* in 1962, Auden returns to themes he sounded in "New Year Letter," *Paul Bunyan*, and the Smith commencement address, of the relation and distance between an idealized vision of America's democratic promise and the sprawling, untidy country he

actually inhabited, with its "horrible Rockettes and the insane salads . . .
[and] the anonymous countryside littered with heterogeneous *dreck* and
the synonymous cities besotted with electric signs . . . [and] radio com-
mercials and congressional oratory and Hollywood Christianity" [*Prose*,
282]. Recalling "Atlantis," where the traveling quester must "become ac-
quainted now / With each refuge that tries to / Counterfeit Atlantis"
in order to "recognize the true" [*CP*, 316], Auden concludes his essay
on James by arguing that America's utopian ideal identity is achievable
not despite its moral and aesthetic failures but *because* of them. Without
the confused and distressingly non-ideal example of real America, with
all its "'democratic' lusts and licenses," he asserts, "the analyst and the
immigrant alike would never understand by contrast the nature of the
Good Place nor desire it with sufficient desperation to stand a chance of
arriving" [*DH*, 322–23]. The path to the Great Good Place, the immigrant Auden suggests, begins right in the chaotic and democratic heart
of America.

James offers Auden a useful, discriminating dialectical counterweight to the all-including Whitmanic narrative of America. In his 1939
essay on Whitman and Arnold, he cites in agreement Whitman's dictum, "Everything comes out of the dirt, everything—everything comes
from the people, the everyday people," but qualifies his endorsement
with a critique: "Whitman was so busy accepting everything, that he
forgot to notice that one thing differs from another" [*Prose*, 12]. And
in *The Dyer's Hand* he observes, "Whitman looks at life extensively
rather than intensively. No detail is dwelt upon for long; it is snapshot-
ted and added as one more item to the vast American catalogue" [*DH*,
288]. Whitman's poetics of "the democratic average and basic equality"
were historically grounded in the bloody divisiveness of the Civil War,
with his sweeping embrace of "everything" aimed at asserting an inclusive narrative of national coherence in the face of the shattered Union.
While Whitman's poems were invested in preserving, in however loose
a form, some kind of nationalist ideal, for Auden, with fascism and the
tragedy of nationalism unfolding brutally across Europe, the ideology of
nationhood itself has become a dangerous, destructive lie. In response,
he adopts Whitman's America-idealizing embrace of democratizing difference to a degree that explodes the very idea of nation as an ideology.
The nation as Auden sees it no longer contains multitudes unified in

an idea of collective aspirational identity. Instead, it becomes a Jamesian Great Good Place, or Atlantis, created by each individual, rather than a constricting narrative imposed by the poet or the state, "the bonds of blood and nation" replaced by "personal confederation," as "New Year Letter" puts it. "America is where you find it," Auden tells his audiences in 1940, in terms that simultaneously echo Whitman's universalizing claim to posterity in "Song of Myself," to be looked for under American boot-soles, and James's own assertion of American distinctiveness: "[I]t seems to me that we are ahead of the European races in the fact that . . . we can deal freely with forms of civilization not our own, can pick and choose and assimilate and in short (aesthetically etc.) claim our property wherever we find it."[19]

Auden asserts a poetics and ethics of choice, situated specifically in an American context. In a 1946 lecture at the Grolier Club in New York, Auden declared his allegiance to a Jamesian notion of the relation between artist and nationality, predicated upon free will and the necessity of choice: "Assuming the artist, the writer today, decides rightly or wrongly, to continue pursuing his vocation, what are his obligations? To this question, Henry James offers, I believe, the correct answers. He must become international and he must stand alone" [*Prose*, 302]. Building on a Whitmanic narrative of inclusive American community but opposing it with a Jamesian view of artistic independence and solitude, Auden arrives, like the quester of "Atlantis," at a poetic vision of America as a different kind of ideal through which artists, by means of their individual dialectical quests, collectively escape and critique the excesses of nationalism. In America, he argues, the absence of the kinds of entrenched, communal, and inherited moral or cultural narratives upon which the European relies for guidance, leaves the American to make his/her own subjective moral choices. For Auden, America is defined by the "awareness of the dialectic" and the inescapability of choice—of action, of belief, of meaning, of identity—that it imposes upon its inhabitants. And the burden of that choice is a heavy and a lonely one, as he argues in his *American Scene* introduction:

> [F]or the individual, it means accepting the lot of the Wandering Jew, *i.e.*, the loneliness and anxiety of having to choose himself, his faith, his vocation, his tastes. The Margin is a hard

taskmaster; it says to the individual: "It's no good your running to me and asking me to make you into someone. You must
choose. I won't try to prevent your choice, but I can't and won't
help you make it. If you try to put your trust in me, in public
opinion, you will become, not someone but no one, a neuter
atom of the public." [*DH*, 321]

In Auden's vision, the American "Margin" (using another capital-
ized Jamesian term), in opposition to the European center, offers no
guidance, only a terrifying freedom that places the obligation of constructing meaning, narrative, or morality in one's existence squarely on
the shoulders of the individual. Here we see a specifically cultural theo-
rization of the same idea Auden expresses in his American art. Just as
in "Atlantis," "New Year Letter," and his précis for the unmade film, the
solitary American hero must arrive by himself at a hard-won, but specifically individual and always provisional insight through the negotiation
with, and choice between, the numberless and intimidating available
options.

◆ ◆ ◆

The specifics of Auden's private life—and, indeed, the personal lives of
those writers whose influential assistance he invoked—are not uncon-
nected to his theoretical diagnosis of either the American character or
the place of his art in his new home. If Auden intellectualized American
identity as existentially lonely, it was also at least in part because Auden
found his own new life in America an extraordinarily lonely one. Even as
he rejoiced in finding his true love less than three months after landing
in Manhattan, both the exigencies of his peripatetic life, which took him
continually from New York to college campuses and lectures and poetry
readings across the United States, and the frustrations of his relationship with the often-absent Kallman, combined to leave him traveling,
tormented and alone much of the time. While he would assemble provisional communities of warmth and personal confederation around him
when he could, as in the months he spent in 1940 and 1941 living in a
rambunctious house at 7 Middagh Street in Brooklyn, in company with
Benjamin Britten, Louis MacNeice, Paul and Jane Bowles, Carson Mc-
Cullers, Richard Wright, and Gypsy Rose Lee among other artists and

lively characters, his temperament and his professional demands often doomed him to unhappy solitude.

In 1941, while teaching as a visiting professor in Ann Arbor, Michigan, a "Middle-West town" like that of the hero of his film, Auden opined colorfully on the relation between private life and American literature to his temporary housemate, a young writer named Charles Miller:

> "Charlie, it's *amazing* that no one has really written about the true America, the land of the lonely! The land of eccentrics and outcast lonelies. "The Lonelies" could be the title of a grand unwritten American novel. I've been told of an unlikely hero, the homosexual 'queen' of Niles, Michigan, you know? Each evening when the New York-Chicago train pauses there to put off a passenger or so, this lonely queen meets the train, hoping to encounter one of his own kind.... Imagine it, Charlie. Imagine such a scene being repeated daily in hundreds of little American towns! Imagine all the small-town queens who have a flat or cottage graced with their few books and records, perhaps some choice pornographic photos. Such queens may speak with an affected accent or lisp, trying for individuality; they idolize New York but never escape the hinterlands.... America *is* one of the loneliest places on this planet."[20]

Auden projects his own experience of itinerant loneliness, of riding trains between countless American towns and cities as he plies his literary trade, onto the entire nation. And significantly, his emblem of American solitude, and the unrecognized subject of the unwritten great American novel, is the forlorn, sad, and somewhat tragicomic figure of an aesthetic-minded homosexual man. The "lonely queen" of Niles, Michigan, trapped in his own "Middle-West" parochial town and seeking and failing to find connection with "his own kind" at the railroad station, is for Auden the epitome of the American experience. While the arrival on that train of someone like the cosmopolitan Auden himself would be, by implication, precisely what the aspirational hinterlands-dweller would most crave, both rootless poet and his overly rooted doppelganger are fated never to connect, their loneliness never to be relieved by true mutual recognition. By envisioning the "unlikely hero" of the essential American story as a lonely gay man, Auden does several things at once. First, he posits his own unique experience in the same "ordinary and universal" terms he asserted of the "average American" hero of his unmade film. If the "lonely queen" is the essence of America, then so is he. Second, he gives a human face to his vision of America defined not by a narrative of unifying nationalism but through a dialectic of "personal confederation" and solitude. "America is where you find it," he says, and where we find it is in lonely and isolated individuals hoping and trying, despite the likelihood of failure, for connection with others. The flickering constellations of "ironic points of light" flashing in the dark "wherever the Just / Exchange their messages" in "September 1, 1939" is Auden simultaneously looking out at America—from his hotel, apartment, or train window—and defining it. And lastly, he, in a sense, queers America itself. His invocation of homosexual writers like James, Whitman, and others like Rimbaud as exemplars to guide him on his American way reveals another narrative of Americanness to stand in dialectical relation to that embodied by his Paul Bunyan, who—interestingly, unlike in any of the previous versions of the story—is given in Auden's opera a wife and a daughter. To the vision of America as the Dynamo of modernity imposing itself upon the Virgin of history and nature (in terms from Henry Adams that Auden explores at length in *The Dyer's Hand*), Auden offers a subversive counter-vision that reads America against the heteronormative grain. What defines America, he provocatively suggests, is its queerness from the rest of the world and from itself. Auden's American, like the lonely man in Niles, Michigan, recognizes "his own kind" precisely in their shared difference from everybody else and, fundamentally, from one another. Auden's opening of the American narrative to include, or even privilege, its queerness will have a significant impact on many younger American poets, who saw his sexual frankness as encouragement to their own efforts to articulate their own American difference, sexual and otherwise.[21]

Auden's American experience and his ambitions for his American art are intimately entwined. As is the relation, pursued throughout this book, between Auden's influence on American poetry and his human presence in postwar American literary culture. "Art and Life agree in this / That each intend a synthesis," Auden writes in "New Year Letter," suggesting that both a person and a poem are seeking the same thing: ideal order and understanding. In his art and his life, Auden finds an image of that order, his Great Good Place, in America itself. In *Paul Bun-yan*, after declaring "America is what we choose to make it," the hero concludes the opera with a statement of self-definition that is also a sum-mation of Auden's new American *ars poetica*:

> "Where the night becomes the day
> Where the dream becomes the fact
>   I am the Eternal Guest
>   I am Way
>   I am Act." [*Libretti*, 46]

The "I" here is doubly dialectical: It is Paul Bunyan and it is Amer-ica, and it is also Auden's poetry and his speaking self. To be at home in America, and in Auden's poems, is to be an "Eternal Guest": always moving, always alone, and always seeking refuge from that solitude. And in that seeking comes self-knowledge, and through that insight comes a kind of action in the world. Looking for an answer to the failure of art to forestall the rise of European fascism and confronting the problem of his new American life, Auden develops a new understanding of poetry as a "Way" of acting and being in the world. In Paul Bunyan, as in the "aver-age American" of his film and in the "Atlantis" quester, we see the literal embodiment of that "way" in a personification of America itself, with America and poetry, person and art, all reflecting upon one another.

In his elegy for Yeats, after asserting in apparent despair that "Poetry makes nothing happen," he immediately offers a profoundly revisionary image of poetry as a river that "survives in the valley of its making." From that point of dark origin, it

> flows on south
> From ranches of isolation and the busy griefs,
> Raw towns that we believe and die in; it survives,
> A way of happening, a mouth." [*CP*, 248]

It is no coincidence that the landscape through which that emblem of poetry's survival flows is a distinctively American one of desolate ranches and lonely towns, since it is in his vision of America itself that Auden found his own poetry's survival. Auden's American poetry knows it can't stop a war but, through its engagement with the idea and reality of America, it discovers it *can* serve as a path, a conduit, a "way," for his reader, and himself, to come nearer to that place of ideal personal, moral, and aesthetic order, whose individual attainment can add to the collective building of that hoped-for Just City. America, at a moment crucial to both his own career and the history of modern poetry, becomes Auden's Atlantis, his life-giving source, his own "way of happening."

PART I

A Way of Happening

Auden's American Presence

In May of 1946, a young American poetry critic offered this enthusiastic review of *For the Time Being*, Auden's second published volume since moving to the United States seven years before:

> Auden's poetry has always aroused much interest, the more so because Auden's personality and technique and opinions have been so flexible. He has been consistently evolving toward disciplined, responsible utterance, and away from slipshod emotional crisis, overconscious penitence, tender despondency and nostalgia. *Another Time* and *New Year Letter* assume power as statements of transition to mastery of personal sorrow and insight into general terror. The tentative accomplishment of this maturity, in *For the Time Being*, set it apart as one of the few great works of poetry of our time, rivalled only by Eliot's last book of poetry and his plays. A definitive review of *For the Time Being* is impossible; it is the kind of book that reviews the reviewer: it is too intelligent in thought and perfected in technique to allow immediate formal judgment. A full appreciation,

exegesis and criticism must be left to the literary studies which will come.

This admiring assessment is illuminatingly representative of its literary moment, both encapsulating Auden's unquestioned importance in the American postwar poetic landscape, and framing a number of the major critical narratives that had assembled around the famous émigré poet in the years following his arrival in New York in 1939. The case for Auden's poetic "flexibility" and his "transition" from the "emotional crisis" of his 1930s lyrics to the "disciplined, responsible utterance" of his new American mode had been fiercely and influentially argued throughout the decade—often with a sharp edge of disappointment and disapproval—by Auden's most committed critic, Randall Jarrell, whose 1941 essay, "Changes of Attitude and Rhetoric in Auden's Poetry," began with a waggish misquoted epigraph from Heraclitus: "We never step twice into the same Auden."[1] The reviewer's assertion of Auden's place as peer and successor to Eliot was similarly by then a critical commonplace, as expressed five years before by Malcolm Cowley, summarizing the literary consensus on the transatlantic trade of the American Eliot for the British Auden: "It's as if we had sent T. S. Eliot to England before the war on a lend-lease arrangement. Now, with Auden, we are being repaid in kind."[2] Louise Bogan had affirmed this ascendancy in the pages of *The New Yorker* in 1945 with the tone of a critic observing the undisputedly obvious: "Auden, it has sometime been apparent, has succeeded Eliot as the strongest influence in American and British poetry."[3] And Karl Shapiro, in his *Essay on Rime* in the same year, noted the same self-evident phenomenon: "The man whose impress on our rhetoric / Has for a decade dominated verse / In London, Sydney and New York is Auden."[4]

Auden's post-immigration "mastery of personal sorrow and insight into general terror," as the 1946 reviewer puts it, further recalls and confirms Delmore Schwartz's hope for Auden's poetic future, anxiously voiced in 1939 just as the world was plunging into war and Auden was embarking on his new American life, that "[I]t may be that with an immense gift for language one can survive social catastrophe, international terror, and the solicitations of the Ego,"[5] while also articulating the mood of the immediate postwar moment in which the terrible "insight into general terror" brought by the war was answered by the fervent wish that its conclusion suggested some larger historical "mastery" over future such horrors. Additionally, the reviewer's confidence that a "full appreciation" of Auden's work would depend upon the academic "exegesis" of future "literary studies" tellingly reflects Auden's prominent place—as critic, contest judge, assigned text, and itinerant faculty member on campuses across the country—in the burgeoning mid-century institutionalization of poetry in the academy, in which a new generation of American students was being introduced to the thorny abstrusities of modern poetry through the rationalizing methodologies and "formal judgment" of the New Critical classroom.

Titled ". . . 'This Is the Abomination,'" taking its quotation from the introduction to the Christmas oratorio "For the Time Being" (one of the two long poems in the book of that name, "The Sea and the Mirror" being the other) in which the Narrator asserts his age's collective dread of the existential "Void," the review's summation of Auden's cultural relevance and influence could have appeared in any number of mainstream literary journals of the time, for whom Auden's importance to the American scene went largely unquestioned. Read through the prism of subsequent literary history, however, the identity of its author acquires a resonant irony. This tribute to Auden wasn't penned by a poet or critic of the then-presiding literary generation of Jarrell, Bogan, Shapiro, John Berryman, Theodore Roethke, or Elizabeth Bishop, each of whom acknowledged in their careers the impact of Auden's 1930s lyrics in particular on their own poetic sensibilities, but who had come to artistic maturity prior to his arrival in America.[6] Rather, it reflects the perspective of a younger generation, one whose poetic education had begun amid the war and its aftermath, during a crucial moment in American poetic history when Auden was both an essential book on the shelf and a very active and powerful living presence in the American literary establishment. Its author? A nineteen-year-old Columbia undergraduate named Allen Ginsberg.[7]

Reading the young Ginsberg in praise of the American Auden's "disciplined, responsible utterance" and rejection of "slipshod emotional crisis" provokes a startling—and amusing—clash of literary stereotypes: Ginsberg, the shaggy antiestablishment rebel whose poems would famously bring defiantly undisciplined utterance and emotional crisis firmly into the literary and pop-culture mainstream, exalting Auden, the high culture, high church, establishment formalist who, in the same year as Ginsberg's review, was telling an audience of Harvard undergraduates to "Read *The New Yorker*, trust in God; / And take short views" [*CP*, 339]. But such disruptions in the settled narratives of literary history, in which presumptively oppositional poles of American poetic culture are seen in surprising alliance, far from being quirks of individual poets like Ginsberg's biography and artistic development, are in fact characteristic—if not definitional—of Auden's role in postwar American poetry. In many ways, Auden served an entire generation of poets like Ginsberg, who grew into their own very distinct voices during his American career, as a "whole climate of opinion," as Auden himself described Freud in one of his earliest American poems. Indeed, it's possible to argue that no writer had as pivotal and wide-ranging an influence on postwar American poetics as Auden. As judge for the Yale Younger Poets contest, Auden shaped national tastes and crowned many of that generation's most important writers. As an openly gay artist of stature, he provided a model for living and writing emulated by many others, including Ginsberg. By critiquing Modernist ideas of the poet's role in society, he forged new ideas about national and individual artistic identity, without which the contemporary American poetic scene, in all its variegated modes and traditions, is almost unimaginable. And his pedagogical and personal connections with countless young poets he encountered in New York, on his summer island home of Ischia, on the lecture circuit, or through his various visiting academic positions at universities across the country, made him a towering, vibrant force throughout American poetic culture from the 1940s through the 1960s. It also illustrates how many of the critical narratives of postwar American poetry—which customarily frame the period in terms of competing camps of formalism versus experiment, establishment versus avant-garde, feminist or gay versus masculinist, West Coast versus East—are complicated by Auden's appearance and influence across all these regional, cultural, stylistic, and gender divides.

When Auden arrived in the United States in 1939, he left behind his public career as activist poet and lyricist of the English Left. The first poem he wrote in America was "In Memory of W. B. Yeats," in which he sounded his famous retraction of an *engagé* and ideological art: "Poetry makes nothing happen." I want to argue that Auden's extensive and largely unexplored impact on the postwar generation of American poets helped not only to define the terms by which these younger poets framed their own work and careers, but also offered a new and influential model for understanding what it meant to write poetry in America after World War II and after Modernism. In particular, Auden's redefinition of his own poetic identity following his emigration from England helped to shape American poetry in terms of what Auden called "the burden of choice": How to select an inheritance from the myriad possibilities opened up in the wake of Modernism's shattering of notions of a unified native tradition. By framing his post-1939 poetry—in the affirmative conclusion of the Yeats elegy—as "a way of happening," Auden inaugurated a poetic vision of post-Modernist America as an open, inclusive text defined not in terms of shared ideals of national, ideological, or historical inheritance, but by the freedom, and necessity, to choose among the kaleidoscopic range of formal, cultural, or transnational poetic identities made available by the collapse of those earlier ideals. Under Auden's influence, both as a maker of poems and as a shaper of careers, the terrain of American poetry expanded to accommodate poetic experiences and voices as diverse as John Ashbery's continental language experiments, James Merrill's Dantean adventures at the Ouija board, and Adrienne Rich's politically engaged insistence on the power of poetry to effect social change, to name just three of Auden's most important and stylistically distinct inheritors, each of whom will be discussed at greater length in later chapters. And as we will see with these three poets, along with Ginsberg and a broad range of other younger American writers who would go on to demarcate the democratic and demotic vistas of American poetry in the second half of the twentieth century, it was with Auden's crucial help that their own individual negotiations with the burden of personal and artistic choice in the wake of Modernism and war allowed them to find their own poetic "ways of happening."[8]

◆ ◆ ◆

One key to how Auden's influence was felt by younger poets can be found in Ginsberg's description of *For the Time Being* as "the kind of book that reviews the reviewer." Among the most notable aspects of Auden's importance for his American successors was the way in which so many of them saw their own multitudinous, very different American selves reflected back at them in the words of this transplanted Englishman. In terms similar to those of Auden's Yeats elegy, in which the dead poet's "words are modified in the guts" of his surviving readers and where the poet's identity is surrendered to those who find part of their own identities in his work, countless poets of every cultural and artistic stripe saw in Auden's poems and persona what they needed to see in order to articulate who they themselves would become. To a remarkable extent, Auden "became his admirers" in the sense that so many of those he influenced found him useful in their own efforts to define themselves, often with widely diverging poetic results. Every younger poet's Auden was different. For some he was, as Ginsberg's fellow poet, friend, sometime antagonist, and Columbia classmate John Hollander would describe him, "[A] clever young uncle . . . holding our hands in the dusk,"[9] a friendly teacher and elder master of the craft who could help point them on their own way. For others, he was a more distant enemy, someone whom they could distinctly and defiantly define themselves against. As the young Robert Creeley would write in 1950 to his ally in establishment-razing, Charles Olson, decrying the embrace of Auden by mainstream voices like Jarrell and Bogan: "[T]he intelligence that had touted Auden as being a technical wonder, etc. lacking all grip on the worn and useless character of his essence: thought. An attitude that puts weight, *first*: on form [. . .] will never get to content. Never in God's world. Anyhow, form has become so useless a term that I blush to use it."[10] For Hollander, Auden's mastery of form and his notion of poetry's moral function made him an important mentor. For Creeley, it was precisely that emphasis on empty form, as he perceived it, as well as Auden's tweedy Englishness, that made him suspect and an embodiment of everything his poetry would oppose. But for each, Auden was *useful*, an important point of reference in their own poetic self-fashioning.

For Ginsberg himself over the course of his career, Auden performed both roles, uncle and enemy, sometimes simultaneously. In that early review, even as he praises Auden's formal detachment, he offers Auden as a kind of vatic voice for the predicament of the times, who can present to those who will listen "the basic psychological facts of the age." These facts include for Ginsberg a state of "formal cultural decadence" that he sees Auden identifying and analyzing and himself enlisting in battle against:

The problems of modern men have little to do with the rather tiring abstractions of facts of historians, the externalized theories of economists, and the bestial rages of moralists, pedants and returning veterans. All theirs are useless uncontrolled reactions, by-products of ruin; at best they have a superficial descriptive value. Perhaps coherent explanation of all this circumstance would be facilitated through some sort of psychoanalytic-anthropology – a discipline which Auden has followed, to judge from his attitude, his vocabulary, and his notes to *New Year Letter*.

In 1931, the twenty-two-year-old Auden had asked, in *The Orators*, "What do you think about England, this country of ours where nobody is well?" [*EA*, 62]. Fifteen years later, the young Ginsberg is asking the same question of his country, in which he detects a similar national pathology, and employs the older Auden to make the diagnosis. Observing Auden's characteristic mode of using the individual-focused insights of psychoanalysis to make broader generalizations of cultural malaise, Ginsberg offers his own effort at a clinical "coherent explanation" for the "ruin" of his age, taking particular note of Auden's first American long poem, "New Year Letter," whose mode of epic, epistolary self-analysis and questing after an ideal of community would find an American heir in Ginsberg's own "Howl" a decade later.

The review was written during an eventful time in Ginsberg's life: He had been suspended from Columbia the previous spring for scrawling obscene slogans on his dorm-room window, though he maintained his editorial position at *The Columbia Review* even while he was no longer officially a student. During that year he had worked as a welder at the Brooklyn Navy Yard, spent a few months as a sailor in the Merchant Marine, experimented with writing under the influence of Benzedrine, and lived and wrote in a chaotic upper Manhattan apartment inhabited off and on by Jack Kerouac, William Burroughs, and assorted friends and eccentric associates who would form the core of the nascent Beat scene. In language that prefigures the tumbling, ecstatic, and angry rhetoric of "Howl," and in images that foretell the countercultural rebellion he would go on to publicly personify, Ginsberg sees in "The Sea and the

Mirror" and the oratorio that gives Auden's book its title, a clear-eyed indictment of the same forces of establishment that had kicked him out of Columbia:

> Alas, the question of the hour is not the conflict between classes, nor that of genius versus mediocrity. All have been so completely intimidated into abdication of responsibility and in ways so obvious and in activities so self-destructive that there is no longer any real chance to face strict problems, to take decisive and valid action; in the general mass and imprecision there is no longer an overt question to precipitate an act, no direct course for a moderate sensible person to take as a choice. And as a result all our healthiest citizens are turning into hipsters, hopheads, and poets.

In a move that reflects the tension Ginsberg felt between his admiration of, and immersion in, the poetic tradition he'd learned from his poet father, Louis Ginsberg, and his Columbia teachers like Lionel Trilling and Mark Van Doren, and his desire to break from those same restrictive cultural and social conventions, his call for a countertradition of "hipsters, hopheads, and poets" is framed by an uncited quotation—"in the general mess and imprecision of feeling"—from that icon of the traditionalists, T. S. Eliot.[11] And his assertion that the "question of the hour" is the problem of "choice" further recalls one of Auden's touchstone poetic themes, articulated in celebrated political poems of the 1930s like "Spain": "What's your proposal? To build the just city? I will. / I agree. Or is it the suicide pact, the romantic / Death? Very well, I accept, for / I am your choice, your decision: yes, I am Spain" [*SP*, 53]. Ironically, Ginsberg seems to envy the kind of excruciating moral and ideological dilemma faced by Auden's generation during the 1930s—"We are left alone with our day, and time is short and / History to the defeated / May say Alas but cannot help nor pardon" [*SP*, 55]—in contrast to the state of existential emptiness he sees all around him, where there is not even the possibility of choosing between difficult, or even outrageous, moral options, ideologies, or actions:

> We have no Orphic creativeness, juvenescent savagery, primitive abandon, not even decadent Satanism to amuse us; we are

faced with no problem to be solved, no god that we can create
or destroy, no ecstasy of our own, no destruction of our own.
Worse than tender sorrow, possible sadism, of spiritual battle,
is this quivering indecision. We are incapable not only of vision
but also of evil, of any authentic emotion. And the complete
statement of the ultimate psychological impasse characteristic of
our age is given by Auden in *For the Time Being*.

Less than ten months after the end of the war, it seems striking that
Ginsberg should be lamenting the impossibility of any "destruction of
our own," suggesting a certain generational anxiety on the part of those
who were too young to have directly participated in the grand narrative
of the times, the heroic and bloody defeat of international fascism. But
Ginsberg's concern with "quivering indecision" also reflects a specific
and new postwar predicament: the precarious and paralyzing stasis of a
world entering into the Cold War, where the anxiety of nuclear annihilation keeps agents of cultural change in check and, as Ginsberg sees it, the
horrors of Hiroshima are the natural extension of a convention-bound
and comfortable citizenry more interested in "remedies for constipation,
his refrigerators and toilets" than in ideas of moral responsibility. As he
puts it, "The awful consummation of this holocaust of hysterical irre-
sponsibility is the Atom Bomb." Inheriting a world defined by his own
generational belatedness and minorness, by the ever-expanding culture
of soul-deadening consumerism, and by what he calls the "nightmare
of repressed anxiety which has culminated in emotional stupidity and
spiritual incompetence," Ginsberg issues—in a college review of a book
of Auden poems—his first literary call for "spiritual battle" against this
"abomination." And he sees Auden as a field marshal in the culture war
he's itching to fight. This is the Ginsberg who is introduced in Kerouac's
first novel, *The Town and the City* (1950), as the poet "Leon Levinsky,"
whose radicalism and sophistication are signaled to his audience by his
bohemian outfit and his ostentatious display of talismanic texts: "He
was wearing a strapped raincoat, a Paisley scarf, and dark-rimmed glasses
with the air of an intellectual. He carried two slim volumes under his
arm, the works of Rimbaud and W. H. Auden."[12]

Auden was of course not Ginsberg's only early poetic guide. Ginsberg's career, from its earliest beginnings, was defined by his search for

elder mentors whose wisdom and influence he could absorb and from whose professional assistance he might benefit, from Kerouac and Burroughs, to his Columbia teacher Trilling, to Ezra Pound, who in 1951 responded from his room in St. Elizabeth's to a letter of inquiry from the twenty-five-year-old Ginsberg with a terse three-sentence rebuff: "Dear Ag / None of yu people have least concept of FATIGUE. / I hv sd it all in print . . . i.e. all answers to yrs. / Cantos no use to people writing shorts."[13] And in 1950 he would begin a correspondence and eventual friendship with William Carlos Williams, whose breath-based metrics and connection to Ginsberg's own hometown of Paterson, NJ would make him his next important influence.[14] But Ginsberg's early poems are shot through with Audenesque language, forms, imagery, and concerns, especially in his first effort at a long poem, never published during his lifetime and written at the same time as his Auden review, called "Death in Violence." Prefaced by an extended quotation from "The Sea and the Mirror" about the revelation to the artist of "the real Word," the poem begins with an address to his fellow poetic questers: "O heroes, hipsters, humanists, Prometheans! / arrange your lives as best you can before the voyage— / sell your mansions of nostalgia, throw away / the playsuits that you frolicked in among the ruins." In the margins of the manuscript of the unpublished poem, next to these lines that both explicitly echo Auden's "Atlantis" and prefigure the efforts of "Howl" at creating through hortatory assertion an ideal community of like-minded outcast artists, Ginsberg has later scribbled an accurate self-critique: "Auden style."[15] Auden would also be one of several dozen friends, allies, enemies, fellow poets, celebrities, and influential tastemakers—including Charlie Chaplin, Pound, Williams, Louis Zukofsky, Jarrell, and Columbia peers and teachers like Hollander, Richard Howard, Trilling, and Van Doren—to whom Ginsberg would send unsolicited promotional copies of *Howl and Other Poems* in 1956.[16] And late into his career, Ginsberg would return in interviews to Auden's double-edged dictum, "Poetry makes nothing happen," as a way of explaining his own "happening"-focused poetics.[17]

But it wasn't just a literary influence that Auden would exert on Ginsberg, and many other poets of his generation. As Ginsberg would recall on the occasion of Auden's death in 1973, the connection was frequently a personal one as well. Ginsberg briskly summarizes his first decade of personal acquaintance with Auden:

We first met at Earl Hall, Columbia, 1945, when he read to
students. I accompanied him on the subway to Sheridan Square,
wondering if he'd invite me to his Cornelia Street apartment
and seduce me. He didn't. Years later in Ischia at a garden table,
1957, I said I thought there was a social revolution at hand,
he poo-pooed it, I drunkenly yelled at him, indignant, "You
ought to be ashamed of yourself discouraging young hope and
energy!" I was outraged, intemperate, tipsy and self-righteous.
Oddly, years later, he apologized to me for having been too off-
handed with me. Actually I'd made pilgrimage to Ischia to see
him and I'd intruded at his restaurant wine leisure dusk.[18]

The Stanford Ginsberg archives include a correspondence in the
summer of 1950 between Ginsberg and Auden's secretary (and onetime girlfriend) Rhoda Jaffe, detailing Ginsberg's repeated efforts to get
Auden to read his poems, and the two poets would eventually establish
a friendly, if occasionally awkward, relationship throughout the rest of
Auden's life.[19] Ginsberg succeeded in getting Auden's advice on the manuscript of *Empty Mirror*, and they would meet on many occasions over
the years in Auden's messy New York apartment, in Oxford, at international poetry festivals, and—as Ginsberg's brief narrative suggests—an
especially memorable encounter in 1957 at Auden's vacation home on
Ischia. Flush with notoriety and visionary bravado following his *succès
de scandale* with *Howl*, Ginsberg had made the trip to Ischia seeking an
audience with his early mentor in the hopes of a poetic communion on
more equal footing. He did not get it. Finding Auden and his friends
drinking at a bar, Ginsberg descended on the party and began to ha-
rangue Auden on questions of social justice, censorship, and the importance of Walt Whitman. Auden, secure in his redoubt and perhaps an-
noyed at the younger poet's poor manners, rebuffed Ginsberg and, after
an evening of fierce and not entirely sober argument, sent the furious
pilgrim off into the night, muttering as he left that Auden and his friends
were "a bunch of shits." [20]
    In light of Auden's documented appreciation for Whitman, his re-
corded admiration for Ginsberg's own poetry,[21] and the cordial friendship that developed between the two poets not long after this meeting,
it is likely that, as Ginsberg's biographer has suggested, this encounter

was more "an example of Auden's having fun with an uninvited guest than a record of his real opinions."[22] It is nevertheless illuminating on several counts: First, it shows that as late as 1957, long after Ginsberg's move toward a radical poetic and political stance, he should still look to Auden for counsel and criticism, suggesting that even in disagreement, Auden exerted a considerable monitory force on younger poets. And second, it serves to illustrate how younger poets took from the older what they needed in order to help forge their own poetic identity. As Ginsberg wrote his father after his unsatisfying Ischia encounter, "All this strengthens the conviction I have had, that the republic of poetry needs a full-scale revolution and upsetting of values (and a return to a kind of imagination of life in Whitman's *Democratic Vistas* that I've been reading in Venice)."[23] For Ginsberg, Auden provided him with a firm springboard from which to leap into what he saw as his own fugitive, anti-traditionalist art. Auden's were the conservative values he would upset, his the republic that needed a revolution. As poetry's Prospero, Auden enabled Ginsberg to play Caliban, learning to curse in his master's language, and gave him the oppositional, yet ultimately civil, role his own poetic vocation required. In his nominal repudiation of Auden, Ginsberg would set the stage for a number of other younger poets whose rejection of Auden's example would amount to a kind of recognition of his role in forming their own poetics. When Auden died, Ginsberg would spend the afternoon in tears, and wrote in his journal, "The aspen grove lost its yellow leaft roof, 'tis the end of September, kind Auden's gone away forever."[24]

When Ginsberg moved to San Francisco in 1954, he went looking for a poetic community and one of the first young local poets he met was Michael McClure. From this encounter would spring the idea and organization for what would become the primal scene of the San Francisco Beats, the Six Gallery reading that featured the dramatic public debut of "Howl" in 1955. The occasion of the meeting of the two young, ambitious, iconoclastic poets was the opening of the San Francisco Poetry Center, founded by the godmother of the San Francisco poetry scene, Ruth Witt Diamant, and which soon became the institutional heart of both the Beats and influential local poets and allies like Robert Duncan and Kenneth Rexroth. And the poet whose reading marked the inauguration of the Center, and whose presence brought both Ginsberg and

McClure together, was Auden.[25] While never intimate, Auden's relation to the rest of the Beats, besides Ginsberg, was also more than an occasional circumstantial proximity. Back in New York, Ginsberg and Kerouac would run into Auden or his partner Chester Kallman at parties thrown by Bill Cannastra, a Harvard lawyer and bon vivant who was a friend of Auden's and whose manic behavior and lurid death is memorialized in "Howl."[26] Harold Norse, a New York poet who was an early participant in the artistic community that would evolve into the Beats and would go on to be the documentarian of the "Beat Hotel" in Paris, where he and Burroughs would influentially experiment with their "cut-up" method of composition, had been romantically involved with Kallman when both were students at Brooklyn College. He was on hand for the first fateful meeting between Auden and Kallman, and served as Auden's secretary and typist in the early 1940s. Another important point of contact between Auden and the Beats was the poet and critic Alan Ansen. A close friend of Cannastra, Ginsberg, Burroughs, and Gregory Corso, and the erudite and cosmopolitan court jester of the Beats, Ansen is memorably fictionalized as the "It"-embodying emblem of the Beat ethos, "Rollo Greb," in Kerouac's *On the Road*, and as the surrealistic joker "A. J." in Burroughs's *Naked Lunch*. Like Norse, Ansen also served as Auden's secretary for a number of years in the late 1940s and early 1950s, and became one of Auden and Kallman's closest friends, eventually serving as Kallman's custodian and companion in Greece following Auden's death—"keeper of the keeper of the flame," as Ansen described himself—and arranging for Kallman's burial in the Jewish Cemetery in Athens in 1975. Auden's 1950 book of essays, *The Enchafèd Flood*, is dedicated to Ansen, and in turn Ansen dedicated his first book of poems in 1959 to his dual mentors, Auden and Burroughs. Ansen wrote a number of poems about Auden and Kallman, including one for Auden's sixtieth-birthday festschrift and a lengthy elegy for Kallman, along with publishing in 1990—in his avowed role as Boswell to Auden's Johnson—a collection of Auden's private conversations and witticisms entitled *The Table Talk of W. H. Auden*.[27] Even Corso, among the most prototypically unschooled and rough-edged of the Beats, had an affectionate relation with the icon of formalism, recounting in a 1958 letter to LeRoi Jones a momentous visit he and Ginsberg had spent with Auden in Oxford: "Also saw Auden twice—he acted like my Shelley at

Oxford—leading us to Christ Church—pointing out the Oxford of his youth—very mellow angel, he."[28] Late in his career, Corso would profess to an interviewer his continued enthusiasm for Auden, along with his notion of the intertwined significance of the poet's work and his social persona: "The poet and the poetry are inseparable. You got to dig the poet. Otherwise the poetry sucks. If I dug the poet, then automatically the poetry worked for me. . . . Pound makes it, Auden made it for me. I mean, Auden is good. I dig Auden, you see. A lot don't." And recalling an early resonant encounter with Auden, he reflected on the elder poet's capacity to encourage and inspire even the least formally academic of his poet-students: "Auden was reading *The Tempest* to me and it sounded beautiful. I was just a kid. Walking down the street, afterwards, feeling good, I was crossing the street when this fucking taxi driver says, 'Get out of the way, you dopey fuck.' Here I am alive with poetry, right? I go home, look in the mirror: am I a dopey fuck? No way!"[29]

Auden expressed a temperamental disdain for the Beats' anti-establishment theatrics—gently scolding Diana Trilling, "I'm ashamed of you," when she told him she'd been emotionally moved by a rambunctious reading given by Ginsberg and Corso at Columbia in 1959[30]—and his disapproval of their emphasis on shock, spontaneity, and solipsism over craft helped contribute to a significant cultural and literary schism among a number of Auden's younger successors, particularly those who knew him as students in New York in the late 1940s and early 1950s. On the one side were Ginsberg and his countercultural allies in what he called "spontaneous bop prosody." And on the other were fellow Columbia poets like Howard, a student friend of Ginsberg's who pointedly reserved judgment on the lasting poetic value of Ginsberg's work in his influential 1969 critical survey of postwar American poetry, *Alone with America*, and Hollander, who was awarded the Yale Younger Poets prize by Auden in 1958 and who notably and negatively reviewed *Howl and Other Poems* in the pages of *Partisan Review* in 1957. For Hollander and Howard and other poets like Louis Simpson (another Columbia student who, despite his poetic differences with the Beats, would end up featured in "Howl" as the man who throws his watch out the window in a rejection of temporality), Anthony Hecht, and Richard Wilbur, Auden offered a model for addressing public themes and private concerns in a form that asserted the implication of the anxious present in the long literary conversation of the past, and in a style that suggested that the chaos of the times hadn't destroyed—indeed, had made more urgent—the need for what Auden in his Freud elegy called a "rational voice." Throughout the postwar decades, this split between those who found in Auden a tutor in the moral and artistic value of form and participation in an ongoing poetic tradition, and those who rebelled against what they felt to be repressive and overly academic convention, would have continuing reverberations and provoke further sometimes bitter poetic skirmishes, including a high-profile clash in the pages of *The New York Times* between Howard and Ginsberg over the merits of Mona Van Duyn's 1971 National Book Award, followed by Howard's dismissal of Ginsberg's *Collected Poems* with a single sentence in the *Boston Review* in 1984. But the serious aesthetic differences that would blossom over the years into furious disputes among his inheritors didn't stop Auden from engaging with the rebellious art of the Beats. And it didn't stop them from seeing him, when they needed to, as an ally in their own efforts at establishing an alternative artistic tradition. Burroughs claimed to have been the first person to give Ginsberg a volume of Auden's poems,[31] and when the influential and Beat-friendly avant-garde magazine, *Neurotica*, was founded in 1947, it was Auden's poem "The Age of Anxiety" that provided the inspiration for its title and editorial ethos of angst and cultural unease.[32] In the 1959 film *Pull My Daisy*, which offers a grittily romantic window into the Beat scene, Kerouac narrates a vignette of Ginsberg and Corso drinking beer and reading their poems to one another in a downtown loft by invoking Auden, along with a number of other American contemporaries, to suggest the literary bona fides of the Beats: "All these poets. Struggling to be poets. Kenneth Fearing and Kenneth Rexroth and W. H. Auden and Louise Bogan, and all the poets. But burning in the purple moonlight if they wanna."[33] And that same year, when Kerouac was trying to market the Beats to a wider public in the pages of *Holiday* magazine, he offered a cinematic catalogue of "the beat night life of New York," complete with parties in artist's lofts, poetry readings in cafes, "Paul Bowles, natty in a Dacron suit, passing through from Morocco," and "the ghost of Herman Melville himself followed by Bartleby the Wall Street Scrivener and Pierre the ambiguous hipster of 1848 out on a walk." And right in the heart of this ecstatic account of avant garde Manhattan, occupying an ambiguous middle ground between the living hipsters and their ghostly literary antecedents, is the legendary elder poet, almost a roving landmark of the scene: "W. H. Auden himself may be seen fumbling by in the rain."[34] Toward the end of his life, walking those same New York streets with a biographer, Ginsberg would echo Kerouac's vision of Auden as an enduring familiar spirit: Pointing out the spot where he had once met Auden, on the corner of Christopher Street in Greenwich Village, Ginsberg observed of the man whose voice had helped him find his own so many decades before, "He has an eternal presence."[35]

◆ ◆ ◆

The symbolic significance of the young Ginsberg's iconic copies of Auden and Rimbaud may seem hard to parse from the perspective of the familiar narratives of postwar American poetry and Auden's customary place within them. A more unlikely pairing of influential poets might seem hard to imagine. Rimbaud, the raging, despairing iconoclastic youth who embarked on his systematic derangement of the senses and repudiated poetry by the age of 21, is seen as the patron of a line of literary art defined by its aggressive experimentalism, non-linearity, and resistance to formal and societal convention: an originator of what Marjorie Perloff has termed a "poetics of indeterminacy," which would include Williams, Pound, Stein, and later poets like Ashbery.[36] Yet in contrast to Jarrell and Bogan's sense of Auden's mid-century omnipresence, if he is acknowledged now to have an American influence at all, Auden is often seen as a conservative emblem of Anglicizing formalism, an "insular Englishman" for whom there was a "brief vogue . . . among Americans who came of age in the 1950s [but whose influence] waned rapidly," in Helen Vendler's words, as younger poets went looking for more adventurous poetic models.[37] One of the ambitions of this book is to argue that, far from enjoying a passing and insubstantial "vogue," Auden's influence was formative and widespread for a startlingly diverse range of poets whose work would go on to define what we talk about when we talk about contemporary American poetry. Part of that project involves suggesting that for many of these poets, as with Ginsberg, the distinctions critics are used to making about competing traditions in American poetry—with often an implied or explicit claim of the superiority of one over another—don't always add up quite so neatly. And that in many important and divergent cases, it is in particular Auden's role in their careers, lives, and poetry that helps to muddy those tidy critical narratives of experiment versus form, radicalism versus traditionalism, political versus quiescent, cosmopolitan ventriloquism versus authentic American song.[38]

In the service of this argument, it's worth pointing out that, for Auden's part, he didn't see himself and Rimbaud in such oppositional terms. Despite Auden's notorious and somewhat theatrical distaste for all things French, Rimbaud was in fact a precursor of iconic significance for Auden. From his earliest work, in "The Journal of an Airman" in *The Orators*, whose final pages constitute a melancholic rewriting of Rimbaud's "Adieu" from *A Season in Hell*, and whose choice of fates for the title character Auden summed up at the time as either "suicide or Rimbaud's declination,"[39] the fiery French renunciator had served as an emblem for Auden's ongoing self-debate about the project and purpose of his art, and the possibility that a poet's most eloquent response to his moment might be silence and exile, as the final lines of the epilogue to *The Orators* suggests: "As he left them there, as he left them there" [*EA*, 110]. In the mid-1930s, Auden cited with approval Rimbaud's dictum, "One must be absolutely modern," as he argued for an artistic and political answer to the question, "How shall the self-conscious man be saved?" [*EA*, 320–21]. And in his first long poem in America, 1940's "New Year Letter," Rimbaud is one of only three poets, alongside Dante and Blake, who preside over the poem's enumerated pantheon of poetic influences, where he is described as "the young Rimbaud guilt demands, / The adolescent with red hands, / Skilful, intolerant, and quick, / Who strangled an old rhetoric" [*CP*, 204]. In that poem, and a year earlier in one of the last poems he wrote before arriving in New York, a sonnet titled "Rimbaud," Auden finds in his rebellious French predecessor an inspirational model for the bold leap he was making as he left his British poetic identity behind and began his new career in America, where he "dreamed of a new self . . . / His truth acceptable to lying men" [*CP*, 182]. The old rhetoric that now needed strangling, in Auden's terms, was that of the 1930s, the "low, dishonest decade" in which demagogic speech, either of dictators or of poets like himself, had shown itself to be either horrifically destructive or, at best, politically futile. And the project of his new American self would be to chart a new course in which poetry's moral and intellectual power would be felt not in its capacity to make something happen but in its ability to allow its readers, in the final lines from Rimbaud's "Adieu," "to possess truth in a single body and soul."[40]

Auden's alliance of himself with Rimbaud's revisionary project was not lost on other younger American poets, including the twenty-three-year-old Frank O'Hara, who in the same year as Kerouac's depiction of Ginsberg flaunting his own devotion to Auden and Rimbaud, would single out for special reverence precisely the same two poets in his poem, "Memorial Day, 1950." In a kind of impressionistic intellectual autobiography, and an ironic commentary on the legacy of the European avant-garde in mid-century America, O'Hara reflects on the impact of painters like Picasso, Klee, and Ernst on his—and by implication, his generation's—imaginative sensibilities, and then lists the poets whose influence was felt with a similar, singular power:

> And those of us who thought poetry
> was crap were throttled by Auden or Rimbaud
> when, sent by some compulsive Juno, we tried
> to play with collages or sprechstimme in their bed.
> Poetry didn't tell me not to play with toys
> but alone I could never have figured out that dolls
> meant death.[41]

Echoing Auden's own imagery of Rimbaud as rhetoric-strangler, O'Hara credits both poets with jolting a generation into an awareness that poetry could be more than the "crap" they had been taught to expect, perhaps in comparison to the work of the experimental painters whose creative demolition of artistic convention, the poem suggests, had provided "shining erector sets" for those who followed them in their ambition to create a new art to reflect the new, war-ravaged realities. Auden and Rimbaud are dually figured as emblems of mythic and youthful strength, as the presumptuous would-be-poets who challenge them in their domain of speech-song end up—like the snakes sent by Juno to destroy the infant Hercules in his crib—getting throttled and dismissed as unthreatening playthings by the hero-poets. The daunting knowledge of poetry's seriousness, difficulty, and power, as wielded by intimidating but inspiring examples like Auden and Rimbaud, suggest for O'Hara, as he puts it a few lines later, "a lesson in utility."

O'Hara had first encountered Auden, on the page and in person, while a student at Harvard in the late 1940s, where Auden embodied one of the opposing poles of fashionable poetic taste on campus. Donald Hall, O'Hara's Harvard contemporary, friend, and fellow poet, describes the poetry scene centering around the college literary magazine: "On the *Advocate* we divided between those who looked back to Yeats and those who looked back to Auden. Ashbery, O'Hara, and [Kenneth] Koch were Auden men: [Robert] Bly and I were Yeats. Adrienne [Rich] was eclectic."[42] Auden had delivered the Phi Beta Kappa poem at Harvard ("Under Which Lyre") in 1946, and O'Hara and Ashbery had met him at a university party after a reading the following year. "All I can remember talking about was asking him whether he liked living in England better than living in America," recalls Ashbery of the occasion. "He said he preferred America, though he preferred the English countryside because it was much tidier looking."[43] Ashbery would write his Senior Thesis on Auden in 1949, and he and Koch, along with O'Hara, would maintain cordial, if distant, social relations with him when they all moved to New York, principally through their friendship with James Schuyler, who, like a number of young New York poets, served a period of apprenticeship as Auden's typist and secretary.

Auden's influence upon O'Hara's poetry was one that O'Hara himself was happy to acknowledge over the course of his career, telling his friend and fellow poet Bill Berkson that Auden had showed him "the possibility of writing down one's metropolitan experiences in a manner that was neither sentimental nor drear."[44] And in April, 1952, O'Hara delivered a lecture on Auden's poetry at "The Club," an informal gathering of artists and writers in Greenwich Village. Characterizing the post-emigration Auden specifically as "an American poet," O'Hara echoes the claim of his poem from two years earlier for Auden's convention-throttling poetic vision: "Auden extended our ideas of what poetry could be; his poems saw clearly into obscure areas of modern life and they provided us with obscure and complex insights into areas which had hitherto been banal." And contrasting Auden's "vernacular" style with Eliot, whose own transatlantic journey had exchanged an American identity for a British one, O'Hara approvingly observes Auden's interest in the intimate exploration of "experiences and expressions of what had been looked down upon by the pretentious estheticism and mysticism of the Eliot school."[45]

O'Hara's "Memorial Day 1950" continues its account of generational artistic awakening with a dismissive double allusion to the Yeats he had rejected in favor of Auden, and to his elder contemporary from the prewar generation, Delmore Schwartz, who had used Yeats's words for the title of his famous 1937 story, "In Dreams Begin Responsibilities": "Our responsibilities did not begin / In dreams, though they began in bed. Love is first of all / A lesson in utility." Schwartz's narrative of an insecure and neurotic son dreaming about watching a movie of his own parents' courtship—and screaming back at the screen, "Don't do it. It's not too late to change your minds, both of you. Nothing good will come of it. Only remorse, hatred, scandal and two children whose characters are monstrous!"[46]—had come to be seen as a defining expression of the pre–World War II generation's anxious relations with its forebears, but O'Hara refuses to align himself with such anxiety. Instead of Schwartz's horror at an imagined primal scene, or Yeats's notion of a self revealed through an engagement with visionary abstractions, O'Hara offers a different ideal of self-conception: self-generation and discovery through erotic exploration. Responsibilities, and an awareness of the relation of one's self to others, are discovered, in O'Hara's model, through the engagement with self and otherness that comes "in bed," through sex. And this vision of erotic education and illumination is explicitly allied to an analogous process of poetic development. The bed of "Auden or Rimbaud," into which the bold ephebe had dared to venture, becomes an erotic and poetic schoolroom. "Love is first of all a lesson in utility," O'Hara suggests, then concludes ten lines later with an epiphanic revelation: "Poetry is as useful as a machine!" Both love and poetry are defined by O'Hara through their utility and their synonymity.

This perspective on the intimate theoretical relation between poetry and eros is one that would prove crucial not only to O'Hara's poetics but to that of many of O'Hara's contemporaries, including, as we will see in succeeding chapters, Ashbery and Merrill and Rich, in their individually distinct ways. And it's not a coincidence that O'Hara should use Auden as his emblem for this model of poetry in which, as he would notably define it a few years later in his mock-manifesto, "Personism" (1959), "The poem is at last between two persons instead of two pages."[47] A "law like love" [*CP*, 262] is the relentless object of Auden's poetic quest, from his earliest poems which "move / Different or with a different love" [*CP*,

29], to the lover of "As I Walked Out One Evening" whose song of eternal love is answered by the cruel facts of time and the fickle heart, to the resonant, doomed assertion of "September 1, 1939" that "We must love one another or die" [*SP*, 97]. And Auden explicitly associated his poems' obsessive expression of erotic yearning to the desire to connect with a reader through writing, as in his 1939 poem in celebration of his new love with Kallman, "Heavy Date":

> When two lovers meet, then
> There's an end of writing
> Thought and Analytics:
>   Lovers, like the dead,
> In their loves are equal;
> Sophomores and peasants,
> Poets and their critics
>   Are the same in bed. [*CP*, 262]

As in O'Hara's later poem, love and poetry are expressions of the same desire whose object is a shared experience of connection, commonality, and engagement of self with otherness. And just as the relationship between Ariel and Caliban, figures of the shaping imagination, is depicted in "The Sea and the Mirror" as that of a pair of squabbling lovers, for Auden, as for O'Hara (and Ashbery, whose Harvard thesis would take that relationship as its primary subject), the erotics of poetry are a touch-and-go affair, grounded in an awareness of the doomed and fleeting nature of the relationship—like all human relationships, bounded either by heartbreak, boredom, or death—between the poet and his promiscuous reader/lover. But its very ephemerality makes it that much more precious and endlessly pursued, even in the face of the inevitable failure of that idealized moment of connection on the page or on the bed. "If equal affection cannot be, / Let the more loving one be me" [*CP*, 584], Auden wrote in 1957, long after Kallman's own promiscuity had crushed Auden's dreams of faultless love, but he's writing about poetry as much as he's lamenting Kallman's cruelty and absence. The poet goes on writing, just as the spurned lover goes on loving, in the vain but eternal hope that the wandering ideal reader/lover will finally hear his call and love him back.

That O'Hara was familiar with both the gossipy details of Auden's bumpy love-life, as well as its relation to his art, is made clear in a poem he wrote a few years before "Memorial Day, 1950," entitled "Mr Auden in Love: Twice." Written in 1947 while still a student at Harvard, and unpublished during O'Hara's life, the poem reflects not only the young O'Hara's sincere emulation of Auden's poetic mode, but also his fascination with the elder poet's biography, personality, and psyche. Presenting itself as two short love-songs in the voice of Auden, the poem is a complex effort at getting inside Auden's head and offers an explicitly Audenesque view on the proximity of love and pain. The poem is addressed to an unnamed "You," who is both the speaker's lover and supreme antagonist, who "tortures" the speaker with malice and indifference, hurting him into poetry: "[W]hile / I watch you wait for advantage over me / my heart speaks / and alone hears its hurt."[48] The poem ends with a single, plaintive sentence:

> You
> who have seized me in your silence
> as the desert wind's desire
>   inflames the dune
>
> when
> simoon's simmer arouses its sands
> to heat that special hades:
>   if you hear
>
> while
> you stand still beneath the bulb's electric stain
> the fine-grained undulation
>   of my love's ululant unbitting
>
> why
> do you remain so reticent of rapine
> even though my blood
>   is blaring to share yours with you?

O'Hara deploys, in a precarious balance between parody and earnestness, a variety of Audenesque rhetorical effects, including Auden's enthusiasm for obscure, exotic vocabulary mined from the *OED* ("simoon," "unbitting"), and the aggressive alliteration of Auden's earliest saga-inflected verse. The "silence" of the resisting or rejecting lover/reader, "reticent of rapine," explicitly recalls one of Auden's first and best-known poems ("From the very first coming down") in which an elusive beloved is characterized, in words that also describe the poetic mode of both the early evasive Auden and the young, mask-wearing O'Hara, as "never . . . more reticent, / Always afraid to say more than it meant" [*CP*, 29]. And the speaker's "ululant" and elaborately figurative love-song, heard but ignored by the lover "beneath the bulb's electric stain," further associates O'Hara's imagined Auden with the singing lover of "As I Walked Out One Evening," who grandiosely proclaims, from a similarly tawdry locale ("under an arch of the railway"), that "Love has no ending" [*CP*, 133]. O'Hara's short Auden-channeling poem functions on at least four distinct levels: First, it emulates one of Auden's most representative poetic modes, the song of "the more loving one" to the unresponsive ideal. Second, we can read O'Hara's poem, as we read so many of Auden's, as the anxious call of the poet to the reader, whose response—or even existence—is a cause of doubt and authorial angst. Third, in its claim of ventriloquism of Auden, it suggests specific knowledge of his tortured relationship with Kallman, whose wanderings and theatrical cruelty to the long-suffering Auden had become, by the time of O'Hara's poem, a well-known piece of celebrity gossip among those who followed Auden's American career closely. And fourth and most suggestively, we can also see the poem as a kind of poetic love-song from O'Hara to Auden himself. By taking on Auden's voice, O'Hara literalizes the desire expressed in the poem's final lines: "My blood / is blaring to share yours with you." The junior poet takes the part of the abject and devoted lover of the indifferent, aloof object of desire, into whose poetic bed he will claim in "Memorial Day, 1950" to have crept, and in doing so makes the scene of seduction a scene of poetic instruction.

This vision of poetic relations, in which younger poets find their own poetic identity through the effort of sharing the blood, or the metaphorical poetic bed, or the voice, of those influences to whom they are attracted and through an engagement with whom they learn the limits of their own poetic self, is one that a number of Auden's inheritors will find useful and enabling. It is an idea of influence based on acknowledgment, emulation, and creative utility, and it is a model that many of his succes-

sors associate explicitly with Auden. And while this influential notion of
influence is not restricted by gender, sexuality, or any particular poetic
ideology, as the broad range of poets who make use of Auden in their
own projects of poetic self-fashioning makes clear, it does have strong
resonances with another specific aspect of Auden's influence, in particular his role as an exemplar for, and champion of, younger gay poets. His
private life, or his attitudes toward sex, were not especially attractive to
the younger gay poets who knew him: "We did not want to live the way
Wystan Auden lived," notes Richard Howard, recalling Auden's unglam-
orous personal manners and habits, including his fondness for Benzedrine, alcohol, rough trade, and urinating in the sink.[49] But for poets like
Howard, O'Hara, Ginsberg, Ashbery, Schuyler, Merrill, and Rich his
significance as a publicly gay poet and intellectual was enormous. And
the vision of poetic influence as a scene of same-sex erotic and intellectual exchange that one finds in poems like Merrill's *The Changing Light
at Sandover* or in Ginsberg's "Supermarket in California," can trace its
origins through, if not directly to, Auden's own homosocial poetics and
his position as a pioneering figure in the burgeoning American gay artistic subculture in the 1940s and 1950s.[50]

◆ ◆ ◆

The identification of Auden with this particularly utilitarian, assimilative construction of poetic influence was one made explicitly by Randall
Jarrell in a major series of lectures on Auden he gave at Princeton in 1951
and 1952. Drawing upon the numerous significant essays he had published on Auden in the previous decade, in his first lecture Jarrell defined
Auden's originality specifically in terms of his exploitation of his own
influences:

> Look into his book at random: there will be, on the first fifty or
> sixty pages, blues; Calypso songs; nursery rhymes; imitations
> of sagas, of Gilbert and Sullivan, of Henry James, of Greek
> choruses, of Lord Byron, Riding, Graves, Joyce, Skelton, Eliot,
> Yeats, Brecht, Perse, Rilke—many a reader must have mur-
> mured wistfully, "I just haven't read enough poetry to know
> *all* the poets Auden is influenced by." . . . Auden's originality is
> plainer than his influences, and he is, very obviously, one of the

most original poets alive. An ordinary poet is controlled by influences—he imitates, is possessed, against his own will or without his own knowledge; Auden consciously and actively *uses* influences, borrows them almost [as] he would borrow a word, a stanza-form, or a plot. . . . The affable familiar ghosts who possessed Yeats's wife announced to Yeats that they had "come to bring him metaphors for his poems"; all the poets of the world seem to be saying to Auden, "We have come to bring you techniques for your poems."[51]

In a later lecture, Jarrell returns to this theme, observing of Auden, "He is unusually skillful at analyzing someone else's work, taking out what he likes, and synthesizing a new style of his own that will include this."[52] As Stephen Burt summarizes Jarrell's thinking, one of his chief objections to Auden's American writing was its move toward what he perceived as a poetry of rationalism that "made too many concessions to the conscious mind." So, with his characteristic love–hate ambivalence toward the poet who had been so important to his own critical and poetic development, Jarrell's analysis comes with a double edge: "Technically, Auden is perhaps the most spectacularly and consciously accomplished poet since Swinburne; and this is rather disquieting to us—we know what we think of Swinburne."[53] But Jarrell makes a telling leap from discussing Auden's own facile use of his influences to speculating on the way Auden's assimilative example could itself influence an imagined younger poet, who might "think of Auden as a Proteus upon whose back he can ride off in all directions."[54] Despite Jarrell's mixed feelings about Auden's American career, his analysis of Auden's utility for future poets was indeed borne out by the careers of a huge range of different poets who used what they found in Auden to ride off in all directions across the landscape of American poetry. And one of the primary imaginative contributions he made to those poets was a sense that, just as he did, they could consciously and actively use their own influences, including but obviously not limited to Auden's own poems, to help discover and define their own poetic projects and purposes. As in Jarrell's list of Auden's omnivorous utilitarianism, ranging from the blues to Greek choruses to Brecht, those influences could come from any place, any tradition, any time, and need not be limited to some abstract or arbitrary notion of what the age or national convention demanded. To be a young American poet in the "Age of Auden," those years during the 1940s and 1950s when Auden presided over the American poetry scene, was to be free—or, as Auden himself would term it, "burdened"—to define oneself in terms of one's choice of inheritance and influence among a bewildering panoply of possible options opened up by the post-Modernist collapse of the notion of a unified native tradition. And Auden was a crucial guide and teacher and example in the act and art of making that choice.[55]

Two decades earlier, one of Jarrell's poetic contemporaries, Elizabeth Bishop, in notes for an unfinished 1937 essay on Auden, observed of influential original poets in general that, "By 'pretending' the existence of a language appropriate to the 'things' it must deal with, the language is forced into being. It is learned by one person, by a few, by all who can become interested in that poet's poetry."[56] For Bishop, Auden's poems are "an excellent example of the power of pretence at work," in that they embody "the tendency, described by William Empson, of what a poet writes to become *real*; the tendency toward 'prophecy'; obscurity, and 'influence,' are all [departments] of this original act of pretence." This creative "act of pretence," as Bishop terms it, whereby a poet's efforts to respond to reality end up giving a shape, structure, and a name to that reality for those who come after them, is a helpful theoretical formulation for the way Auden's poetry, and his ideas about the making of poetry and poetic identity, affected his American inheritors, particularly in the generation after Bishop and Jarrell's own. When Bishop is writing in the late 1930s, she credits him principally with being "the founder of the 'forsaken factory' school of literary landscape painting," but her notes conclude with a quotation from D. H. Lawrence that suggests in broader terms the way Auden offered a model in whom his successors could find their own distinctive and divergent identities usefully reflected: "It provides an emotional experience, and then, if we have the courage of our own feelings, it becomes a mine of practical truth." It was Auden's poetic pretensions—in the etymological sense of stretching in order to contain—toward the political, cultural, and private confusions of the 1930s, written from the perspective of a poet anguished but optimistic at the possibility of poetry's power to diagnose and heal "this country of ours where nobody is well," that asserted themselves most strongly over the generation of Bishop, Jarrell, Shapiro, Bogan, Berryman, and Roethke, each of whom adopted in differing ways some of the pre-immigration Auden's rhetorical strategies to help address their own generational experience. But it was Auden's responses to his new American career and life that helped set the terms for those who would come to their artistic maturity after his arrival in the United States. For them he would serve, in Bishop's terms, as "a mine of practical truth" for developing their own poetic identities in the wake of war and international Modernism. James Merrill would pursue Bishop's metaphor—and connect it with Auden's well-known affection for old mining machinery—in *The Changing Light at Sandover*, in which Auden—"our mine of good sense" [*CLS*, 306]—serves as his Virgilian guide in that epic Dantean descent into the underworld of the human psyche, poetic tradition, and the process of achieving poetic originality through exploiting and refining the imaginative ore of one's influences.

Auden's role in postwar American literary culture also went beyond providing a lexicon from which younger poets could quarry their own poetic resources. His practical omnipresence in the lives, educations, and careers of countless poets was another essential aspect of his influence. For the Jarrell/Bishop generation, he was both a celebrity and an elder peer, as suggestively illustrated in the well-known photograph at the Gotham Book Shop on the occasion of a birthday celebration for the Sitwells—showing Auden perched brashly and unselfconsciously on a ladder above a gathering of American poets including Jarrell, Schwartz, and Bishop. Auden wrote Guggenheim recommendations for Bogan, served on prize committees with Lowell, and was the best man at Roethke's wedding and loaned him his Ischia retreat for his honeymoon. For the younger generation of O'Hara and Ginsberg, he was a canonized icon, an enthusiastic teacher, and an institutionally powerful figure in their early careers. Maxine Kumin credits Auden as her greatest influence—"Almost everything I know how to do with the line, I learned from absorbing Auden," she notes—and recalled for an interviewer the significance of both his frequent public readings and the utility of his example for younger women poets in the 1940s and 1950s: "I probably attended a dozen readings he gave, in and around Boston, in his carpet slippers. I worshipped him from afar. Today, it must seem a strange influence—an Anglo-American male. You'd expect I would say—I don't know—some woman role model. There really was no one at that time."[57]

In 1982, years after that early exposure to Auden's personal and textual authority, Kumin would reflect in verse, from her honored position as Consultant in Poetry to the Library of Congress (a title renamed three years later as U.S. Poet Laureate) on the lessons learned:

> Poetry
> Makes nothing happen.
> It survives in the valley of its saying.
> Auden taught us that.
> Next year another
> Consultant will sit
> under the hand with the arrow
> that props the door ajar
> for metaphor.
> New poets will lie on their backs
> listening in the valley
> making nothing happen
> overhearing history
> history time
> personal identity
> inching toward Armageddon.[58]

A distinguished poet now herself, Kumin reframes her Audenesque inheritance while troubling the same questions that prompted Auden's influential assertion forty-three years before: What can poetry do in a world where history, time, and personal identity are slipping into despair and confusion? Her answer is to dwell in the semantic ambiguity of Auden's phrase, where the "nothing" that poetry "makes happen" is both an acknowledgment of art's political futility and a positive assertion against a tide of darkness. A poet actively makes "nothing" happen; she creates a space of solitude and thought, like her quiet Library of Congress office, and offers at least a dialectical counterweight to the terrifying somethings ("Weeks apart / a president and pope are shot") being made to happen all around us by the same forces that hurt Auden into his American poetry.

Sylvia Plath, like the young Kumin, experienced the impact of the American Auden as a pedagogical, self-defining one. As she records in her college journal on the occasion of Auden's teaching-visit to Smith in the spring of 1953, it was not only through his books and poems that he made his influence felt:

> Auden tossing his big head back with a twist of wide ugly grin-
> ning lips, his sandy hair, his coarse tweedy brown jacket, his
> burlap textured voice and the crackling brilliant utterances—
> the naughty mischievous boy genius, and the inconsistent white
> hairless skin of his legs, and the short puffy stubbed fingers—
> and the carpet slippers—beer he drank, and smoked Lucky
> Strikes in a black holder, gesticulating with a white new ciga-
> rette in his hands, holding matches, talking in a gravelly incisive
> tone about how Caliban is the natural bestial projection, Ariel
> the creative imaginative, and all the lyrical abstrusities of their
> love and cleavage, art and life, the mirror and the sea. God, god,
> the stature of the man. And next week, in trembling audacity, I
> approach him with a sheaf of the poems. Oh, god, if this is life,
> half-heard, glimpsed, smelled, with beer and cheese sandwiches
> and the god-eyed tall-minded ones, let me never go blind, or get
> shut off from the agony of learning, the horrible pain of trying
> to understand.[59]

In the eyes of the twenty-year-old Plath, "the stature of the man" rests on Auden's human presence, a "god-eyed tall-minded one" with hairless legs and stubby fingers, as much as it does on the greatness of his poems. And it is the human encounter with the benevolent, eccentric genius that sends her into poetic paroxysms and affirms her ambitions to make a life in, and of, poetry. For Plath, as for many of her contemporaries, accounts of Auden's influence are never simply a matter of recording their appropriation and adaptation—or even repudiation and rejection—of his characteristic poetic modes and forms and ideas. His impact was felt as both person and poet, in both the lives and the poems of young poets. Auden was, to his inheritors as well as to himself, in the words of the title of his first American volume, a "double man." In a letter home that same spring, Plath reflects this doubleness, pledging fealty to both the charismatic man and his art: "The great W. H. Auden spoke in chapel this week, and I saw him for the first time. He is my conception of the perfect poet: tall, with a big leonine head and a sandy mane of hair, and a lyrically gigantic stride. Needless to say he has a wonderfully textured British accent, and I adore him with a big Hero Worship. I would someday like to touch the Hem of his Garment and say in a very small adoring voice: Mr. Auden, I haveapome for you: 'I found my God in Auden.'"[60]

An even younger student poet than Plath, Marilyn Hacker, recalls amusing and inspiring encounters as a teenager with middle-aged Auden in their shared New York neighborhood in the early 1960s. She recounts in a sonnet an early visit to Auden's notoriously disheveled East Village apartment in 1961 in response to an "invitation to tea":

> We sit in a cold room. A. pours the tea.
> A gaudy twilight helps us hide ourselves.
> I try to read the titles on the shelves
> and juggle cup and saucer on my knee.
> A. tells me anecdotes that I have read.
> I poise a studied ambiguity.
> A. wonders will I turn my head and see
> The crumpled blue kimono on the bed.
> I pick up a crystal ashtray to watch
> its slow rotation slap a waterfall
> of iridescent limbs across a wall,
> fumble with cigarettes. A. strikes a match
> as the enormity of darkness swells
> upward in a cacophony of bells.[61]

Auden's double identity as literary celebrity whose small-talk is already familiar from books and interviews, an eccentric occasionally awkward human being, sitting in a cold gloomy room and pouring tea, is manifest in Hacker's poem, as is her projection of the Auden poems she has read upon his living breathing person. As he strikes a match to light a cigarette in his dim apartment, he enacts before her in both literal and humbly quotidian fashion one of his most resonant poetic images, showing an affirming flame in the darkness for a young poet looking for connection and guidance. Auden's willingness to serve as avuncular mentor to younger poets, on college campuses or in his home, was a crucial aspect of his American influence. And the prospect of meeting the powerful yet available literary lion, showing him their work, and learning what they could from him, was an opportunity many younger poets

eagerly pursued. And as Richard Howard remembers, Auden's pedagogical function wasn't limited merely to private encounters or formal
readings and lectures:

> We were all very aware of him as part of our New York educa-
> tion. . . . I remember [going] to the first performance of "The
> Cocktail Party" by T. S. Eliot . . . and that moment in the second
> act when Henry Harcourt Reilly suddenly assumes the aspect of
> quotation and says those lines from "Prometheus Unbound." The
> audience rustles plaintively—they know they're hearing some-
> thing but they don't know what it is . . . And Wystan Auden was
> sitting maybe six rows in front of us, and he turned around to
> the whole of the mezzanine and he said, "Shelley, my dears!" He
> really sort of felt that he was still at Gresham's School and he was
> telling us things that we ought to know. There was that capacity.
> He had that quality of educating us.[62]

Anthony Hecht, along with Hollander, Howard, and Richard Wilbur, an avowed inheritor of an Audenesque vision of the aesthetic and
ethical value of form, and who would end up spending summers on
Ischia with Auden after the war, remembered in particular Auden's frequent book reviews in *The New Republic*, *Partisan Review*, and elsewhere
as a crucial part of his and other poets' literary education: "I think I was
almost never disappointed in a discovery of Auden's. His taste, his acu-
men, was as near to infallible as one could want."[63]

Though older than poets like Hecht, Plath, Kumin, or O'Hara,
Robert Hayden's early career also evolved under Auden's explicit pedagogical and professional influence, especially during the years Hayden
studied with Auden at the University of Michigan in the early 1940s. It
was Auden's instruction in formal discipline and the handling of disparate poetic materials that helped Hayden develop the complex polyvocal, transhistorical schematic of his most important early poem, "Middle
Passage," along with other crucial poems from his prize-winning *Black
Spear* project.[64] "I think he showed me my strengths and weaknesses as a
poet in ways no one else had done before," Hayden observed.[65] William
Bronk, another poet of Jarrell's generation whose career flowered late,
and one not often considered in relation to Auden, reflects on Auden's
constructive professional presence in postwar literary culture, even as he

recognized their aesthetic differences: "I don't know that Auden influenced me at all, but I liked his work, and I had known for a long time someone who has also known Auden. . . . Auden was the judge for the Yale Series, and I guess that was when the personal contact started. . . . I sent him *My Father Photographed with Friends*, and he didn't choose it, but he wrote me a very nice note and said that if I came to New York sometime, he would be receptive if I wanted to come see him, and I did."[66] And even a poet like Charles Bukowski, who embodies a certain vivid strain of antiestablishment American poetics, could list Auden among those who helped him do his literary work: "[T]he best of Auden / the best of Jeffers / they helped immensely."[67]

As Bronk's recollection suggests, it was probably in his role as judge for the Yale Younger Poets Prize that Auden exerted his most notable institutional influence on the shape of the postwar American poetic canon. From 1946 to 1958, Auden selected ten unpublished poets—in two years of his judgeship he deemed none of the submitted manuscripts worth publication—many of whom would go on to establish distinguished and distinctive careers that would mark out much of the terrain of postwar American verse. Among the innovations of Auden's tenure was to open up the contest—at that point one of the few major institutional avenues for publication by younger American poets—to poets who wrote in English, regardless of their country of birth, as attested by his first selection, the London-born Joan Murray. His choice of Murray, who had died at age 24 in 1942, marked a break with the kind of poetry published by the series in other ways as well, not least in its aggressive difficulty and interiority, along with pointing up the extent to which Auden's textual influence intersected with his personal professional influence, since Murray may have been among his students at the New School in New York in the early 1940s.[68] In the succeeding years, Auden published and wrote introductions for the first books of Robert Horan, Rosalie Moore, W. S. Merwin, Adrienne Rich, Edgar Bogardus, Daniel Hoffman, John Ashbery, James Wright, John Hollander, and William Dickey.

Auden's introductions were characteristically idiosyncratic, often reflecting whatever particular intellectual hobbyhorse he was riding at the moment of its composition, but nonetheless illuminating of both the poets' general poetic projects and the extent to which they did or did not follow his own personal sense of aesthetics. The extent to which

Auden's choices reflected a startling catholicity of taste can be seen in
the juxtaposition, for instance, of Horan's and Moore's ecstatic and
Hart Crane–influenced verses (especially in light of Auden's own statements of his distaste for Crane), with the wry understatement of Bogardus. And against the claims, occasionally made, that Auden's selection
amounted to an effort to replicate his own formalist mode and stifle divergence from convention, can be placed the careers of poets like Rich
and Wright whose poetics would evolve in notable and important ways
from the formalism of their early books. Auden's method of selection
could itself be somewhat unconventional, including—most famously—
his direct solicitation of manuscripts from Ashbery and O'Hara in 1955
when he found the manuscripts from which he had been asked to choose
unsatisfactory. As he wrote from Ischia to his editors back in New Haven, "What bothers me particularly is that a young poet (John Ashbery)
whom I know personally told me he was submitting a manuscript this
year. I have reservations about such of his poems as I have seen, but they
are certainly better than any of the manuscripts which have reached
me."[69] Auden wrote to both Ashbery and O'Hara to send him their
poems, putting the close friends in direct competition with another—
a contest that Ashbery eventually won. Auden elaborated avuncularly
on his "reservations" about both of the younger poets' work in his letter
of gentle rejection to O'Hara, observing, "I think you (and John too,
for that matter) must watch what is always the great danger with any
'surrealistic' style, namely of confusing authentic non-logical relations
which arouse wonder with accidental ones which arouse mere surprise
and in the end fatigue."[70] Auden's contributions to the books he published often went beyond mere selection and admiring introduction. It
was his decision to title Ashbery's now-famous first book *Some Trees*,
and in letters to Merwin in 1951 about his prize-winning manuscript,
he suggests not only which poems could be dropped to make the text a
manageable length, but also recommends specific edits of poems: "If you
will forgive my saying so, I feel that both the 'Anabasis' poems and 'Rime
of the Palmers,' which I like very much, could be improved by extensive
cutting. One has to be very careful with lyric stanzas to be certain that
every stanza, however good and interesting in itself, is essential to the
structure of the poem as a whole. Look how you improved 'Epitaph,'
by suddenly reducing the whole thing to four lines!"[71] In quintessential

schoolmaster mode, he even corrects Merwin's prosody ("by the way, 'systole' is a 3 syllable word"), and in another letter he advises cutting "the repetition of 'A dropping stone' which I feel is a rhetorical device without, in this particular instance, an emotional justification." He does eventually drop the pedagogical role, however, expressing his frustration with the formal demands of his job as judge: "As you probably know, the Yale Press idiotically insists on an introduction by me which is embarrassing for both of us. If there are any facts about yourself which would be useful to me in writing the damned thing or anything you would like or not like to have said, please let me know."[72] He also offers to write Merwin a fellowship recommendation and gives him advice on renting a cheap London flat.[73]

♦ ♦ ♦

Writing from his New York City deathbed in 1935, an elderly Edwin Arlington Robinson advised a friend on new trends in poetry: "I doubt if you would care much for Auden or Spender. They are for the youngsters."[74] Robinson's wry alertness to Auden's appeal and utility to the next generations of American poets, as well as his ambivalence about the value of that influence, suggests a tension that would characterize much of Auden's American critical reception in the years after his arrival in America. While prewar "youngsters" like Jarrell, Bishop, Shapiro, and Bogan found his voice a seductive and sometimes overpowering presence in their own work, and the postwar generation of poets like Ginsberg, O'Hara, Ashbery, and Rich found in him a Proteus, as Jarrell foresaw, upon whose back they could ride off in all directions, Auden's impact on American poetry was by no means an uncontested one. For many younger poets and critics Auden represented an unwanted and negative presence in the American poetic landscape. William Carlos Williams, just twelve years younger than Robinson, was a powerful voice of principled opposition to what he saw as both Auden's "obscurity of purpose"[75] and his rationalist "error" in suggesting "that all writing is an instrument."[76] Using Auden as a foil to articulate his own influential ideas on the relation between living language and poetic form, Williams asks in 1941, "How can an intelligent man say to himself that he will take some line, some arbitrary or convenient stanza, and that he is going to use it and make the words fit? He may even succeed but if he does it will be only at the cost of missing his MAJOR opportunity, as Auden obviously does and a whole train of copyists in his train. The major imperative is to make the line fit the language, not the language the line, and to discover there the new structural integer, completely new, forged under the hammering of contemporary necessity to make a more comprehensive and significant structure."[77] For Williams, Auden is a misguided inheritor and transmitter of an Eliotic notion of poetic impersonality and formal detachment, leading "a whole train of copyists" into error. And Auden's original sin, for which no amount of craft and effort can compensate, is his Englishness. In a 1948 lecture that would prove a central text for the students in Williams's own poetic train, "The Poem as a Field of Action," he again uses Auden as a cautionary example of what American poetry should not become, and foregrounds Auden's country of origin as a poetic dead-end from which his departure for America could not save him: "Auden might have gone to France or to Italy or to South America or following Rimbaud to Ceylon or Timbuctoo. No! He came to the United States and became a citizen. Now the crisis, the only crisis which could drive such a man, a distinguished poet, to that would be that he had come to an end of some sort in his poetic means—something that England could no longer supply, and that he came here implicitly to find an answer—in another language. As yet I see no evidence that he has found it."[78] The exhaustedness of the English poetic well, in contrast to the vigor of the flowing American fountain, is explicitly allied to the issue of Auden's formal mastery, which, as Williams sees it, betrays an allegiance to a dead and empty conventionalism that keeps true human vitality forever beyond the reach of his art: "Look at his poems with this in view—his very skill seems to defeat him." Williams nationalizes the question of poetic form: America as the open discursive field of action versus England as a closed and backward-looking island of self-conscious etiolated technique. Auden's importation of that poetic toxin into the American poetic bloodstream is for Williams an unfortunate sequel to the Anglophilic and cerebral "great catastrophe" of Eliot's "The Waste Land."[79]

The harshness of Williams's polemical rhetoric exceeded any personal animus the two poets actually felt, as Auden allied himself immediately upon his arrival in 1939 with a group of other prominent writers and artists, calling themselves "Les Amis de William Carlos Williams," that dedicated itself—on the five occasions it actually met during its brief existence—to advocating on behalf of Williams's under-recognized contributions to American poetry.[80] And in 1946, Williams wrote to the poetry archivist Charles Abbott of the news of being offered an honorary degree, asking in disbelief, "Did you say Auden had something to do with this? Now, I know he's really intent on becoming an American. If true, the situation as it concerns him would be really very touching. It does him also honor."[81] And Williams felt sufficiently admiring of Auden's poetic skill ("more skillful than I am though I feel not the slightest jealousy toward him") to invite him in 1947 to join with him in convening a high-level private summit-meeting on the state of contemporary verse: "[F]our or five men, 'master' poets such as Auden and myself might profitably get together here, at my house, over a week-end to discuss the technical advances that had been made in the writing of poetry in modern times." Through the expert study by these "masters" of a representative group of poetic texts, including Milton's *Samson Agonistes*, Pound's *Cantos*, and Eliot's *Four Quartets*, Williams reasoned, "Reams of incompetencies could be wiped out in a day and some sort of basis for a true criticism of poems as technical constructions could be arrived at."[82] Despite pitching the idea to Auden twice, the meeting never happened, though a few years later in 1952, in a letter to Robert Lowell, Williams hinted at the warm personal feelings between the two "master" poets: "I wish I could go to Ischia next year. Auden offered me or us his villa there, but I did not take him up. I am a little afraid of it, but it would be marvelous if we could get ourselves to do it."[83]

But while Williams may have felt himself to be Auden's amicable professional antagonist, the force of his polemic carried considerable weight with other younger poets who saw in Auden an icon to be smashed rather than emulated. In 1950, three days before O'Hara would write worshipfully of Auden in "Memorial Day 1950," Robert Creeley was lamenting Auden's malign influence in a letter to Charles Olson:

Other things: had whacked at [friend and publisher Jacob] Leed this morning abt the biz of the new romanticists, etc., Rule Britannia, etc. I.e., cannot think that they are the ones to bring guts back to the wasteland, etc. Cannot think that anything 'but great clarity can cut thru. . . .' [quoting Pound] Do not think

they have it. To be sure, now&again something to admire & wd
that good intentions & a love: cd buildmore than claptrap. To
hell with that. Wd make use of what was of use: there anywhere:
but wd not 'subscribe' to that out. To hit them: as the 'noo' sav-
iors: is to forget that a constant opp has been up against Auden
& co etc. For many yrs. If only these: the dr, stevens, moore, ep,
etc. THEY carried the weight and useless to shift it at this late
date to a bunch of sun daft daisy pickers.[84]

Like Williams—"the dr" in the list of weight-carrying opposers of
the "Rule Britannia," along with Wallace Stevens, Marianne Moore, and
Pound—Creeley sees "Auden & co" as part of an unwanted British inva-
sion of gutlessness and "claptrap" that threatens a more authentic and
vigorous native strain of American verse. Creeley's description of Auden
and his admirers as "a bunch of sun daft daisy pickers" also evocatively
dismisses them in terms that suggest disdain beyond mere national chau-
vinism. To be an Audenesque poet is to be feckless, myopic, and effete,
in contrast to the weight-lifting far-seeing action-poets of the American
opposition. It is tempting, if perhaps a little unfair to read too much
into Creeley's offhand remark, to speculate that part of the resistance
to Auden's influence on American poetry stemmed for some from an
uncomfortable (and perhaps unconscious) association and conflation
of Auden's poetic style with his very public sexuality, in which a native
American tradition is figured as a field of masculine action and expan-
siveness, with fastidious Audenesque craft representing a feminizing
threat to that virile self-definition. A narrative that frames the ideological and formal conflicts in postwar American poetry in terms of sexual
anxiety is, of course, complicated not only by Whitman's foundational
role in the American tradition championed by Williams and Creeley,
but also by a poet like Robert Duncan who, being no fan of Auden's
influence on his contemporaries, also found no discordance in his own
work between a Williams-derived open form and a gay poetic perspective.[85] But the complex of identities represented by Auden—English,
formalist, rationalist, intellectual, gay—certainly seemed to combine
into a profile that was seen to be at odds with what some of Auden's an-
tagonists felt it authentically meant to be, as Williams influentially put
it, "in the American grain."

Auden's Englishness was also a point of professional irritation for some who resented the fashionability of exotic expatriates on the burgeoning poetry-reading circuit, where reputations were made and honorariums earned. As Charles Olson complained to the Canadian poet Irving Layton about having been bumped from a reading at McGill in favor of Auden and two other notional Englishmen: "[B]y god, if you mean what you say abt us Americans (EP WCW & CO, say, not to speak of Creeley etc) how come you find the till empty just now??? How come the money got spent on Auden (Eng) Campbell (Eng) Viereck (*Eng*)?"[86] Despite Roy Campbell's South African origins, and Peter Viereck being born in New York and educated, like Olson and Creeley, at Harvard, their alienness from the anti-formal tradition of Williams and Pound along with perhaps their unapologetic political conservatism, gets them lumped in with Auden as presumptively "English," taking scarce poetry dollars out of the pockets of "American" poets like Olson ("CO") himself.

The emphatic presence of Pound ("EP") next to Williams in both Olson's and Creeley's genealogies of authentic American poetry (as well as their shared Poundian shorthand epistolary style) points both to his own crucial importance and influence over the development of American poetry, but also to the fascinating parallels between Pound and Auden as perceived icons of rival traditions. In her own study of Pound's American poetic legacy, Marjorie Perloff asks, "What is it in Pound's oeuvre that has made such a difference in the poetry of the later twentieth century, a difference that transcends, in curious ways, the local differences between individual poets?"[87] As this discussion of the huge and diverse range of postwar poets who owe artistic debts to Auden should make clear, we can ask much the same question of Auden as well. And Perloff herself, as she traces the Poundian influence on poets as diverse as Louis Zukofsky, the Black Mountain School, and Robert Lowell, also notes Auden's significance as a contending alternative to the Pound-focused narrative of American poetry, observing that Auden's poetry "represents a variant on the Pound model that has had great influence on such poets as James Merrill and John Ashbery," while further pointing to theoretical affinities between Auden and Pound-identified poets like Zukofsky and Jerome Rothenberg.[88]

Both poetic and biographical ironies surround the cultural positioning of Pound and Auden as American literary antitheses, including the obvious fact that, as Perloff suggests, many younger poets—like Ginsberg, Hollander, Merrill, and many more—found both elder writers important to the development of their own artistic identities and projects. Richard Howard's *Alone With America*, for instance, prominently announces its dedication, "To Ezra Pound and to W. H. Auden."[89] It's also amusing to note that in his 1936 introduction to the *Oxford Book of Modern Verse*, Yeats chastises Auden for his inattention to poetic form and blames Pound as the chief influential source for "that lack of form and consequent obscurity which is the main defect of Auden, Day Lewis, and their school."[90] And though the specifics of their lives and politics couldn't be any more different, in general poetic profile Pound and Auden share a surprising amount in common. They each stand as complementary and representative emblems of a twentieth-century literary economy that saw American poets in the first part of the century traveling to Paris and London to internationalize themselves and establish their reputations, followed by the postwar shift in the centers of the international poetic establishment back across the Atlantic to the United States. Both were seen as the charismatic centers of their literary moments, the namesakes of "The Pound Era" and "The Auden Generation," while employing their vast systematizing erudition to serve, in Gertrude Stein's term, as a "village explainer" for their times. Both were tireless mentors: Auden in New York, on college campuses, and on Ischia; Pound in London, Paris, and later in St. Elizabeth's Hospital in Washington, D.C., where he made himself gruffly available to an enormous range of younger American poets, from Bishop to Zukofsky. The idiosyncratic evolution of their careers, including Pound's slide into ugly racist dementia and Auden's later devout and public embrace of Christianity, proved similarly flummoxing or distressing to some of each poet's most ardent admirers. And at different points in their careers, both saw their art as a way of participating actively in the political world, and each embodied a model of poetic identity achieved through the appropriation of the varied voices of the poetic tradition, making it new through the studied translation of the transnational past.

Their lives and careers intersected in significant and resonant ways as well. After Pound's arrest in Italy in 1945 for treason, Auden's publisher, Random House, wanted to exclude Pound from its anthology of American verse until informed by Auden that if they dropped Pound he would find a new publisher for his own work.[91] Auden also served as a judge on the committee that awarded the first Bollingen Prize to Pound in 1949, provoking a furious national controversy and echoing in very public fashion the assertion in his first American poem that Yeats's troubling private politics, like that of Kipling and Claudel, stood insignificant next to the poems in the judgment of time, which "Worships language and forgives / Everyone by whom it lives; / Pardons cowardice, conceit, / Lays its honors at their feet" [SP, 82]. Further recalling crucial lines from 1940's "New Year Letter"—"Art in intention is mimesis / But, realized, the resemblance ceases; / Art is not and cannot be / A midwife to society" [CP, 201]—Auden justified his selection of Pound for the Bollingen in the pages of the Partisan Review by pointing to the power of poetry not to shape society through propagandistic rhetoric (like Pound's wartime broadcasts), but to impose an engagement with individual interpretive and moral choice upon the reader: "One may . . . hold . . . [a] theory of art, that, in intention, at least, it is a mirror in which the spectator sees reflected himself and the world, and becomes conscious of his feelings good and bad, and of what their relations to each other are in fact. . . . An art which did not accurately reflect evil would not be good art."[92] Auden would pay tribute to Pound's immense poetic, rather than ideological, legacy in a Yale University radio broadcast in honor of Pound's seventieth birthday in 1955: "There are very few living poets, even if they are not conscious of having been influenced by Pound, who could say, 'My work would be exactly the same if Mr. Pound never lived.'"[93]

The pairing of Auden and Pound, finally and importantly for the purposes of this study, also helps frame some useful questions about the relation between poetic and national identity, and about Auden's complicated place in narratives of American poetry. The paradoxes of Pound's xenophobic internationalism and Auden's American-identified continentalism open up intriguing fissures in the landscape of postwar American verse and suggest both why it has proven so difficult to map coherently and why those efforts at mapping so often divide into contentious factions of critical cartographers screaming at one another. The grounds of these debates are almost always competing visions of what it means to be an "American" poet, with individual poets and poetic traditions conscripted into opposing authenticist camps, or, if a poet doesn't fit a particular critical framework of artistic nationality, excluded from the anthologies and histories. It's a particular irony of literary canon-making that Pound, whose entire career was predicated upon a rejection of philistine America and the "mass of dolts" who inhabited it, culminating in an embrace of European fascism and anti-semitism, can be held up as an icon of a native American tradition, while Auden, who tried to enlist during the war and eventually served with the United States army on a postwar intelligence mission in Germany, became an enthusiastic citizen in 1946, and spent the second half of his career reinventing his own poetic identity while reshaping the American poetic landscape, can be rejected as insufficiently authentic to qualify for inclusion in most anthologies of modern American poetry.[94] And even when Auden's influence on younger poets is acknowledged, it can still often be derided as ultimately inconsequential, a "brief vogue" as Vendler puts it. Harold Bloom and David Bromwich, whose choice of modern American poetic progenitor is not Pound but Wallace Stevens, sound a characteristically dismissive note: "Poets who had their beginnings in Auden, and whose early work can often be mistaken for Auden's, have by whatever route found a resting place in the native tradition."[95]

Perloff, drawing upon Pound's admonitory *ABC of Reading*, describes Pound's legacy in terms that similarly presuppose a connection between poetic practice and national identity: "[T]he thrust of the Poundian poetic is that poetry *matters*, that it is *important*, that 'if a nation's literature declines, the nation atrophies and decays.'"[96] Auden's legacy, to the enormous range of poets who learned from him in the 1940s and 1950s, was likewise a lesson in the moral and civic importance of poetry: that it could be, indeed, a "way of happening."

However, unlike that of Pound, Auden's influence was felt not as an effort at defining American poetry in terms of some prescriptive notion of what it should be, or in terms relating poetry to ideals of native authenticity. Rather, Auden's great contribution to his American-born successors was a model of American poetry that eschewed the idea of poetic nationalism entirely. As Nicholas Jenkins has argued, "Almost all critics have overlooked the depth and thoroughness of Auden's critique of that most modern marker of personal identity, nationality."[97]

In his public career, in his private interactions with countless younger poets, and in the verses of post-immigration poems like "In

Memory of W. B. Yeats," "New Year Letter," "The Sea and the Mirror," and "The Age of Anxiety," Auden provided a vital example in writing poetry that can best be described as "post-national."[98] The poetry Auden wrote in the shadow of the global catastrophe of World War II offered a new vision of how to write poetry in a world where the idea of nationalism itself had been proven, conclusively it seemed, morally, politically, and artistically bankrupt. Auden's American legacy is a characteristically paradoxical one, reflecting the difficulty critics seem to have in accounting for Auden's place in American poetry. Auden defined America, and American poetry, as an absence of—or more constructively, as an escape from—the idea of national identity itself. To be an "American" poet after Auden was to be able—or more dialectically, to be burdened by the necessity—to choose any poetic identity one liked, from any time, any place, or any tradition, unfettered (or unassisted) by notions of native authenticity. Auden helps his inheritors see poetic identity not as an obligation to be defined according to some essentialist national narrative, but as a product of choice, of desire, and of the unanxious assimilation of influences that help the poet say what he or she needs to say. One could be a formally trained Jewish-Buddhist transnational visionary bard, like Ginsberg, or a Francophilic analyst and aesthete of the ephemeral and the urban, like O'Hara. One could be a passionate archivist of cultural history, like Hayden, or a cold-eyed anatomist of the brutal psychic interior, like Plath. Each has an equal claim to American poetic authenticity, and each owes notable debts to Auden's useful example and assistance. If, as Charles Olson observed in his notebook in 1945, Pound taught American poets to "Write as the fathers to be the father,"[99] I want to argue for Auden's analogous pedagogical role in American poetry, but with this nuanced but significant difference: Rather than teaching poets to use the past to replace, or triumph over, their predecessors in a notional native tradition, Auden taught American poets to write as their poetic fathers—and mothers and cousins and lovers and friends and fleeting acquaintances and occasionally himself—to become their distinctive and diverse postwar and post-Modernist American poetic selves.

PART II

Father of Forms
Merrill, Auden, and a Fable of Influence

For Auden's sixty-fifth birthday in 1972, James Merrill contributed a poem called "Table Talk" to a festschrift marking the occasion. In keeping with the festive moment celebrating Auden's presence and influence on the American poetic landscape for more than three decades, Merrill's poem describes a lavish, lively dinner party. Presided over by "Charles," a character who shares his name with Merrill's famous financier father and who appears in a number of his poems as a kind of super-refined fictive version of Merrill himself, the poem begins with the host discoursing to his guests upon the hazards of a sophisticated palate:

> "Food!" exclaims Charles. "Each new dish I have tried
> Moves me more strangely than the last.
> Often my hostess, as an aproned bride,
> Will enter to a blast
> Of burning biscuits, and her screams
> Shake the red, gas-lit theatre of my dreams.

> "Those nights, the marquee spells out plenitude:
> SARAH BERNHARDT IN HEARTBURN HOUSE.

The opening speech ("If physic be the mood
Of love," said by the Doctor to his spouse)
Quite glues me to my seat.
"More, please!" I clamor. We are what we eat.[1]

Recalling Auden's homely digestive image for the appropriation
of an artist's work by his audience in the Yeats elegy, in which "the
words of a dead man are modified in the guts of the living," Merrill's
poem frames Charles's ornate meals as emblems of art: theatrical performances of skill and imagination whose appreciation is marked by
the guests' hearty appetites (and occasional indigestion). And it is in
that nourishing consumption of art that the eater becomes a theater
and performs his own identity, with the range of entrees, from "burning biscuits" to hot dogs whose "full-fleshed and sizzling nudes" are
"unsurpassed by anything in Brecht," adding girth to his literary gut:
"We are what we eat." All of these dishes, Charles tells us, from the
"lowliest tuber" to the "opaque cabochons" of chestnuts, obey the artistic oracle, "Transfigure and Redeem." All art, he suggests grandly,
from the lowest to the loftiest, has the power to feed and transform its
audience. Lost in his own metaphoric reveries, he forgets the meal he
is himself serving:

"While just to think of bittersweet
Oranges veiled in flickering blue rum,
Or—but you must be starving! Shall we eat?"
He goes. And from an inner room
Brings out the bird a-crackle in its nest
Of spices, asks who will have leg, who breast.

Here the poem reveals that the meal is, in fact, a Thanksgiving dinner, complete with an elaborately prepared "bird a-crackle in its nest of
spices." Charles's flashy production of the bird from an "inner room"
(*The Inner Room* is the title of one of Merrill's books), and his witty but
self-involved observations on the art of living and on living through art,
prompt in the previously silent narrator some critical ruminations on
the value of artistic self-absorption:

Charles is a marvelous cook. Still, there are meals
He serves that make me wonder, as tonight,

What it all means, and what my neighbor feels.
Somehow I cannot touch a bite.
If only Wystan, like a jolly priest,
Were here to tell me: *Go ahead, my son, enjoy the feast!*

For the narrator, struck by the narcissism of Charles's performance, this Thanksgiving proves a hollow one. He feels an absence of purpose and emotion in Charles's sumptuous meal, causing him to wonder "What it all means, and what my neighbor feels." He personifies this absence in the likeness of Wystan Auden, whose fatherly benediction he seeks. At Charles's table of self-conscious aestheticism, the speaker wishes for Auden's sensible and jovial presence.

In "Table Talk," the image of Auden serves Merrill as a vehicle for poetic self-critique. Amid the divided consciousness of the poem, split between Charles's artistic self-cultivation and the engaged rationalism of the narrator, Auden stands as a figure of reconciliation between the two. Viewed in the context of Merrill's career in 1972, we can see a poet anxious about the narrowness of his poetic scope—which up until this point had been limited to gem-like lyrics of astonishing craft but relatively little human feeling—and casting about for a way to expand his range. With Auden's help, Merrill suggests, he could begin to write poems that would successfully combine both aspects of his poetic ambition, poems whose aesthetic refinement wouldn't preclude an involvement with the world outside them. He looks to Auden as the guide who can instruct him and encourage him to enjoy the feast of the full range of poetic modes. Just under two years later, Merrill would begin that instruction, starting work on a new project that would aim to unite craft and sentiment, aesthetics and engagement, and whose vast ambition would more than encompass "what it all means, and what his neighbor feels." That project was *The Changing Light at Sandover*, the poem that would rewrite Merrill's identity as a poet of epic scope and vision, and the schoolmaster in *Sandover*'s classroom and a central figure in the composition and narrative of the poem, is Auden.

"The Book of Ephraim," the first installment of what would become *Sandover*, begins in January, 1974—just over three months after Auden's death on September 29, 1973. While readers of the complete poem discover the crucial role Auden eventually plays as Merrill's guide through the spirit world, his presence in "The Book of Ephraim" is narratively slight. He appears—with the exception of a quotation of a resonant fragment of "As I Walked Out One Evening" in section "Q," and a passing allusion to the triumphant Venetian premiere of *The Rake's Progress* in section "V"—only twice: First, in the list of "Dramatis Personae" in section "D," and then in a brief, inconclusive episode in section "Y" recounting the elder poet's stern disapproval in life of Merrill's occult experiments, and upon his recent death his somewhat disoriented reemergence on the other side of the Ouija board:

> During one of our last conversations
> (Wystan had just died) we got through to him.
> He sounded pleased with his NEW PROLE BODY
> And likened Heaven to A NEW MACHINE
> But a gust of mortal anxiety
> Blew, his speech guttered, there were papers YES
> a box in Oxford that must QUICKLY BE
> QUICKLY BURNED—breaking off: he'd overstepped,
> Been told so. Then the same mechanical,
> Kind, preoccupied GOODNIGHT that ended
> One's evenings with the dear man. [*CLS*, 87]

While neither of these early appearances fully suggest Auden's eventual significant role in the rest of the poem, leading Merrill through *Sandover*'s celestial "Lessons" and proposing appropriate verse forms for transmitting otherworldly wisdom as poetry, each notably marks the poem's epitaphic relation to Auden. In section "Y," the poem signals the fictive moment of its composition as following hard upon Auden's passing into the world of those reachable only via the Ouija board—"Wystan had just died"—and, at the head of the cast of "Dramatis Personae," his name and death-date appear as if inscribed on a recently erected tombstone: "Auden, W(ystan) H(ugh), 1907-/ 73, the celebrated poet" [*CLS*, 11]. Among *Sandover*'s many overlapping generic identities—occult epic, autobiographical memoir, supreme poetic fiction—it is also, from the beginning, both an elegy for Auden and a celebration of his importance to the development of Merrill's own poetry.

In fact, the inception and composition of *Sandover* are marked historically by the deaths of two of Merrill's principal poetic influences,

Wallace Stevens and Auden. Stevens died in August, 1955, the same summer that Merrill and his partner David Jackson began the sessions at the Ouija board that would culminate in the writing of *Sandover* almost twenty years later, when the transcripts of those sessions would find their final form in verse, during the same winter as Auden's death.[2] If, as has been argued by numerous critics, Stevens served as Merrill's first major poetic influence, it seems fitting that Merrill's major poem should find its beginnings in the elegiac moment of his first mentor's passing.[3] It is likewise fitting that the actual composition of the poem, the forging of inspiration into words, should occur in the shadow of the death of Auden, Merrill's great teacher of poetic craft, his "father of forms" [*CLS*, 135]. The deaths of the two elder poets seem to have served as watershed moments for Merrill, as if it were only in their absence and loss that he could begin to hear their voices clearly and begin to incorporate and assimilate their respective legacies in poetically productive ways. The occasion of *Sandover* is death, and one of its chief subjects is literary inheritance and the construction of poetic identity.[4] And it is Auden's death in particular that Merrill's poem commemorates, and uses—in a remarkably literal way—as a catalyst for establishing and asserting his own artistic self. The poem begins in the shadow of Auden's death and ends with Auden's shadow itself instructing Merrill in the relationship between his own living poetic voice and those of his dead precursors. In "New Year Letter," Auden assembles the tribunal of his own influences from whom he learns how to build his new American poetic identity. In *Sandover*, we see Merrill assimilate Auden's example, while placing Auden himself at the head of his own gallery—or festive dining table— of influences who help him find his own poetic voice. *Sandover* enacts the wish of "Table Talk"—"If only Wystan were here"—and offers up a poetic thanksgiving of its own for Auden's permanent constructive presence in Merrill's work.[5]

◆ ◆ ◆

The mystery of selfhood's debt to inheritance is perhaps the central theme of Merrill's life and his work. Throughout Merrill's career, from his early poems and his first novel, *The Seraglio*, to later texts written in the light of *Sandover*'s lessons like "The School Play" and "Prose of Departure," we find him puzzling over the question of the relation between identity and influence, a theme of obvious relevance to the anxious child of "The Broken Home" and the heir to the massive fortune of his financier father. And as a poet who exchanges a life of inherited indolence for the laborious life of art, the question of what the artist owes to his poetic forebears looms especially large in his writing. In 1959, in his second volume, *The Country of a Thousand Years of Peace*, Merrill published a sonnet called "Marsyas" that explicitly addresses the question of the poet's relationship with his precursors:

> I used to write in the café sometimes:
> Poems on menus, read all over town
> Or talked out before ever written down.
> One day a girl brought in his latest book.
> I opened it—stiff rhythms, gorgeous rhymes—
> And made a face. Then crash! my cup upset.
> Of twenty upward looks mine only met
> His, that gold archaic lion's look
>
> Wherein I saw my wiry person skinned
> Of every skill it labored to acquire
> And heard the plucked nerve's elemental twang.
> They found me dangling where his golden wind
> Inflicted so much music on the lyre
> That no one could have told you what he sang. [*CP*, 96]

The myth of Marsyas, as we know from Ovid, tells of a satyr who challenges Apollo to a test of musical skill. When Marsyas loses, Apollo hangs his flayed body from a tree. We also know—from the first Canto of the *Paradiso*, where Dante invokes Apollo to "breathe into my bosom . . . as when Marsyas by thy hand was dragged / Forth from his limbs, unsheathed"[6]—that there is considerable precedent for employing the skinned satyr as a figure for the condition and consequences of poetic inspiration.[7] While Merrill follows Dante by similarly placing himself in the position of Marsyas the aspiring artist—thereby transforming a brutal image of overweening ambition justly punished into a positive trope of selfless and uncompetitive submission to the muse—he alters Dante's formula by replacing Apollo with the figure of another poet. Here, it is the "gold archaic lion" of the elder poet who, when conjured from the pages of his "latest book," breathes "his golden wind" into the bosom of the young aspirant, producing new song.

While one might detect a certain anxiety here in the image of the young poet being skinned by a god-like senior bard and turned into a kind of Aeolian harp singing with the other's breath, the significance of this poem goes beyond a simple allegory of a beginning artist being overmastered by a powerful predecessor. Importantly, "Marsyas" demonstrates that, even early in his career, Merrill had formulated a representation of poetic voice in which the poet achieves originality by having other poets speak *through* him. "No one could have told you what *he* sang," says Merrill of the elder poet, implying that while it is the "archaic lion" whose breath is powering the song, it is Merrill's voice—the vocal cords, as it were, of the harp—that we hear. It is an identity affirmed by the forms of his elders. It is in reading the book that the young poet's face is "made"—in the older poet's "look" he sees himself.

"Marsyas" was written during the moment of Auden's greatest American cultural celebrity and authority, and it takes little effort of imagination to see the famous author of 1955's *The Shield of Achilles* in the figure of the prolific literary lion in "Marsyas," writing his characteristic "stiff rhythms and gorgeous rhymes." Merrill had visited Ischia in 1951 and there had absorbed the legend of the eccentric poet presiding like Prospero over the island, and dominating the table talk of the café-world evoked in the sonnet. He had also been in the audience at the 1951 premiere of *The Rake's Progress* at La Fenice in Venice. As Merrill would recall more than forty years later in his memoir, *A Different Person*, his youthful excitement at the prospect of the premiere had been acute, and he and a friend had bought the score and memorized it the afternoon before the opera's feted debut: "The work promised to embody what most attracted us in the collaborators, Stravinsky's neoclassical vein (a cannibal in a top hat, as somebody put it) and Auden's lyrical, cabaret-haunted glamour." The experience made a profound impression on the young aesthete: "From this pinnacle the rest of the twentieth century would be all downhill."[8]

Auden's "Good-Bye to the Mezzogiorno," which publicly closed and commemorated the Ischian café-haunting period of his life, was published the year before Merrill's poem, and "Marsyas" indicates further formal and thematic allegiances to other contemporary Auden poems, among them a sonnet called "The Song" that Auden published in 1956. That poem likewise presents a figuration of an aspiring poet—traditionally troped, in this case, as a songbird—whose "rebellious wing" carries it aloft over a morning landscape, racing and seeking to "better its obedient double" reflected on the surface of the lake below. The final stiffly rhythmed sestet reads,

> Climbing to song it hopes to make amends
> For whiteness drabbed for glory said away
> And be immortal after but because
> Light upon a valley where its love was
> So lacks all picture of reproach it ends
> Denying what it started up to say. [*CP*, 625]

Here the songbird, like the cocky Marsyas in his café, aspires to artistic immortality through a song whose originality derives from its oppositional stance to the tradition. Not only does it challenge its earthbound peers—its "obedient doubles"—but it takes on its predecessors as well. Its ambition is to "make amends" for the inadequate songs of those who have come before, songs whose drabness and garrulity, perhaps, have obscured and squandered the "whiteness" and "glory" they were meant to be about. But the wind-borne bird learns a similar lesson to the "wind-inflicted" Marsyas. Just as Marsyas finds his authentic voice through the abdication of self, the songbird discovers, through the "light" of "love," that its song of unfettered ego is an inadequate and inauthentic one. Instead, it recognizes that "whiteness" and "glory" are achievable, not through the heroic melody of Shelley's soaring skylark—singing "In profuse strains of unpremeditated art" such that "the world should listen" and be "wrought / To sympathy with hopes and fears it heeded not"—but rather through selfless, harmonious singing. The bird finally understands that it must abandon its high-flying Romantic ambition, perhaps to rejoin what the poem calls "tribes of a beauty which no care can break"—the birds he had left behind in his ascent, birds who achieve beauty without ambition ("care") and through a tribal collective concord. The poem ends with an affirmation, via a denial, of the virtue of poetic selflessness and, as in "Marsyas," with the singer himself unable to tell you what he sang.

Merrill was a devoted reader of Auden's most influential critic, Randall Jarrell (copies of all of Jarrell's books were in Merrill's library at his home in Stonington, Conn.), and it is also possible that a reading of Jarrell's contemporary criticism of Auden lies in part behind Merrill's choice of imagery in "Marsyas." In 1955, in *The Yale Review*, Jarrell reviewed *The Shield of Achilles*, and described the evolution in Auden's verse in terms of the appearance of Auden's "irrevocably, inexorably middle-aged" face: "And the change in the Auden of the poems prepares us for the change in the everyday Auden, who is no longer a lank, towheaded, slouching boy, but who looks at you with a lined, sagging, fretful, consciously powerful old lion's face."[9] A decade earlier, in Jarrell's well-known 1945 essay, "Freud to Paul: The Stages of Auden's Ideology," published in the *Partisan Review*, Jarrell discusses the "magic" of some of Auden's poetry explicitly in terms of the Marsyas myth: "But in our culture how much (like the flaying of Marsyas) goes on under—far under—the level gray gaze of Reason and Taste; just as Apollo, when he was not occupied with Knowledge, Art, and Light, slithered under the pillars of his temples in the person of a hunting snake, and was called by his worshippers the Mouse-Slayer."[10]

Auden is, of course, not the only influence to be felt by the early Merrill, as even Merrill's apparently Auden-"inflicted" poem makes clear.[11] As Stephen Yenser has suggested, one can also find trace elements of Stevens, who died four years before the publication of Merrill's poem, in "Marsyas."[12] Beyond Yenser's recognition of Stevens's "modern poet 'twanging a wiry string,'" we might also identify in the poem such characteristically Stevensian images as the lion, or find lyrical echoes of Peter Quince ("Susanna's music touched the bawdy strings / Of those white elders; but, escaping, / Left only Death's ironic scraping"[13]) or the inscrutable song of the singer at Key West ("The song and water were not medleyed sound / Even if what she sang was what she heard, / Since what she sang was uttered word by word"[14]). Mark Bauer has further found the poem an important index of the influence of Yeats on Merrill's imagination.[15] But the multiplicities of poetic precursors whose faces appear in the old lion's face in Merrill's poem only illustrate in very literal terms the idea of influence posited by the poem itself, in which the elements of the tradition itself combine to breathe new song through the medium of the inheritor poet. It is a model of the relation between the tradition and the individual talent that will find its fullest exploration and expression in *Sandover*, in which the figure of Marsyas will once again appear, including in an important exchange between Merrill and the spirit of

Auden on the ways younger poets can turn the tables by incorporating their influences rather than surrendering to them. And it is precisely this sense of what Merrill calls the "composite voice" of *Sandover* that is one of Auden's legacies to the poets like Merrill who follow him. The claim is not that Auden is the only significant poetic influence on Merrill, but that one of Auden's chief contributions to his own inheritors was an approach to the poetic tradition and poetic identity that allowed them to see their precursors as instrumental, in an almost literal sense, in shaping their own poetic identities and projects. With Auden's help, younger poets like Merrill learned that they could take from Yeats, from Stevens, and from Auden himself, what they needed to sing their own songs. It is, then, in the words of one of *Sandover*'s lessons, "No Accident" that it is the "gold archaic lion" of Auden—who shows Merrill/Marsyas how to find his own voice by using the voices of his masters—who ends up being figured as head tutor in *Sandover*'s school of the ages.

◆ ◆ ◆

In a 1977 poem called "The School Play," midway through the composition of what would become the completed text of *Sandover* (the first section, "The Book of Ephraim" was published in 1976, with "Mirabell" and "Scripts for the Pageant" following in 1978 and 1980), Merrill addresses, with his characteristic eye toward metaphor and personal fable, the role of influence in shaping identity. Staging the drama of the tradition's relation to the individual talent in terms of a remembered schoolboy theatrical production of *Richard II*, Merrill affirms the poetic virtues of artistic self-surrender, and the role of the work of past "masters" in helping younger artists, in the words of the poem, "find themselves":

> "Harry of Hereford, Lancaster, and Derby,
>   Stands here for God, his country, and..." And what?
> "Stands here for God, His Sovereign, and himself,"
>   Growled Captain Fry who had the play by heart.
> I was the First Herald, "a small part"
>   —I was small too—"but an important one."
> What was not important to the self
> At nine or ten? Already I had crushes
> On Mowbray, Bushy, and the Duke of York.

Handsome Donald Niemann (now himself,
According to the Bulletin, headmaster
Of his own school somewhere out West) awoke
Too many self-indulgent mouthings in
The dummy mirror before smashing it,
For me to set my scuffed school cap at him.
Another year I'd play that part myself,
Or Puck, or Goneril, or Prospero.
Later in adolescence, it was thought
Clever to speak of having found oneself,
With a smile and a rueful headshake for those who hadn't.
People still do. Only the other day
A woman my age told us that her son
"Hadn't found himself"—at thirty-one!
I heard in the mind's ear an amused hum
Of mothers and fathers from beyond the curtain,
And that flushed, far-reaching hour came back
Months of rehearsal in the gymnasium
Had led to: when the skinny nobodies
Who'd memorized the verse and learned to speak it
Emerged in beards and hose (or gowns and rouge)
Vivid with character, having put themselves
All unsuspecting into the masters' hands. [*CP*, 422]

In a combination of the pedagogical and the theatrical that mirrors its most complete exposition three years later in the "Scripts for the Pageant" of *Sandover*, composed of a sequence of lessons on the nature of poetic creation and originality, this poem construes the creation of identity as a process of construction through emulative performance. The figure of the poet remembers the "small part . . . but an important one" played by his experience as a first-grader, acting for the first time in the annual Shakespeare play at St. Bernard's School in New York, in the evolution of his artistic identity. In "Education of the Poet," a prose account of his own poetic development, Merrill describes the scene:

We at St. Bernard's were too young to know what many of Shakespeare's lines meant. When Richard II said, "Wanting the manage

of unruly jades," he could have been talking not about horseman-
ship so much as an earthquake in a Hong Kong curio shop. But
once the line was said with proper stresses, there was little more
to ask of the child who wore the crown. [*CPM*, 10–11]

It was at this age, "nine or ten," as Merrill recalls, that he first began
writing poetry, and "The School Play" offers an originary moment when
the poet first glimpses the truth that one "finds oneself" in the words of
others. Those first words he declaims on the school stage in the persona of
the "First Herald" herald, as it were, the kind of artist he will become.

From the self-assured perspective of one who has, as a mature artist, long since "found himself" (with a smile and a rueful headshake for
those who haven't), Merrill looks back four decades to present a portrait
of the artist as an extremely young man and to suggest the manner in
which he started on the path to that mature identity. For the young poet
and his thespian peers, it is the hard work in the "gymnasium"—suggesting the dual senses of exercise and school—of getting the text of the play
"by heart" that allows them to see the possibilities for their own identities. The experience of memorizing the verse and learning to speak it is
framed as a productive surrender of identity to one's influences, as they
"put themselves / All unsuspecting into the masters' hands." In Merrill's
poem, the notion of being influenced becomes synonymous with being
taught, as the plural "masters" encompasses both Shakespeare and the
teachers of St. Bernard's who are directing the students in the play. Both
language and form are essential in the construction of poetic identity, as
it is both Shakespeare's words and the teachers' instruction in saying the
lines "with the proper stresses" that results in artistic metamorphosis.
Metaphorically reproducing *Richard II*'s narrative of usurpation, Merrill
recounts how the young actors are usurped by Shakespeare's words, and
in the process come into their own, transforming from "skinny nobodies" into bold new personages, "vivid with character."

In another echo of *Sandover*'s homoerotic fable of poetic inheritance and collaboration, Merrill explicitly relates the creation of artistic
identity to the experience of erotic attraction. "Already I had crushes /
On Mowbray, Bushy, and the Duke of York," he writes, giving a different
meaning to the notion of knowing the play "by heart." The figure of the
young poet finds himself in love, not with his young classmates, but with

the Shakespearean characters they are inhabiting. To be in love is to engage with a fiction, and—in a Merrillian reversal—to engage with a fiction is to be in love with it. In fact, it is the refusal of "Handsome Donald Niemann"—"now himself," in the 1977 present of the poem—to fully surrender his own personality to that of the character which keeps the nine-year-old Merrill from setting his "scuffed school cap at him." Niemann's "self-indulgent mouthings in / The dummy mirror" denote for Merrill not the conceit of the title character whom Neimann is supposed to be playing, but Niemann's own. The true artist must relinquish the self in his art, not indulge it. Niemann's imaginative failure is also an erotic one: his incapacity to give himself over to Shakespeare's fiction suggests a similar incapacity to reciprocate love. "Finding oneself" in a text is, for Merrill, directly analogous to finding oneself in another person.

But the young poet learns from Niemann's error, just as he learns from his own, incorporating past roles into future performances. "Another year I'd play that part myself," he writes, and readers of Merrill can see something of Richard, the double-minded poet-king ("His face still combating with tears and smiles," in Shakespeare's words[16]), in the poet of love and loss Merrill would become. Over the course of his career Merrill would perform his share of mirror-gazing ("Mirror," "The Book of Ephraim"), mirror-smashing (the conclusion of "Scripts for the Pageant"), and—as in "Matinées," another narrative of incipient poethood, set around the same time as "The School Play"—grandiose self-dramatization: "The point thereafter was to arrange for one's / Own chills and fever, passions and betrayals, / Chiefly in order to make song of them" [CP, 269]. He would play other poetic roles as well, from Puck, delighting in playful metaphoric transformations in poems like "The Transfigured Bird" and "To a Butterfly"; to Goneril, the resentful child of an errant father, in "Scenes of Childhood" and "The Broken Home"; to the enchanter Prospero, a "master" now himself, orchestrating the metaphysical masque of Sandover. Across his poetry Merrill incorporates multiple personae in his poetic identity, enacting Richard II's theatrical self-description, "Thus play I in one person many people,"[17] and framing his career in terms of a narrative of education in the art of self-construction. "Years have gone by," Merrill summarizes in Section Y of "Ephraim," years during which he'd lived and loved and learned and, in particular, listened for thirty years to the voices from the other world—

Auden's most prominently among them—teach the lessons of putting himself productively into the shaping hands of the poetic past: "Young chameleon, I used to / Ask how on earth one got sufficiently / Imbued with otherness. And now I see" [*CLS*, 89].

In "Prose of Departure," from 1988's *The Inner Room*, Merrill extends and expands on this idea, placing the notion of poetic inheritance once more within a performative, theatrical model. Merrill's prose poem includes an account of a performance of the classical Japanese art of *bunraku*, in which extremely lifelike puppets enact traditional dramas, each major character manipulated by three puppeteers who stand in full view of the audience, and accompanied by a vocalist who recites their lines:

> Seldom do we the living . . . feel more "ourselves" then when spoken through, or motivated, by "invisible" forces such as these. It is especially true, if, like a puppet overcome by woe, we also appear to be struggling free of them. (Lesser personages make do with two manipulators, or only one.) [*CP*, 556]

Here Merrill places the artist in the role of the puppet, manipulated by forces invisible to him, yet visible to others. Those forces, like influential ghosts, act upon him in concert, giving life to him through their artifice. This notion of artifice is important, since it implies an element of craft while also suggesting a sense of fictionalized self-presentation. Even the attempt to escape the manipulation of the invisible forces is itself seen as artificial—one only "appears to be struggling free of them." It is a dramatized fiction, an aesthetic perception, not an agonistic conflict. One may be aware of one's desire to break free from those influences, but one can never escape them. In fact, the recognition of that very desire is one of the manifestations of their influence. For the puppet—and the poet—everything he does, his entire persona, even his voice, is the product of the combined influence of others who stand behind him, unseen, in the dark. It is their craft, their artistry, that make him who he is.

This is a powerful metaphorical analogue for the complex fiction of personal and poetic identity that Merrill presents in *Sandover*, a fiction perhaps best summarized in the words of Merrill's own fictive avatar, Francis Tanning, in his early semi-autobiographical novel from 1957, *The Seraglio*:

Each of us here on earth is looked after, cared for by an individual patron . . . Our lives are not ends but means! The soul begins as an insect, an animal, pig, dog, cat. The cat sees in the dark, sits on the wall, waiting to become human. The soul does become human at last, is helped through one incarnation after another until found worthy of the first of the other world's nine stages. Once that happens, the patron moves to a higher stage, and *you* become a patron!... Far below on earth a tiny savage soul is born, in Naples or the Brazilian jungle. It is yours to care for and lead towards wisdom. [*CN*, 235]

The model for the tradition that this passage offers, in its account of the influence of the "patrons" of "the other world" on our lives, ties in neatly with Merrill's later *bunraku* conceit. We are, in Ephraim's words, "representatives" [*CLS*, 8] of those ghostly forces, representations crafted by their skill. The poet, then, is the product of his "patrons," the text, in a sense, that they have written, just as *Sandover* is a text "written" by Merrill's influences, a poem "all by someone else" [*CLS*, 261] as "JM"— *Sandover*'s fictive representation of Merrill—complains to Auden in "Mirabell." He is their "composition," composed of and by them. The poet is the puppet of his influences.

But Merrill's metaphor is characteristically double-sided. A puppet is both actor and acted upon. It is the puppet's personality, his expression and his plight, that the audience sees and sympathizes with, not that of the puppeteers. The fictional self that the puppeteers successfully create takes on an agency and identity that appears to transcend their influence. It comes alive, and struts upon the stage, to the amusement of the appreciative audience. Just as, in Francis Tanning's account, the "representative" in time becomes a patron, the puppet becomes a person who can elicit genuine emotion and intellectual engagement from his audience. Thus, the poet achieves an authentic identity, despite the artificiality of its construction. He gains a voice that is uniquely his own, even as others are speaking through him. As the spirit of Auden tells JM, echoing both "New Year Letter" ("The powers / That we create with are not our own" [*CP*, 241]) and his own 1939 elegy for Ernst Toller ("We are lived by powers we pretend to understand" [*CP*, 250]), "I BELIEVE WE SHALL DISCOVER / THEIR POWERS ARE IN US QUITE AS MUCH AS OVER" [*CLS*, 345].

This double nature allows Merrill a multiple role in *Sandover*. He shows JM to be a doubly mediated figure: not only the fictive "representative" of the "real" James Merrill, but the subservient medium for others' voices as well. Yet Merrill himself retains his own authenticity and authorship. It is he, James Merrill, who has summoned these disparate voices and arranged them into a coherent poem, and whose name is printed on the cover. He is the one who manipulates the characters of his poem, who pulls the strings of the poets of the past, who are never more vigorous than in their ghostly representations. He is both puppet and puppet-master, both creature and creator. He gives a poetic body to voices of the past, who work in the service of his own identity and ambition and success. He is the poetic tradition incorporated.

The metaphor of incorporation is a rich one for Merrill, as one might expect of the son of the founder of Merrill Lynch & Co. When Merrill autographed copies of *The Changing Light at Sandover*, he sometimes signed them "James Merrill & Co."[18] and the gentle joke goes beyond the simple recognition that the book was written with the help of "voices from the other world," not to mention David Jackson, Merrill's companion and partner at the Ouija board (referred to in the poem as "DJ," or "the Hand"). For a poem that seems to take place so completely beyond the world of money and capitalism, *Sandover* is a highly corporate enterprise. Apart from a passing reference to the banker and art patron Otto Kahn [*CLS*, 55], there is not a single reference in the entire poem either to the world of commerce or to people whose "densities," or talents, might lead them to prefer business over art or the investigative sciences. And even Kahn's inclusion in the poem's afterlife carries with it a literary resonance, given Kahn's role as the financier of Hart Crane's *The Bridge*, a poem whose own visionary glimpse of "Atlantis" serves as just one of the many precursor texts that haunt *Sandover*. Much of the imagery of *Sandover* comes from the world of big business, from the hierarchy of the bureaucracy in heaven, to the Research Lab in which new products—like man—are developed. Industrial images like stripmining and nuclear power are deployed as poetic metaphors and even the vision of metempsychosis seems more capitalist than anything else, with the billions of animal- and vegetable-density souls serving and being consumed by an elite of merely two million high-flyers. Even among the elect there is a kind of anxiety akin to that of the employee up for his job performance evaluation. Those without a sufficient work ethic get drummed out of the *corps*: Immortality, *Sandover* tells us, "IS THE GIFT MAN EARNS (OR NOT) WITH HIS LIFE" [*CLS*, 315].

The structure of *Sandover* unearths the capitalist pun latent in the famous phrase of Crane—another poet-son of American commerce— for poetic communion, "the visionary company." Merrill's is a company in which he serves as chief executive, with "the Five," or the Angels, constituting a kind of Board of Trustees. The poet employs his laborers of spirits and voices, delegates his authority to them, and reaps the profits of their collective toil. He is also the figurehead of their communal enterprise, their "representative" in the world, much as CEOs are seen as the human incarnations of their companies. Further, like any corporation, *Sandover* has a purpose, a mission, a product to sell. It has "V Work"—*vie* work, life work—to do. "THE SCRIBE'S JOB IS TO HELP SPEED ACCEPTANCE / OF THE 5'S WORK," as Mirabell says [*CLS*, 143]. Part of that work is the transmission of *Sandover*'s unmistakable social message—its warning against the use of nuclear energy— which Mirabell tells them must "SLOWLY INFILTRATE" [*CLS*, 124] man's consciousness. In a very literal way, the poem sets up a kind of intellectual economy. The more skillful the craftsmanship of the poet and his employees, the more likely is the poem to be well-received by the public. The more sympathetic readers it acquires, the more people will hear its message. And the more who hear its message, the more likely it is to be heeded, and the poem's "V Work" will have been accomplished, not unlike a product whose success earns it a dominant market share.

An episode in *The Seraglio* can shed some light on this aspect of Merrill's notion of poetic work. Francis Tanning, the scion of a wealthy business family, is meeting his brother-in-law, Larry, who is the chief executive in his father's brokerage house and is in charge of Francis's trust fund. Francis has decided to give up his inheritance and has marched into Larry's Wall Street office to demand that the safety net of his own wealth be eliminated, on the grounds that "One has to *work* for one's life." When Larry offers him a job at the brokerage firm, Francis rejects it, saying, "No, no, I was talking metaphorically. . . . You should know I'd do anything before working *here*. That is . . . being the son of—," he breaks off. "To work *anywhere*, for me, wouldn't be real," he resumes. "I shouldn't need to do it, I'd be inventing a life" [*CN*, 96]. In the end, he accepts Larry's decision to leave his trust fund intact.

If one reads the protagonist of this *roman à clef* as a stand-in for Merrill, one sees here a kind of transference of vocation from business-man to poet. Born into wealth, Francis, the would-be-artist, can see no purpose in working for its own sake. Since he does not need the money he would earn, it would be false, play-acting, unreal. So when Larry's re-fusal to disinherit him "dooms" him, as he puts it in the novel, to a life of "unreality," he must find another way to "work for his life." For Francis, as for Merrill, that "work" would be his art. If working in the "real" world of business condemns him to artifice, to "inventing a life," he would turn that unreality into a source of power and embrace the artificial, the aes-thetic, where inventing a life is one's job. In art, the invented life becomes real—just as the puppet comes to life—and the real becomes fictive—as James Merrill becomes "a different person," JM. The realm of art, of poetry, is itself, in Merrill's words, "the other world," a shadowy domain that is both real and unreal, where fact is fable. It is a looking glass world and the "real" world it reflects is, for Merrill, the world of business that he rejected to become a poet. Poetry for Merrill is thus more than simply his life's work, his "*vie* work." Rather, it is real *work*: labor with a utility in the world. This fact has dual implications, both of them distinctively Audenesque. First, it defines poetry as a job, a profession. Auden was seen by younger poets as the paragon of the modern professional poet. Very little was romantic about his vocation: He was a highly trained, highly skilled craftsman who kept regular hours and earned a living from his work. Second, and significantly, it asserts that poetry—at least within the supreme fiction of *Sandover*—is indeed a way of happening. In the Yeats elegy, after apparently acknowledging poetry's worldly impotence, Auden revises himself: "It survives / In the valley of its making where executives would never want to tamper" [*CP*, 248]. In *Sandover*, Merrill further revises Auden, reclaiming poetry for those executives, suggest-ing that the world of commerce and the world of poetry may not be so far apart. In a very literal sense, he is a poetic executive (from the Latin meaning to follow or carry out): He assembles his workforce of influ-ences, represents and gives them a voice and a mouth, employs their vari-ous skills for his own imaginative profit, and directs their collective work out into the world to provide a real service for his poetic consumers: to help them "survive." "We must improve the line / In every sense, for life" [*CLS*, 91], he writes in *Sandover*, yoking technical craft and poetic product development with human survival: "Measures, furthermore, had been defined / As what emergency required" [*CLS*, 2]. For Merrill, poetry is a very serious business.

◆ ◆ ◆

The composite Auden–Stevens–Yeats figure of "Marsyas" recalls the "familiar compound ghost" of "Little Gidding," Eliot's spirit of "some dead master / Whom I had known, forgotten, half recalled / Both one and many" and with whom readers have identified principally Yeats, but also Dante, Milton, Swift, and numerous others.[19] In the same spirit, Merrill's parenthetical aside in "Prose of Departure"—"lesser personages make do with two manipulators, or only one"—offers a whiff of the same aristocratic air that blows through Eliot's famous observation in "Tradition and the Individual Talent" that "Only those who have personality and emotions know what it means to want to escape from these things." Eliot's spectral trope, as well as his actual ghost and personality-filled voice, reappear in *Sandover*—not least in the poem's description of the polyvocal Ephraim as its "Familiar Spirit" [*CLS*, 4]. And as Robert Polito and Piotr Gwiazda have noted, Eliot's ideas about the relation between the individual poet and the tradition also feature prominently in Merrill's epic.[20] The Ouija board conversations with past poets, and Merrill's apparent abdication of his pen to their voices, literalize Eliot's well-known notions regarding poetic impersonality and how the "best [and] most individual parts of [a poet's] work are those in which the dead poets . . . assert their immortality most vigorously."[21] But Eliot's ghostly presence in *Sandover*, and the relation between his theories of poetic originality and influence to the model enacted in Merrill's poem full of dead poets, allow us to see both how Auden served as a figure of transition and pedagogy for poets of Merrill's generation, and how Merrill's poem dramatizes in almost theatrical fashion Auden's function for younger poets as a liberating intermediary between Eliotic Modernism and a postwar vision of American poetic identity. Auden's ideas about the relation of influence to identity build upon Eliot's famous formulation, but it is Auden's theoretical refinement of Eliot's ideas that shows

Merrill and other poets of his generation a way of writing that acknowledges their own belatedness, yet still allows them an original voice. From
Auden, poets like Merrill learn how to move through and beyond Eliot's ideas and poetics to reflect a world where being modern no longer
means "making it new" and where the prospect of shoring fragments
against ruin no longer seems tenable in the wake of global war and the
looming shadow of nuclear annihilation. Anthony Hecht, a friend and
poetic contemporary of Merrill's, has observed, "I think it was easier to
learn from Auden, for the poets of my generation, than from Eliot."[22] In
Sandover, we see Auden's generational pedagogical function acted out
on the stage of JM's Ouija board.

Auden advances upon Eliot's formulation of poetic influence by introducing the question of choice, one of his touchstone themes. "Originality," writes Auden, "means a capacity to find in any work of any date
or place a clue to finding one's authentic voice. The burden of choice and
selection is put squarely upon the shoulders of each individual poet and
it is a heavy one" [*DH*, 80]. Poetic authenticity is defined for Auden, not
simply by Eliot's "continual surrender of himself"[23] to the tradition, but
by the poet's ability to find and appropriate voices that will serve what he
has to say. Poetic originality, says Auden, is achieved through conscious
choice and skillful selection of poetic mentors. Like Merrill's *bunraku*
puppets, it is a state of doubleness in which the poet both surrenders
himself to the voices of others while retaining an agency that makes
the performance his alone. It is as if the puppet were able to choose his
puppeteers, selecting one manipulator for his skill in handling feet and
hands, another for his mastery of expression, and another for his ability
to communicate narrative. Just so might a poet choose one precursor for
his metrical facility, another for his expressiveness, and another for his
content, the combined influence of whom adding up to something entirely original. The poet may surrender himself, but he carefully chooses
to whom he surrenders, and it is that choice that defines him. The tradition, then, becomes a tool for the poet's construction of identity, just as
poetic form is a tool for self-discovery. The poet can deploy the voice of
a predecessor in exactly the same way that he would choose a particular
rhyme scheme or formal structure to suit his subject.

In "New Year Letter," Auden does precisely this in his efforts to write
a poem that would reflect the kind of American poet he wants to be. His

assembled "summary tribunal" of past poets literalizes Eliot's vision of the dead being present in the minds of the living, but it also demonstrates a process of choice and selection. It isn't a universal convocation of dead poets, a babel of voices all straining to force themselves into his poem. Rather, poets appear, as they will in the ballroom at Sandover, by invitation only:

> There Dryden sits with modest smile,
> The master of the middle style,
> Conscious Catullus who made all
> His gutter-language musical,
> Black Tennyson whose talents were
> For an articulate despair,
> Trim, dualistic Baudelaire,
> Poet of cities, harbors, whores,
> Acedia, gaslight and remorse,
> Hardy whose Dorset gave much joy
> To one unsocial English boy,
> And Rilke whom *die Dinge* bless,
> The Santa Claus of loneliness. [*CP*, 204]

Dante, Blake, and Rimbaud preside over the poem, chosen as visionaries and iconoclasts by a poet embarking on a *vita nuova* that would repudiate his earlier career. But Dryden, Catullus, Tennyson, Baudelaire, Hardy, and Rilke are also in attendance, each invited for the particular contributions they might make to Auden's project. Dryden, for instance, is chosen as a model of the "middle style"—neither bombastic and high-flown, nor pedestrian and low-brow—toward which Auden was aiming in his poem. Thus each predecessor adds something to the living poet's voice, helping him to achieve through this "composite voice" originality and artistic success. Auden's catalog is therefore more than simply an acknowledgment of past poetic influences. Rather, it is a marshaling of resources, through whom the poet both discovers and displays his poetic self. Thus it is no surprise to hear Auden, from beyond the grave, exhorting JM, "Think what a minor / Part the self plays in a work of art" compared, he says, to the "great givens" of poetic forms and what he calls "the family" of past poets, the

SWEET WILLIAMS & FATE-FLAVORED EMILIES
THE DOUBTING THOMAS & THE DULCET ONE

(HARDY MY BOY WHO ELSE? & CAMPION)
MILTON & DRYDEN OUR LONG JOHNS [CLS, 262]

It is through the concerted effects of these resources, these "givens," that the poet gains his powers and it is through them that the poet's identity and voice are incorporated and given body in the text.[24]

For Auden, as for Merrill, the question of poetic professionalism is also intimately related to the question of poetic originality. That is to say, in the wake of Romanticism, when the soaring strains of Shelley's skylark have been reduced to the "'Jug Jug' to dirty ears" of Eliot's Philomel, when the welter of Modernist experimentation and allusion have left the would-be poet wondering what poetry could or should be, and when war and holocaust have rendered the poet's Icarus-like aspirations to fight human suffering through art an unimportant and ignored failure, Auden determines that the only avenue to originality available to the poet who knows that he comes too late is through the exercise of a professional discipline. By accepting limitation—moral, intellectual, and formal—the poet gains access to an undiscovered country of the self. In moral terms, the acceptance of the fact that words can't stop a war and that "Poetry makes nothing happen," encourages the poet to explore more private ways in which poetry can make a difference and can be "a way of happening, a mouth." Intellectually, the acknowledgment of one's belatedness allows the poet to dispense with his Romantic anxiety and explore the complexities and instabilities of the self in a new way. And technically, the seemingly stodgy constraints of traditional forms actually become liberating, allowing the poet to go places he would never have imagined, had he not been prodded by the demands of artifice. In each case, as Auden shows, the poet discovers freedom in necessary limitation. As JM remarks in Sandover, dramatizing Auden's pedagogical influence, "Dear Wystan, thank you for reminding me / The rock I'm chained to is a cloud; I'm free" [CLS, 462].

Originality, then, for Auden and for Merrill, becomes a matter of technique, expertise, taste, self-knowledge, education, will, and choice. In the words of Sandover's Maria, in the "other world" of poetry, "ALL THINGS ARE DONE . . . IF YOU HAVE TECHNIQUE" [CLS, 104]. This is a distinctly professional and un-Romantic conception of originality, in which one achieves authenticity not through some sublimated

poetic agon, but through conscious, diligent craft. It is an idea of originality that, far from being anxious about poetic influences, instead acknowledges, appreciates, and consciously utilizes them.[25] The anxiety an
Audenesque poet feels in the face of the "intense interrogation [of] the
summary tribunal" of past poets is not the burden of the past, or the
fear that his belatedness deprives him of originality. Rather, it is the burden of choice, and the fear that his selection of voices, of influences, will
prove wrong and result in an inauthentic, dishonest poem.

As in "Marsyas," Merrill grappled early on with the notion that
originality is achieved through borrowed voices, and throughout his career he attests to the value of forms, poetic choice, and the authenticity
that comes from self-effacement. "Form's what affirms," he says in "The
Thousand and Second Night" [*CP*, 185], and to an interviewer in 1981
he remarks,

> I by and large put my faith in forms. The attention they require
> at once frees and channels the unconscious, as Auden kept
> reminding us. Even if your poem turns out badly, you've learned
> something about proportion and concision and selflessness.
> And at best the form "received" by the next poet to use it will
> have taken on a new aspect because of what you learned there.
> [*CPM*, 143]

Here, in short, is a primer on Auden's poetics, as Merrill himself acknowledges. First, poetry is work, and requires attention and diligence.
Second, formal limitation frees the self. Third, poetry is pedagogical and
teaches both poet and reader about the relation between self and world.
Fourth, selflessness is a path to true poetic expression. Fifth, poetic voice
inheres in forms. Sixth, poets inherit and employ the voices of their predecessors. And seventh, poets construct their own voices out of those
they receive from the tradition.

In another interview, in 1967, Merrill professes his faith in the Audenesque process of finding oneself through the refinement of existing poetic resources:

> Some poets actually say they don't revise. . . . They say their
> originality suffers. I don't see that at all. The words that come
> first are anybody's, a froth of phrases, like the first words from

a medium's mouth. You have to make them your own, and only
then begin to efface yourself. [*CPM*, 61]

Again Merrill offers an Audenesque formula for poetry. The least
original voice is the one unmediated by technique and revision, while, in
a characteristic doubleness, authenticity comes from the effacement that
follows the recognition of one's own voice. The reference to the "first
words from a medium's mouth" points to the project of *Sandover* and
suggests a way of looking at Merrill's role amid the "froth of phrases" of
that poem. Once again, like the *bunraku* puppets, the poet's position is a
dual one. He maintains an agency, "making his own" the words from the
medium's mouth, while simultaneously abdicating it by relying on the
medium for the words in the first place and then effacing himself further.
In *Sandover*, Merrill literalizes Auden's idea of artistic selflessness—and
recalls the "Marsyas" sonnet—with his notion of the "stripping process."
In Ovid, Marsyas cries out to Apollo, who is ripping the skin from his
body, "Why are you stripping me from my self?"[26] The spirit of JM's
friend Robert Morse, as he is about to be reborn as a composer—and, in
the process, lose any awareness of his past self—echoes his homonymic
predecessor by telling JM that self-effacement and surrender are necessary requirements before the artist can achieve individual agency and
originality. The "callus of the self," he says, must be "ALL STRIPPED
OFF / BEFORE ANOTHER TINY MARSYAS / CAN STAND UP TO
APOLLO, FLUTE IN HAND" [*CLS*, 538].

This image is in turn related to another of Merrill's literalizations
of Auden, specifically Auden's conception of how aspects of past poets
are put to constructive use. In *Sandover*, poets like Stevens and Auden
himself are literally "mined" for their poetic densities, an experience the
otherworldly Auden, who has "GIVEN HIS PINT," comically describes
as "AN ODD SENSATION LIKE MISSING NOT ONLY MY SPECS /
BUT THE MEMORY OF WHAT IT WAS I MISSED." To which JM responds, "The 'pint' being Inspiration?" Auden replies, "TOO GRAND A
WORD / FOR THE FLEET IMPULSE TO JOT DOWN A THOUGHT /
& JUST AS WELL: IVE LOST MY STUBBY PENCIL." "Lead left in it,
we hope, for the next user," cracks JM, simultaneously echoing Auden's
idea of how past poets are used, while making a bawdy joke that inscribes

this conception of poetic influence within a specifically homosexual milieu [*CLS*, 189].[27] The trope of "mining" is appropriately associated with Auden, whose poems are notorious for their obsession with mining machinery, while the implicit pun here on "mind" suggests, yet again, that it is no accident the angels refer to Auden as their "platinum poet," recalling as it does Eliot's shred of platinum in "Tradition and the Individual Talent," which he likens to the mind of the poet. JM's reference to Auden as his "mine of sense" [*CLS*, 129] also subtly affirms the idea that one's poetic identity involves a sense of exploitation and possession of one's influences. Auden, says Merrill, is *mine*, reflecting back Miranda's villanelle from "The Sea and the Mirror" ("My Dear One is mine as mirrors are lonely" [*CP*, 421]), learning in practice through engagement with Auden the theory of individual talent posited by Eliot at the end of the poem: "THESE WORKS . . . THAT OTHERS 'WRITE'/ ARE YET ONE'S OWN" [*CLS*, 557].

◆ ◆ ◆

When Randall Jarrell panned Auden's "The Age of Anxiety" in the pages of *The Nation* in 1947, he reserved his most vituperative denunciation for a passage at the beginning of that poem establishing its dramatic scenario in which four strangers meet by chance in a New York bar, fall into conversation, and in doing so commence an elaborate masque on belief, grief, love, and the malaise of a war-torn world. Addressing the noisy radio, one of the poem's four interlocutors announces:

> Listen, Box,
> And keep quiet. Listen courteously to us
> Four reformers who have founded—why not?—
> The Gung-Ho Group, the Ganymede Club
> For homesick young angels, the Arctic League
> Of Tropical Fish, the Tomboy Fund
> For Blushing Brides and the Bide-a-wees
> Of Sans-Souci, assembled again
> For a Think-Fest: Our theme tonight is
> *HOMO ABYSSUS OCCIDENTALIS*
> *or*

A CURIOUS CASE OF COLD FEET

or

SEVEN SUPPERLESS AGES [CP, 464]

Calling these lines "abominable" with a "dreary facetiousness that would embarrass a comedian on the radio," Jarrell witheringly rejects the entire eighty-page poem as "worth neither indignation nor dismay, but only a line or two of indifferent dismissal."[28] Readers of *Sandover*, however, may find them familiar and resonant and further suggestive of Merrill's explicit engagement with Auden's poetic example. Auden's lengthy "baroque eclogue," like his "New Year Letter" and many other poems, finds itself incorporated and revised in Merrill's own epic meditation on private and collective cultural anxiety. From the dramatic framework of four characters enacting a visionary exploration of existential truths, to the campily witty salon-room discourse of the four-sided "Think-Fest," we can see Merrill reflecting Auden in his own poem's mirror. Auden's poem is set on "the night of All Souls" [CP, 451], it grapples with the traumatic memory of war ("Many have perished; more will" [CP, 457]) and fear of worse to come ("Do I love this world so well / That I have to know how it ends?" [CP, 510]), and its themes of "Homo Abyssus Occidentalis" and the Ages of Man rhyme with Merrill's own Purgatorial descent and metaphorical narrative of existential progress and recurrent dooms. In a passage suggestive of the perils of atom-splitting, Auden offers lines that seem to summarize *Sandover*: "Man has no mean; his mirrors distort; / His greenest arcadias have ghosts too; / His utopias tempt to eternal youth / Or self-slaughter" [CP, 452]. And while Jarrell may have hated the poem, we learn via the Ouija board that Psyche herself—"TWIN SISTER OF OUR GOD BIOLOGY" [CLS, 407]—gave it her approval, kissing Auden's cheek as he came up with its now-iconic title [CLS, 411]. Even the "Box" whose silence is demanded at the beginning of Auden's poem makes a mirror-distorted reappearance in Merrill's, at the moment of Auden's first communication from beyond the grave, telling JM and DJ to "BURN THE BOX" [CLS, 87] he'd left behind in Oxford, presumably containing letters since Auden instructed all his friends to destroy his correspondence to forestall a biography. And it is JM's pondering of Auden's ghostly command that prompts him to consider, then in the final section of "Ephraim" to decide against, burning the transcripts from the Ouija board that provide the raw poetic material for *Sandover*. So in a very literal sense, *Sandover* has its origins in a reading and a rewriting of Auden.

Another of Auden's theatrical texts, the 1960 operetta, *Elegy for Young Lovers*, also finds its echo in the themes and structure of *Sandover*, and add a further frame to its elegiac function. The operetta, which Auden co-wrote with his partner Chester Kallman, is loosely (and somewhat slanderously) based on the life of the subject of Auden's first American poem, Yeats, and explores the consequences of the Yeatsian dictum, "The intellect of man is forced to choose / Perfection of the life or of the work." It tells of a writer and his manipulations of those around him toward a disaster that feeds his own artistic inspiration. As Auden and Kallman summarize the action, "Our hero, Mittenhoffer, is a great poet. Throughout the opera he has been working on a poem; in order to complete it successfully, he (morally) murders two people and breaks the spirit of a third" [*Libretti*, 247]. The opera concludes with Mittenhoffer alone on a theatrical stage reading his poem aloud before an aristocratic and admiring audience. In the words of the final stage directions,

> He opens the manuscript book and begins to read, solemnly and with hardly any gestures. We do not actually hear any words, but from behind him come one by one until they are all together, the voices of all who contributed to the writing of the poem:

> HILDA with her visions, CAROLINA with her money and management, DR REISCHMAN with his medicines, TONI and ELIZABETH with their illusory but rhymable love.

> The lights fade until there is nothing but a spotlight on MIT-TENHOFFER. His poem is written. The opera is over. [*Libretti*, 243–44]

The parallels with "The Ballroom at Sandover," the final section of the poem in which Merrill reads aloud the poem to, and in the voices of, "all who had contributed to the writing of the poem," are clear. And the echoes between Auden's operatic fable of authorship and Merrill's own also sound a number of significant resonances with other poetic concerns. First, it theatrically rehearses two tensions involving Yeats and

Auden, one in their own careers and one in Merrill's. The highly unflattering depiction of Yeats in Auden's opera (he makes it almost explicit
in the accompanying synopsis that Mittenhoffer is based on Yeats) reflects the same deep ambivalence manifested in Auden's elegy for the
Irish poet and in the dueling perspectives of his prose staging of a trial,
"The Public Vs. Mr. W. B. Yeats," written at the same time as the elegy, in which the recently dead poet's many perceived faults get a full
hearing as well as a defense. This ambivalence, and rivalry, gets written
into *Sandover* itself, where Yeats is revealed as the silent spiritual force
behind David Jackson's guiding "Hand." When Yeats finally emerges
from DJ's hand to speak in his own voice toward the end of the poem,
JM exclaims, "Mr Yeats, you who have always / Been such a force in
my life!" [*CLS*, 492]. To which the ghost of Yeats, presumably stung by
Auden's critiques of him and resentful of Auden's large dramatic role
in the construction of Merrill's poem, replies with a sidelong smack at
Auden: "WYSTAN, U HEAR?" To which Auden demurs with studied po-
litesse and "the straightest of faces," "MAITRE, I HAVE EVER HEARD /
THE GOLDEN METER IN YOUR WORD, / AND KISS YOUR HAND." The
decorous squabble between the two elder poets, with Auden's attitude
described by the witnessing spirits as a "SOUPCON OF A GLOAT / AT BE-
ING TEXT TO WBY'S FOOTNOTE" [*CLS*, 527], keeps the poetic debate
between the two of them comically alive beyond their own deaths, and
also points more seriously to the tension Merrill himself felt between
the two different poets' influences upon him: Yeats the eternalizing
aesthete versus Auden the humanizing rationalist, each contending for
dominance in Merrill's poetic identity. Yeats is the only poet besides
Auden to appear in the "Dramatis Personae" section of "The Book of
Ephraim," setting up a tension that takes more than 500 pages to play
out. That Auden apparently wins the battle of *Sandover* doesn't settle
the ongoing war, and speaks perhaps most pointedly to Auden's pedagogical role: Auden's function in the poem, as in Merrill's career, is to
teach him how to productively make use of all his influences, including and especially artists besides himself.[29] It also suggests that the final
leave-taking of Auden in the poem, when JM and DJ shatter the mirror
that sends him back into the physical world, marks a moment of meta-
elegy, where the poem honors and bids farewell not only to Auden's
own influence on Merrill and the poem, but to all the other influences,

from Yeats back to Homer (greeted by Auden as "IMMORTAL BARD, YOU WHO CREATED ME!" [*CLS*, 355]), who contributed to Merrill's mature poetic identity—an identity that takes confident center-stage as the poem concludes.

There is one final, poignant echo of Auden's *Elegy for Young Lovers* in Merrill's poem. The opera, like *Sandover*, was written in collaboration between two partners, with Auden claiming that Kallman had written 75 percent of the libretto. The opera's story of what happens to those who are consumed by the poet for the purposes of his own art has strong ironic implications for the domestic relationship between Auden, the "great poet," and Kallman, the less talented beloved whose life and misbehavior provided much of the anguished erotic inspiration for Auden's American poetry. In their life together, Kallman was notorious for his self-destructiveness and petulance, stemming, it was assumed by his friends, from his sense of having lost his own identity in the shadow of Auden's genius and fame. Merrill knew Kallman well when they both lived in Athens, and Kallman's unhappiness in life is mirrored in Merrill's poem, in which he is depicted as a rather sad and bitter figure in the afterlife, throwing tantrums, making scenes, and complaining that even among the dead he has to play second-fiddle to Auden: "JUST LIKE LIFE / THOSE YEARS WITH WYSTAN ONCE A BACKSTREET WIFE / ALWAYS A BACK STREET WIFE" [*CLS*, 106]. For David Jackson, who had his own artistic ambitions as a novelist but whose career languished amid Merrill's increasing success, the parallels with Kallman would be disturbing. And even in the poem itself, Jackson, whose hand is helping to guide the cup over the letters of the Ouija board, is revealed by those letters to be deemed celestially inferior to Merrill, the "Scribe," whose density of divine gifts is numerically accounted as significantly greater than his own. And it is Merrill's name and initials on the cover of *Sandover*, not Jackson's, however much he contributed to its composition. In a sad literalization of both Auden's opera and the lesson of his life with Kallman, then, it comes as an almost overdetermined conclusion to learn, as we do in later Merrill lyrics like "Clearing the Title," that the thirty-year relationship between Merrill and Jackson, which *Sandover* celebrates and commemorates, doesn't long survive the poem's completion and publication: "*Our* poem now. It's signed JM, but grew / From life together, grain by coral grain. / Building on it, we let the life cloud over..." [*CP*, 408]. So, like the poem's staging of the consumption of its poetic influences followed by a farewell to their role in its creation, the poem also enacts a similar elegiac, self-knowing farewell performance to the central influence on the poet's domestic life for three decades. Without Jackson's influence, the poem would not exist, but the cost of that influence, like the "stripping process" by which poetic influences like Auden's are "mined" in the poem, is his own effacement at the hands of the consuming artist. In its foreshadowing of Jackson's fate, *Sandover* becomes an elegy about and for influence itself, both for the poetic sources used and necessarily left behind for the poet's own self-assertion in the world, and for the young lovers that once were Merrill and Jackson.

Along with giving voice to a range of new "posthumous ephemera" that will "keep [Auden's] fans and critics on their toes" [*CLS*, 246], enacting the notion that the poet possesses his influences, *Sandover* also incorporates many other pre-posthumous Auden poems into its poetic body. JM describes a line from "For the Time Being" ("The concept Ought would make, I thought / Our passions philanthropic") as one of his "Touchstone stanzas" [*CLS*, 164], "Law Like Love" serves as a motto for celestial jurisprudence [*CLS*, 252], Miranda's villanelle of mirrors, loneliness, and high green hills offers totemic and imagistic inspiration [*CLS*, 273], and *The Rake's Progress*, whose score is playing during Nature's fete in "Scripts for the Pageant," gets rewritten as a fable about atomic energy [*CLS*, 485]. Auden's "Atlantis" also emerges in multiple aspects of *Sandover*, from Merrill's identification of the doomed Utopia before human time with the same mythic emblem of an elusive ideal, to Robert Morse's reflection of the dialectical quest of Auden's poem in his melancholy summary of his own life as "AN ATLANTIS / SUNKEN AND PERFECT AND DOOMED" [*CLS*, 384]. Auden's spirit also recalls his own "poetic vision" of Atlantis, announcing the abstract metaphor behind Merrill's story of the destruction of the verdant home of prehistoric centaurs, unicorns, and bat-wing angels: "I SEE ATLANTIS AS IDEA, A FIRST / PASTURE TO INNOCENCE, AND RAPED BY IT" [*CLS*, 322]. In life, Auden had also seen Atlantis as an idea, an idea of a dialectical poem-America, and placing Auden's America-inflected Atlantis next to Merrill's opens up a reading of Merrill's poem as engaged in a similar national figuration, with his narrative of self-destroying Atlantis serving as a fable of American naivete and pride leading to its own annihilation. And when Auden offers a critique from beyond the grave of his later work, he does so in terms that frankly echo the lesson of his own "Atlantis," amid "stone and snow, silence and air," to "Remember the noble dead / And honor the fate you are, / Travelling and tormented, / Dialectic and bizarre": "FOR IS IT NOT OUR LESSON THAT WE COME / EACH TO HIS NATURE? NOT JUST ANY VAST / UNIVERSAL ELEVATION, JUST / EACH TO HIS NATURE PRECIOUS IF BANAL" [*CLS*, 308]. JM responds to Auden's lesson by connecting this "Atlantis"-derived vision of a humble existential ideal, framed by Auden's elemental metaphor, to the structure of *Sandover* itself: "It's as we were told at the outset—every grain / Of dust, each waterdrop, to be suffused / With mind, with *our* minds. This will be Paradise" [*CLS*, 308]. Auden's imaginative fate in *Sandover* is to return to earth in mineral form— "BACK TO THE GLABROUS CLAYS / THE OILS AND METALS MY FIRST LOVES" [*CLS*, 303]—through which he will finally achieve the ideal his "nature" sought and suffuse himself within the "stone and snow, silence and air" such that their elemental identity is one with his, prompting the meta-elegy for Auden as "our mine of good sense" as he prepares to depart the poem to become "the glinting faithful heart of stone" [*CLS*, 306]. Auden's function within the poem's narrative is to suggest how this fable of realized identity is a figuration, or mirrored reflection, of the process of achieving poetic identity. Just as Auden's reincarnated self offers an image of ideal identity in which he and the wider world become reflections of one another with every grain of dust or waterdrop suffused with his mind, *Sandover* offers an image of poetic identity in which the poet and his all-including encyclopedic text, full of others' voices, achieve a kind of dialectical unity. The poem may be comprised of the words and identities of others, but they are suffused with *Merrill's* mind. *Sandover* is, then, more than a poetic vision of an imagined or metaphorical Atlantis/ Paradise beyond actual human accomplishment. It defines itself, in terms that Auden provides in his poems and in his persona in Merrill's poem, as an articulation of ideal poetic identity: a "dialectic and bizarre" union of tradition and the individual talent.

Over and over again in *Sandover*, Merrill presents similar pedagogical moments, combining the didactic mode of "New Year Letter" with the masque form of "The Age of Anxiety" to stage scenes of instruction between Auden and himself that theatrically enact Auden's own influence on his poetics and serve as elegiac homage to the way in which

Auden helped him, like the young Shakespeareans in "The School Play," to find his own artistic identity. The interaction between the characters of Wystan, the teacher whose "intellect begins to light the way" [*CLS*, 131], and his pupil JM dramatize the process by which Merrill schooled himself on Auden's poetic example. "FACT IS IS IS FABLE" [*CLS*, 263], Auden tells JM, imparting the central dialectical theme of the poem and pointing to its function as both a fiction and literal demonstration of influence. Auden's role in the poem as the provider of rhyme schemes and stanza forms, and his tutelage in the way in which influences can be exploited, reproduce in fabular fashion Auden's historical role as Merrill's "father of forms," the "gold archaic lion" to his Marsyas. One such scene of instruction explicitly invokes Marsyas, reflecting back on the poem from twenty years before in which Merrill had posited a vision of influence that, with Auden's help, *Sandover* would literalize and epically make manifest. Following the grand revelation toward the end of the poem that his old friend Maria is actually the reincarnation of Plato, JM inquires after the historical Socrates. Auden's spirit informs him that Plato's literary depiction of Socrates was more an inspired rewriting—"AS, OH, TO MILTON THE DROWNED LYCIDAS / SO SOC TO PLATO"—than a reflection of the actual Athenian dialectician, but that in exploiting him for his own purposes the younger philosopher had given new significant meaning to his precursor, turning him from mere man into myth:

> THE SOCRATIC MASK
> BECAME THE FACE OF THE GOAT GOD SILENUS
> WINEBAG FLUTE INVENTING COUNTERPART
> TO MICH/APOLLO IN THE DAWN OF ART
> To be flayed by him like Marsyas? OF COURSE
> BUT WHAT WERE SKINS TO SUCH A MYTHIC FORCE!
>   [*CLS*, 473]

Auden teaches Merrill, and Merrill constructs Auden teaching him, that the relation between inheritor and influence goes—like so much else in the poem—both ways. And in so doing, Merrill reproduces Plato's act of rewriting his precursor, memorializing and transforming the wrinkled old poetic lion into an elemental and eternal mythic force.

The Gay Apprentice

Ashbery, Auden, and a Portrait of the Artist as a Young Critic

It is a well-rehearsed episode in the history of postwar American poetry that W. H. Auden selected John Ashbery for the Yale Younger Poets
Prize in 1956, inaugurating the younger writer's public career as the most
honored and influential American poet of his generation. What is less
well-known by readers and critics, however, is that Ashbery had chosen
Auden more than a decade earlier. While critical accounts of Ashbery's
poetics have often, and justifiably, emphasized his connections to Wallace Stevens, Ashbery himself claims Auden as his most significant poetic model. "He was the first big influence on my work, more so than
Stevens," he has said, contra Harold Bloom, his earliest and most influential critical champion, who has prominently placed Ashbery in the
lineage of what he calls the "American Sublime" line of Emerson, Whitman, and Stevens.[1] "Auden was the most important because he came
first," Ashbery has continued to remind interviewers.[2] Indeed, on one
occasion, when asked about the importance of Auden to his own poetry,
Ashbery responded with a chuckle and his best imitation of one of his
friend Bloom's characteristic oracular pronouncements: "Once, when I
pointed out to him that he sort of ignored Auden's effect on me, Har-

old told me, 'Nonsense, darling. You only *think* you were influenced by Auden. But it's Stevens who made you who you are.'"[3]

As with many other poets of his generation, Auden's influence on Ashbery—Bloom's protestations notwithstanding—was profound. By looking at the development of Ashbery's career through the prism of his early apprenticeship to Auden, and by taking Ashbery's claims about his own poetics seriously, I want to challenge some familiar critical presumptions about Ashbery, prompted by a few basic questions: What are we to make of the disparity between how Ashbery sees himself and how he is seen? What is the responsibility of critics toward authorial claims of self-knowledge and intention? Is there something to be learned by *listening* to this poet and his poems, rather than reading through or against them? What does it mean to read Ashbery as a self-conscious inheritor of Auden's civic tradition, rather than heir to the various Romantic traditions—from Wordsworth to Whitman to the High Modernisms of Stevens or Eliot—with which he is customarily linked? Is there an understanding of poetic influence itself that can accommodate Ashbery's acknowledgement of Auden's role in the development of his poetry that doesn't reduce either to trivial allusion- or echo-identification, or to competing claims of supposed poetic priority and authenticity? In the end, my goal is less to reject prior understandings of Ashbery than to augment and complicate them, and suggest that in doing so, we discover a poet who is even richer—both more familiar and more strange, more conventional and more radical—than we may have seen.

This other Ashbery traces his beginnings to 1944, when he was 17 and, upon the suggestion of a family friend who taught poetry at the nearby University of Rochester, started reading Auden intensely. "She was the only person I knew who'd read any poetry and she told me I should read a lot of Auden's poetry," Ashbery recalls, "So I did and I found myself seeming to understand it and became mad about it."[4] A year later, in an essay entitled "Recent Tendencies in Poetry," written for his high school English class and preserved on a few tattered notebook pages in Harvard's Houghton Library, the precocious poet-to-be singled out Auden as one of the two most important young poets (alongside Stephen Spender) since Eliot, whose "poems are complex because they must spring from a mind which has been made complex by its double-existence—its social responsibility and its inward enigma."[5]

Ashbery's enthusiasm for Auden's poetry, and his attention to its dualistic tension between "social responsibility" and "inward enigma," continued during his years at Harvard, even as he was being introduced by teachers like F. O. Matthiessen to the more recondite mysteries of Stevens's work, and was honing his craft in the company of friends and fellow Harvard poets Frank O'Hara and Kenneth Koch. Auden's impact on the young poet is clearly evident in early poems like "The Painter," written in the summer of his junior year in 1948,[6] whose form finds its origin in Auden's sestinas, "Have a Good Time" and "Paysage Moralisé," and whose subject, an iconoclastic artist thrown by his audience into the sea, recalls the Icarus of "Musée des Beaux Arts." "Illustration," written a year later, about a novice who jumps from a building to her death, also echoes the protagonist of the "The Second Temptation" of "The Quest" sonnet sequence from *The Double Man*, who leaps from a university tower "And plunged into the college quad, and broke" [*CP*, 288].[7] The "reticent" lovers whose "accents seem their own defense" in "Some Trees"—written during Ashbery's senior year, and the title-poem of the volume to which Auden would award the Yale Younger Poets Prize seven years later—also bears an unmistakable Auden stamp, as John Shoptaw has suggested, in its echoes of his anxious lovers, "Always afraid to say more than it meant."[8] In many of these early poems, we find Audenesque figures torn between the claims of society and the "inward enigmas" of their own private art and desires.

But the lasting significance of his youthful engagement with Auden's work finds its most compelling articulation not in one of his early poems, but in a piece of literary criticism he wrote at the same time, his Harvard undergraduate Senior Honors Thesis, written in 1949 and entitled "The Poetic Medium of W. H. Auden."[9] As an undergraduate analysis of Auden's English and early American career, this fascinating document, also in the Harvard archives and for the most part unstudied by Ashbery's critics, demonstrates considerable sophistication in Ashbery's early skills as a sympathetic reader of another poet's work. But it is as a record of Ashbery's own nascent poetics that it offers the greatest interest and insight. If, as Ashbery would later observe, "Poets when they write about other artists invariably talk about themselves" [*RS*, 106], then Ashbery's account of Auden's poetic medium provides his readers with a singular perspective on the development of his own work. In what amounts to a poetic manifesto—a rare thing in the career of the famously evasive poet he would become—the undergraduate Ashbery offers the initial formulation of ideas and themes that will come to seem, over the course of his career, characteristic of his own poetics.

Looking at Ashbery as a young critic accomplishes a paradoxical double task: First, it shows us in embryo the Ashbery familiar to us from his later poetry, and suggests ways in which his practice as a critic contributed to the formation of his poetic identity. But it also shows us a newly unfamiliar Ashbery, an Audenesque Ashbery whose attentions are directed outward at the world and not exclusively in toward the self, and who sees poetry as exerting a moral influence on that world. Through his poetical and critical engagement with his first and most important influence, we can also hear and trace Ashbery's Audenesque ideas about the relation between a poet and his precursors, as well as his thoughts on the relation between poetry and consciousness.

But perhaps most importantly, in his reading of Auden we can see Ashbery developing a conception of poetry as what the elder poet calls "embodied love" [*CP*, 272], a notion that is crucial in understanding Ashbery's poetic ambitions. Like Auden, Ashbery sees poetry as concerned with the ethical relation between private people and construes the relationship between poet and reader as a romantic, even erotic one, founded on a desire for contact, communication, and community. For both poets, poetry serves as an expression of longing in the face of loss, and as a space of hopeful exchange in a world of alienation and isolation. It is in this space of exchange between himself and Auden that we see the young Ashbery taking the first steps in the direction of the poet he will become: a poet whose own poems reach out hopefully to the reader, like a lover yearning for an ideal partner, even as those poems both acknowledge and enact the difficulty, if not impossibility, of that ambition. The difficulty of an Ashbery poem, with all its evasions, revisions, and misrepresentations, is the same difficulty shared by Auden poems like *The Orators*, or "Caliban's Address to the Audience" from "The Sea and the Mirror": It is the difficulty of the wounded, and therefore necessarily guarded, lover whose desire for the beloved manifests itself in a reticence that is also a challenge. The poet's withdrawal demands a pursuit, and the true lover/reader is the one who takes up the challenge, who senses the rewards amid the defensive misdirections, who is willing to work to understand him and, in so doing, reach that place of true contact and communion. With the promise that the labors will be worthwhile, the speaker of an Ashbery poem asks the reader to *work* at it, thereby simultaneously proving the reader's love while earning his. And as we will see, and as Ashbery addresses in his essay, this idea of his poetry as "embodied love" might also prove to have intriguing consequences for how Ashbery's readers and critics—those willing to do the hard work of listening to him, and of attending to his glinting, deceptive surfaces—construe their relation to the poet and his work.

Interestingly, Ashbery's undergraduate response to Auden's work also marks, to a certain extent, the high-point of Auden's influence on him. Ashbery has said on a number of occasions that he stopped reading Auden seriously after "The Sea and the Mirror"—the primary critical focus of Ashbery's essay—as Auden's poetry turned increasingly domestic, conservative, and prosaic, in keeping with his developing religious, cultural, and aesthetic perspective. But this early engagement with Auden has an impact that will echo through his entire career. In many ways, the Ashbery we know was formed in response to the Auden of the decade between 1939 and 1949, the years when Auden was redefining himself as an American poet and when Ashbery was reading—and writing through—him most intensely. Reading the young Ashbery reading Auden we see a self-portrait of the future artist, reflected in the elder poet's mirror.

Indeed, the very first lines of Ashbery's essay set the terms for this future Ashbery, and begin the argument for seeing the Ashbery we know as a product of his engagement with the example of Auden. Ashbery opens his study with a declaration of critical and poetic independence reflecting the bravado of a confident twenty-two-year-old undergraduate, but significant in its implications for his later work:

It is often said that we read so-called "intellectual" poetry for its style rather than its content; anthologists and instructors assure us that Pope's *Essay on Man* contains not a single fresh idea; that its saving feature is the vigor and grace with which it expresses old ones. Such a false division between form and content presupposes two boxes, one of which contains old, hashed-over

ideas which everyone assimilated years ago, and from which the
poet takes whatever he needs to "stuff" his poem; and the other,
brand-new, unthought of ideas, to which the philosopher re-
sorts when seeking inspiration. But there are no new ideas, any
more than there are any old ones; there are merely old and new
ways of looking at the world. Every new poem is a fresh discovery, and Pope stands acquitted on the charge of commonplace
subject matter; "what oft was thought but n'er so well expressed"
might as well be what n'er was thought for those who, but for
the poet, might have understood the idea but not been able to
apply it within their realm of experience.

In the space of this single introductory paragraph, we see, *ab ovo*,
notions of poetics that will find expression throughout his own mature
poetry, and reflect Ashbery's Audenesque inheritance. Beginning with
an attack on what would become one of his favorite targets, literary critics, Ashbery styles himself as a brash iconoclast, not unlike the Painter
of his sestina, by setting up the "anthologists and instructors" of his Harvard classes as the straw men for a defense of poetry that acknowledges
the power to be gained from belatedness and bases its claims for poetry's
value on its capacity to help people apply poetic truth "within the realm
of their own experience." This claim, which is echoed in the final line of
the thirty-two-page essay in which Ashbery stakes Auden's importance
on his achievement in having "brought innumerable people closer to
the world in which they live," signals Ashbery's inheritance of an Audenesque notion of poetry's place in the world. Like the newly American
Auden of "In Memory of W. B. Yeats," written soon after the poet's arrival in the United States in 1939, the young Ashbery asserts poetry's
power not to make something happen, but to be a way of happening in
which the experience of reading the poem serves as what Auden elsewhere called a "rehearsal for living" [*EA*, 311] offering the reader access
to ideas he "might have understood but not been able to apply." Poetry,
for the young poet—as it was for Auden—is essentially didactic, if not
in content then in effect.

And this is not simply the idealistic position of the unsophisticated
twenty-two-year-old budding poet, later to be abandoned as he matured
into the jaded, postmodern ironist familiar to us from our own "anthol-

ogists and instructors." Thirty years later, the now-established Ashbery is still reaffirming his claim as an inheritor of Auden's post-emigration vision of poetry's power to effect change, telling an interviewer,

> [T]here's a celebrated line from Auden: "poetry makes noth-
> ing happen." It doesn't, but its value is precisely the fact that it
> doesn't, because that's the way it *does* make things happen. The
> pleasure that you get, if you love poetry, is a pleasure that's going
> to cause you to act, it forces you back into life. Poetry is in fact—
> I was just reading a quotation from Hazlitt—not a branch of
> literature, but life itself. So that an intense poetic experience for
> me causes me to want to, you know, go out and be with people,
> perhaps join a political demonstration, which I have done and
> did during the Vietnam war. I did this somewhat dubiously
> because I felt that poetry makes nothing happen, neverthe-
> less, here was a case where I felt that even though this is true,
> maybe people will, by the nature of my non-political poetry, be
> persuaded to become more *people*. I mean a person will become
> more of a person and will therefore do these not only politically
> helpful and constructive things, but things that will make him
> more aware of his own life and the people around him and will
> influence his actions on a number of levels, not just one.[10]

In the history of Ashbery's critical reception, little attention has been paid to this aspect of his poetics, namely its insistence that the experi-ence of reading his poetry ought to—and indeed, does—have a didactic, constructive, even moral effect on the reader.[11] He is more often seen, under Bloom's guidance, as a figure of "triumphant solipsism,"[12] lost in the discursive drama of himself: "Like his master, Stevens, Ashbery is es-sentially a ruminative poet, turning a few subjects over and over, know-ing always that what counts is the mythology of the self, blotched out beyond unblotching," says Bloom.[13] Or, he is proposed as a disengaged representative of late capitalism, whose "intractable" poetics, as another critic summarizes it, "confirms the opinion that poetry does not make any difference, unless, perhaps, it markets difference."[14] Ashbery's insistence that poetry is "not a branch of literature, but life itself" and can make the reader "more aware of his own life and the people around him and will influence his actions on a number of levels," argues strongly against his many critics who find in Ashbery the paradigm for a contemporary poetics of detachment, fragmentation, and Stevensian philosophical solipsism.[15] Ashbery is less the Stevensian man on the postmodern dump than an Audenesque love poet with a vision of poetry's constructive, moral power as "a way of happening." For Ashbery, the knowledge of the world's difficulty, and its expression in his difficult poetry, is not the verdict to which we surrender in existential despair, but the inhospitable terrain in which we, self-aware, continue to strive, and act, and hope, even in the face of probable failure. Like his mentor Auden, who saw in poetry the power to "make a vineyard of the curse," Ashbery sees his poetry as an act of hopeful cultivation: Amid the decay of the dump or the stony rubbish of the wasteland, the poet can still bring forth life.

♦ ♦ ♦

In that first paragraph of his Honors Thesis, and throughout the rest of the essay, Ashbery sets forth a number of Audenesque notions that, reading back through the history of his poetic career, will come to define his own poetics. Perhaps the most pronounced of those features that would later become familiar to his readers is what Auden called, in a critique of Romantic poets, an "awareness of the dialectic" [DM, 118]. Ashbery announces himself immediately as a writer distinguished by a relentlessly dialectical perspective. From his initial observations about "'intellectual'" poetry, whose ironizing quotation marks imply a dubiousness about its presumed antithetical relation to its "emotional" opposite, to his remarks about the "false divisions" between style and content, between new ideas and old ones, and between poet and philosopher, the young poet-critic's opening flourish bursts with dialectical pairings. And in each case, these pairs are shown to be more complexly related than a simple antinomial relation: "There are no new ideas, any more than there are any old ones; there are merely old and new ways of looking at the world."

As every reader of Ashbery's poetry soon discovers, his is a poetics defined by its dialectical vision.[16] As Ashbery himself asks in his double-columned poem "Litany," calling attention to the interplay between the competing voices of the opposing lines of verse, "Who can elicit these rubbery spirals / Antithesis chirping to antithesis?" [AWK, 8] Like the Auden of *The Double Man* (whose "tedious dialectical obscurity" Ashbery chastises, but assimilates, later in the thesis), and the doubly conscious Auden of Ashbery's high school essay, divided between "social responsibility and inward enigma," Ashbery refuses to take sides, continually seeking what Auden, in "New Year Letter," calls "the gift of double-focus." For the young Ashbery, as it would be for the older, the challenge of seeing the world truthfully is the challenge of seeing it from contending perspectives, and trying to make sense of, and live within, each: "A kind of fence-sitting / Raised to the level of an esthetic ideal," as he would wryly put it in "Soonest Mended" [*SP*, 88]. With these introductory remarks, Ashbery embarks on his reading of Auden—and, in a very real sense, the "new way of looking at the world" that would manifest itself in his poems—armed with that old dialectical gift, inherited from Auden himself.[17]

For Ashbery, as for Auden, the ultimate space of dialectic in human experience, and therefore in poetry, is the tense dialectic of *eros*, as lovers continuously seek or resist the stability of their union. In one section of Ashbery's essay we see him staging the poetic transmission of this idea, in a scenario full of erotic implication—between younger and elder poet, between poet and his reader, and even between poet and his critics. While devoting most of his critical attention to "The Sea and the Mirror," Ashbery reserves his highest praise for one portion in particular, "Caliban's Address to the Audience," calling it "probably the most brilliant writing Auden has ever done." Ashbery has acknowledged in interviews the formal influence of Caliban's Jamesian prose upon his own work, in particular his prose *Three Poems*, but this poem's significance and utility for Ashbery extends beyond his later adoption of its form. Ashbery's choice of emphasis in his analysis is telling, as he focuses special attention on Caliban's remarks not to the audience but to the "strange young man" who has come to the performance "not to be entertained but to learn" [*CP*, 430]. To this figure of the younger artist, the "gay apprentice in the magical art who may have chosen this specimen of the prestigiditory genus to study this evening in the hope of grasping more clearly just how the artistic contraption works, of observing some fresh detail in the complex process by which the heady wine of amusement is distilled into the grape of composition" [*CP*, 430], the worldly Caliban recounts the history of his own artistic career, including his tempestuous relationship with Ariel, his doppelganger and muse. This relationship, in Caliban's account of it and in Ashbery's pointed summary of it, reaches a crisis when Ariel, the imaginative spirit upon whom Caliban the artist had depended for his art, the bodiless inspiration who could be summoned and dismissed at will, suddenly insists on his own freedom, identity, and corporeality:

> Striding up to him in fury, you glare into his unblinking eyes
> and stop dead, transfixed with horror at seeing reflected there,
> not what you had always expected to see, but a gibbering fist-
> clenched creature with which you are all too unfamiliar, for this
> is the first time indeed that you have met the only subject that
> you have, who is not a dream amenable to magic but the all too
> solid flesh you must acknowledge as your own. [*CP*, 433]

Throughout Caliban's address to the young artist, Auden characterizes this multifaceted dialectical artistic relation—between Caliban and Ariel, between the artist and his muse, between body and spirit, between the self and its alienated other, between himself and the "gay apprentice"—as being an explicitly romantic, and erotic, one: "At last you have come face to face with me, and are appalled to learn how far I am from being, in any sense, your dish" [*CP*, 433]. Caliban details the stormy nature of this romance, including the charged and angry nights spent "wrestl[ing] through long dark hours," and the drunken days spent "jump[ing] naked from bed to bed," as the fractious duo repeatedly spurn, then return to one another. That Auden has in mind a specifically homoerotic—and therefore culturally risky—model of relations is made clear by Caliban's ironic observation, "Such genuine escapades, though, might have disturbed the master at his meditations and even involved him in trouble with the police" [*CP*, 434]. But the pair, like an old couple whose wild-oats-sowing days are behind them, eventually settle down into something resembling domestic harmony, or at least non-conflict:

> From now on we shall have, as we both know only too well,
> no company but each other's, and if I have had, as I consider, a
> good deal to put up with from you, I must own that, after all, I
> am not just the person I would have chosen for a life companion

myself; so the only chance, which in any case is slim enough, of my getting a tolerably new master and you a tolerably new man, lies in our both learning, if possible and as soon as possible, to forgive and forget the past, and to keep our respective hopes for the future within moderate, very moderate limits. [*CP*, 435]

In portraying the relation between the artist and his muse not unlike his own turbulent yet domesticated partnership with Chester Kallman, Auden offers a humble but powerful metaphor for his vision of the dialectical nature of poetic art, governed by the "hidden law" of love. For Auden, as for Ashbery, the relation between the poet and his muse, like the relation between the poet and his reader, is a manifestly difficult, tension-filled one: Poetry, like love, is hard repetitive work and requires significant amounts of patience, forbearance, acceptance, and trust to make it work, however imperfectly. The question implicit in this difficulty is whether we, as readers, are willing to commit, as it were, to the demands of this relationship.

Ashbery, in his essay, opts not to comment explicitly on Auden's homoerotic construction of his poetics, or on the possible implications of Auden's term for the student artist as the "gay apprentice," even though, as Shoptaw has pointed out, "Ashbery remembers first hearing the word 'gay' as 'homosexual' at Harvard in 1946," and had used the word suggestively in his own undergraduate poems.[18] This omission—apart from making perfect sense in the less-liberal environment of 1949 Harvard[19]— would be, for Shoptaw, further evidence of what he has helpfully termed Ashbery's "misrepresentative poetics," in which Ashbery's rhetoric of evasion simultaneously masks and enacts its "homotextual" perspective.[20] But it also suggests Ashbery's ambition to reach out, not just past the limits of self, but past the limits of gender as well, toward a vision of civil, equal relations built on individual, often intimate and private, mutual acknowledgment. Ashbery, who has resisted being read as a "gay poet," assimilates Auden's notion of the erotics of poetic relation—itself formed in the context of, if not in response to, Auden's own homosexuality—and responds to its vision of homoerotic relations as a trope for all hopeful human relations. Ashbery's poetic love, like Auden's, while emerging from a homoerotic context, reaches out to any and all who might respond.[21]

Ashbery expands on the pathos and difficulty inherent in this dialectic, and emphasizes his rejection of the absolutist's insistence on an
either/or choice, in his essay's comments on Caliban's closing remarks, in
which Ashbery discusses (citing the poet/critic Henry Reed's own reading of Auden) "the two false paths" his reality-seeking audience might
take: "The one is an attempt to discover a world of false childhood, a
world of looking to others for comfort, a world conceived as free and
without responsibility . . . ; the other a state of false adulthood which
achieves a state of disregarding the separate existence, a world likewise
free and irresponsible." Ashbery's "solution"—and Auden's—to over-
coming these equally tempting, solipsistic falsehoods is a self-aware recognition of one's "very moderate limits," an acknowledgment of mutual
dependence, and a confession of love:

> The only solution is seeing ourselves as we are—actors in a
> *completely unconvincing and unbeautiful drama*, "the greatest
> grandest opera rendered by a very provincial touring company
> indeed" (Caliban's detailed description of it is magnificently
> adequate). Only by realizing how "indescribably inexcusably
> awful" it has been, by seeing ourselves as we truly are, can we
> succeed in gaining the "full bloom of the unbothered state," the
> "sounded note" of the "restored relation." Last of all, Ariel's song
> comes as the "sounded note," begging Caliban to "Weep no
> more but pity me . . . helplessly in love with you" and reassuring
> him that "I will sing if you will cry . . . *I*." [emphasis Ashbery's]

This scene, of the conflicted traveler facing the choice of forking
paths and seeking a "solution" that will resolve them, reappears throughout Ashbery's poems, including "The System," one of Ashbery's Caliban-
influenced *Three Poems*:

> That's the way it goes. For many weeks you have been explor-
> ing what seemed a profitable way of doing. You discovered that
> there was a fork in the road, so first you followed what seemed
> to be the less promising, or at any rate the more obvious, of the
> two branches until you felt you had a good idea of where it led.
> Then you returned to investigate the more tangled way, and for
> a time its intricacies seemed to promise a more complex and

therefore a more practical goal for you, one that could be picked up in any number of ways so that all its faces or applications could be thoroughly scrutinized. And in so doing you began to realize that the two branches were joined together again, farther ahead; that this place of joining was indeed the end, and that it was the very place you had set out from, whose intolerable mixture of reality and fantasy had started you on the road which has now come full circle. It has been an absorbing puzzle, but in the end all the pieces fit together like a ghost story that turns out to have a perfectly rational explanation. Nothing remains but to begin living with this discovery, that is, without the hope mentioned above. Even this is not so easy, for the reduced mode or scope must itself be nourished by a form of hope, or hope that doesn't take itself too seriously. [*TP*, 90]

Here, the traveler's "solution" lies—as it does for Caliban—neither in choosing one path as "more practical" than the other, nor in successfully achieving some grand transcendent synthesis between the two. Rather, resolution comes from complete self-awareness, total consciousness of the "intolerable mixture of reality and fantasy" that compels the artist to set out in the first place. The two paths are not options to be chosen between, but are in fact part of the same road: "this place of joining was indeed the end, and... the very place you had set out from." The "end"—the "purpose"—of Ashbery's poetry is to reach this "place of joining" and the pathos-filled "solution" for achieving this end is the painful recognition that we are always already there without knowing it, and are destined to go on not knowing it. Poetry's purpose is to communicate, however inadequately, that knowledge, that instantaneous self-awareness, so that we can try to "begin living with this discovery."

It is a melancholy knowledge, "how indescribably inexcusably awful" our fate is, in Caliban's words, to keep seeking that which we already have but can never grasp, yet from this knowledge comes, as Ashbery puts it in "The New Spirit," the first of his prose poems, "A strange kind of happiness within the limitations" [*TP*, 27]. This happiness is achieved, says Ashbery, only by "seeing ourselves as we truly are," a phrase he repeats twice in his essay and a third time, with a slight variation, in the first line of his first book, "We see us as we truly behave." Our journey must be, as Ashbery significantly describes Auden's poem, an "epic of self-consciousness." Only by seeing ourselves as "actors in a completely unconvincing and unbeautiful drama," as travelers through an "intolerable mixture of reality and fantasy," can we succeed in reaching that "place of joining," or, as Ashbery paraphrases Auden, "in gaining the 'full bloom of the unbothered state,' the 'sounded note' of the 'restored relation.'" That "sounded note" is the note of love, the "restored relation" where both understanding and consolation are found. Ariel's love song to Caliban, "Weep no more but pity me...helplessly in love with you," and their mutual acknowledgment of their dependence—"I will sing if you will cry . . . I"—signals that ideal moment of self-knowledge which comes, paradoxically, through an awareness of otherness. As Auden defines it in *The Orators*, which Ashbery has called one of his favorite poems: "Awareness of difference—love" [*EA*, 75].

This awareness is everywhere to be found in Ashbery's own poetry. He is, as surprisingly few of his critics have observed, in every sense an Audenesque love poet.[22] From the brief early lyric "Some Trees," whose trees tell the reticent lovers that "soon / We may touch, love, explain," to grander projects like "A Wave," which figures love itself as the giant wave that propels the poem, it is easy to claim, as Ashbery does of his long poem, "Fragment," "Like maybe all of my poems, it's a love poem."[23] Ashbery has even teasingly offered his critics a foundational biographical moment that places the origins of his poetic ambitions in a specifically erotic context, telling one interviewer that, as a boy, "I fell deeply in love with a girl who was in this [painting] class but who wouldn't have anything to do with me. So I went to this weekly class knowing that I would see this girl, and somehow this being involved with art may have something to do with my poetry."[24] Ashbery's intriguing placement of the erotic origins of his poetic career at a moment of heterosexual desire both subtly disputes his critics' attempts to read him as a "gay poet," and reinforces his (and Auden's) notion that poetry, like love, is the expression of the yearning for connection between people, regardless of sex. For Auden, love is both the genesis and the revelation, the conception and the consummation of poetry, and, as is made clear in poem after poem, Ashbery shares Auden's notion that the fundamental dialectic at the heart of poetry is the dialectic of love. Indeed, the last lines of "A Wave" itself offer a rewriting of Caliban's account of his final

domestic arrangement with Ariel, in which the artist/muse partners—
who are also the aspects of the divided self, the artist and his audience,
the poet and his "gay apprentice"—settle into a stable, loving relationship grounded in their own differences: "And so each of us has to remain
alone, conscious of each other / Until the day when war absolves us of
our differences. We'll / Stay in touch. So they have it, all the time. But all
was strange" [*SP*, 343].

To be in love, as Roland Barthes suggests, is to desire affirmation,[25]
and the continuous dialectical voices in Ashbery's poems are continually
seeking affirmation, from one "erotic double" to another: "Thank you.
You are a very pleasant person. / Thank you. You are too" [*AWK*, 82].
The double columns of "Litany" enact this erotic dialectic as one column
first affirms, then dismisses the other—"It was nice of you to love me /
But I must be thinking about getting back" [*AWK*, 44]—while its partner plaintively looks for support, as in the poem's final lines which pointedly ask: "Would you / Try?" [*AWK*, 68]. Ashbery has described the
two columns as "like two people I am in love with simultaneously,"[26] setting up a love triangle between the poet and the dual voices of his poem.
Ashbery becomes Caliban's figure of the "master," while the squabbling
yet dependent columns again re-create the roles of Caliban and Ariel,
the dialectical constituents of his poetic identity.

In "As I Walked Out One Evening," Auden depicts a solitary lover
singing "under an arch of the railway" of his eternal devotion, claiming
"Love has no ending" and that his love will last "till the ocean / Is folded
and hung up to dry / And the seven stars go squawking / Like geese across
the sky" [*CP*, 133]. His love, the amorous singer asserts, is "The Flower of
the Ages / And the first love of the world." But "all the clocks in the city,"
Time's stern representatives, correct the young lover, telling him "O let
not Time deceive you / You cannot conquer Time." Love, they tell him,
at least in the real world of "crooked neighbors" with "crooked hearts,"
is never eternal except in mutability. Worldly love is a fickle, changeable,
confusing thing, and in the war between Love and Time, Time always
wins. In "Thank You for Not Cooperating," Ashbery updates Auden's
singing lover: "Two lovers are singing / Separately, from the same rooftop: '*Leave your change behind*, / Leave your clothes, and go. It is time
now. / It was time before too, but now it really is time'" [*SP*, 308]. The
single lover has become two, not "under an arch of the railway" but up

on "the same rooftop." These are lovers who have already learned the lesson of the clocks. They are singing together, but "separately," and they know that what defines their relationship is "change." In fact, the only way to "leave [their] change behind" is to part, and rather than trying to conquer time, they welcome its decision: "It is time now."

In Ashbery's poems, the lovers already know that their love is doomed by time, but they go on loving anyway. Ashbery's lovers, like the "human" and "faithless" lovers of Auden's early poems, begin with the knowledge that love is mortal and always moving: "It's they can tell you how love came and went / And how it keeps coming and going, ever disconcerting, / Even through the topiary trash of the present, / Its undoing, and smiles and seems to recognize no one" [*SP*, 336]. Love doesn't conquer time, but actually shares some of its properties: "Love is different. / It moves, or grows, at the same rate / As time does, yet within time" [*AWK*, 56]. In Ashbery, love "moves" and "grows" and, like time, is inescapable.

In "Late Echo," Ashbery develops this idea of love's "difference":

Alone with our madness and favorite flower
We see that there really is nothing left to write about.
Or rather, it is necessary to write about the same old things
In the same way, repeating the same things over and over
For love to continue and be gradually different. [*AWK*, 88]

Ashbery here defines love by its cyclicality, its repetitiveness. Paradoxically, in order for "love to continue and be gradually different," the lovers must "repeat the same things over and over." In "A Love Poem" he makes the same point, as the lovers write "notes to each other, always repeated, always the same" [*AWK*, 101]. In the quotidian context of a romantic relationship this makes sense, as we can recognize the aspect of repetitiveness that goes into a relationship of any duration while also recognizing that to a certain extent it is the very stability of doing these "same old things / In the same way" that allows that "love to continue." As with Caliban and Ariel, domestic harmony often comes at the expense of "difference." But in terms of poetry, this definition of love has other implications.

In both "Late Echo" and "A Love Poem," Ashbery equates love with the act of writing itself: The poet must "write about the same old things" for "love to continue and be gradually different." Under the guise of a domestic love-lyric, Ashbery is making a startlingly bold—and Auden-esque—claim: For love to survive, we need poetry. Poetry, which, as we recall from Ashbery's introduction to his Thesis, repeats the "same old" truths of our existence ("There are no new ideas, any more than there are any old ones; there are merely old and new ways of looking at the world"), is "necessary"—using Auden's own abstracted term for the ines-capability and obligations of love—to the world of human relations. In "And *Ut Pictura Poesis* Is Her Name," Ashbery writes,

> Something
> Ought to be written about how this affects
> You when you write poetry:
> The extreme austerity of an almost empty mind
> Colliding with the lush, Rousseau-like foliage of its desire to
>   communicate
> Something between breaths, if only for the sake
> Of others and their desire to understand you and desert you
> For other centers of communication, so that understanding
> May begin, and in doing so be undone. [*SP*, 235]

Ashbery here reverses the formula from "Late Echo," and follows the example of Caliban, in describing poetry in the language of a romantic relationship. Poetry is defined as an economy of "desire": the poet's "de-sire to communicate something...for the sake of others," and their "desire to understand...and desert [him] / For other centers of communication," or other poets. The relation between poet and audience is figured here, as in Caliban's address, as an erotic one. Poet and reader "desire" one another, and "desire to understand" one another, but the relationship, like any romantic relationship, is likely a doomed one. With time, they will "desert" each other. But with this separation comes a kind of "under-standing." For Ashbery, "understanding" is what Auden in "New Year Letter" calls "a process in a process / Within a field that never closes" [*CP*, 208], an endless cycle of setting out and coming home, of seeking and abandonment, whose meaning comes through repetition, not reso-lution. "Understanding" is the dialectical process itself, always seeking and never finding, yet worth continuing nonetheless. Love, too, works this way—"coming and going, ever disconcerting, / Even through the

topiary trash of the present, / Its undoing, and smiles and seems to recognize no one"—yet is somehow necessary.

Both poetry and love seek "understanding" and both are subject to
time and the frustrations and contingencies of existence. As Ashbery
puts it in "A Wave," "What were the interruptions that / Led us here and
then shanghaied us if not sincere attempts to / Understand and so desire
another person" [*SP*, 337]. In Ashbery's terms, to "desire another person"
is to "attempt to understand" them. "Desire" and "understanding" are,
for Ashbery, the same thing. Poetry and love are unified in their shared
ambition, and their shared pathos. As he puts it in "Litany," "The essence of it is that all love / Is imitative, creative, and that we can't hear it"
[*AWK*, 66]. Ashbery's poems, then, are love songs: "imitative, creative"
songs of desire and understanding to himself, to lovers, to the reader, to
the world. The pathos and anxiety of the poet—and the lover—is that
these songs of himself will go unheard, that there will be no Ariel to echo
his Caliban-cry of "*I*." The title of one of Ashbery's books is *Can You
Hear, Bird* and this—with an implied emphasis on "hear"—is Ashbery's
continual question, and plaint, to his readers: Can you *hear*—as opposed
to talk over, or project onto—me? For readers of Ashbery, looking for
hidden significances and latencies, or observing the fragmentations and
evasions, is, in some sense, the easy part—it's the simple listening that is
difficult. It's hard work, but Ashbery asks us, "Would you / Try?" It's an
earned intimacy that while it may become familiar, never becomes any
easier—like love, like life. And if poetry is love, and if to read a poet is
to love and be loved in return, then, in the history of Ashbery's poetic
affairs, Auden stands as his first, never-to-be-forgotten romance.

♦ ♦ ♦

In Ashbery's undergraduate essay we see the young poet achieving what
Auden calls, in his own essay on the importance of Hardy to the development of his poetics, a "literary transference," as the young artist identifies and assimilates aspects of his mentor that will help him become the
poet he wants to be. The relation between the "gay apprentice" and the
elder artist is figured as both a relationship of love and a relationship of
convenience and utility, and suggests that these two relationships need
not be mutually exclusive. The young Ashbery *uses* Auden to become
the future Ashbery: a poet who, in welcoming the difficult world into

his consciousness and reflecting it in his poetry, hopes in some way to transform it.

Auden's range of discursive reference, from science to popular songs, suggested to Ashbery a kind of cultural democratization that would serve useful in his own poetry. He cites at length and with approval a 1935 *Poetry* review that contrasts Auden favorably with Eliot and declares, "Allusiveness in Auden . . . tends to be on a lower, more generally comprehensible plane" that offers "the opportunity to catch poetry in the act of returning from the remote realms of symbolist subtlety to the workaday world of proletarian experience, refreshed with new powers." Ashbery adds his own encomium: "No other poet at this time, I feel, has a comparable medium for expressing the ideas which are common to most modern poets. Eliot, it is true, did much of the ground work for Auden. But his poetry as a whole, though it introduced the idea that the everyday world is part of the province of poetry, remains allusive and refined, lacking in the immediacy and concreteness which Auden gives to all he touches." He concludes with a peroration on Auden's poetic pluralism and utility:

> His poetry is, as Hindemith describes his own music, "for use";
> its beauty as poetry functional, though surpassing whatever
> "pure" poetry we have today. He has absorbed certain common
> techniques of thought (the cataloging, the characterizing by
> denoting an unusual quality) and rhythms (those of the cabaret,
> the birthday card, the political broadsheet) which are very much
> a part of our life, using them to convey ideas which matter very
> much to us. If he is not a great poet, a decision which must be
> made by time, he has brought innumerable people closer to the
> world in which they live.

For Ashbery, the poet whose own range of allusiveness stretches from the Marvell of "Picture of Little JA in a Prospect of Flowers" to the Popeye of "Farm Implements and Rutabagas in a Landscape," Auden served as the crucial link between "the remote realms of symbolist subtlety" and the "poetry of the everyday world" that he wanted to write. Auden consolidated and synthesized Eliot's innovations in allusion and the incorporation of the demotic into poetry, "using them to convey ideas which matter very much to us" and making them available "for use." Poetry, as he will later say, "is not a branch of literature but life itself," and can be a vehicle to carry people back more forcefully and engagedly into that life.

Evidence of Ashbery making *use* of Auden's poetry to articulate his own poetics is everywhere to be found in his undergraduate essay. Ashbery's notion of the crypt word, which Shoptaw has shown to be a defining feature of Ashbery's poetics, finds its first expression in his analysis of the first lines of "The Sea and The Mirror" in which the Stage Manager sets the dramatic mood in expectation of the night's performance: "The aged catch their breath, / For the nonchalant couple go / Waltzing across the tightrope/ As if there were no death / Or hope of falling down." Comparing Auden's use of the metaphor of the tightrope-walker with its less-effective use by a minor contemporary poet named (felicitously enough) Walker Gibson, Ashbery remarks on Auden's provocative and productive substitution of an unexpected word in the formula of a cliché: "In his poem he has made this 'hope of falling down' a happening as ordinary as the 'fear of falling down.'" This was a lesson the young poet would take to heart, making a habit throughout his own work of revealing the hidden freight carried by words in familiar combinations, from this "mooring of starting out" of his own career to the "mourning forbidding valediction" [*HL*, 114] of his later books.

Ashbery also tellingly observes Auden's penchant for list-making: "Instead of a traditional presentation and examination of an object, its illumination through metaphor and simile, Auden gives us lists of objects interesting and significant without description; which are, indeed, often only named, and then draws or allows to be drawn the poetic conclusion." Identifying this mode as "a special kind of poetry which Auden has created," he goes on to theorize its relevance to the contemporary moment:

> Such a poetic theory seems peculiarly of our time. In the first place, when we think of the ubiquity of the list, the sheet of tabulations, in almost every category of modern life; in science, business, even in popular poetry—think of the numerous popular songs in which the beloved is designated by lists of desirable objects ("You're a Paris hat, a month in the country, a hot fudge sundae," etc.) it is not surprising that a poet so completely contemporary as Auden should have absorbed the process.

Secondly, our age seems to be characterized as well by a rapid drawing of conclusions from certain particulars—one thinks of scientists, technicians, and even our present-day conversation, which, in growing more sophisticated has tended to make a code of all that can be observed easily or rather easily, and is able to adduce particulars immediately when a name, a quality is mentioned.

From early poems like "Popular Songs" (the second poem in *Some Trees*), whose disjointed romance narrative ("He continued to consult her for her beauty") is spiked with evocative song titles like "The Gardens of the Moon" [*ST*, 22], to later works like "Daffy Duck in Hollywood," with its "mint condition can / Of Rumford's Baking Powder, a celluloid earring, Speedy / Gonzales, the latest from Helen Topping Miller's fertile / Escritoire, a sheaf of suggestive pix on greige, deckle-edged / Stock" [*SP*, 227], Ashbery's work repeatedly enacts Auden's "poetic theory" of lists. In "And *Ut Pictura Poesis* Is Her Name" Ashbery explicitly addresses this theory, asking "Now, / About what to put in your poem-painting: / Flowers are always nice, particularly delphinium. / Names of boys you once knew and their sleds, / Skyrockets are good—do they still exist?" [*SP*, 235], and in *The Vermont Notebook* he writes a book of lists, consisting almost entirely of obscurely defined catalogs like, "Front porches, back porches, side porches, door jambs, window sills, lintels, cornices, gambrel roofs, dormers, front steps, clapboards, trees, magnolia, scenery, McDonald's, Carrol's, Kinney Shoe Stores" [*VN*, 25]. If this is a "special kind of poetry which Auden has created," then it is a kind Ashbery has made his own.

Elsewhere in his essay, Ashbery relates this idea of Auden's poetic inclusivity, accumulation, and utility specifically to the question of poetic influence itself. In a discussion of Auden's play, *Paid on Both Sides*, which takes its inspiration from Auden's beloved Icelandic sagas, Ashbery observes:

It is rather futile to talk about "influences" in *Paid on Both Sides*, as it would be to discuss influences on Joyce in the "Oxen of the Sun" (hospital) episode in *Ulysses*. A literary influence usually implies an unconscious or semi-conscious assimilation of authors which slowly alters a writer's style into something new. Auden, like Joyce, has gone out of his way to imitate many styles, and if, in doing so, he has finally achieved stylistic detachment, he has reached that state fully conscious of the direction in which he was traveling. At any rate, the many styles which occur throughout the early *Poems* and throughout the individual poems themselves are drawn from many sources: besides the saga language, we find technical and scientific terms, contemporary *argot*, Shakespearean rhetoric, satires on occasional, "family" verse, and the clumsy meter and rhyming of the political broadside, all jostling each other, yet in most cases seeming to form a unified and satisfactory whole. It is our task to discover how and with what justification, what purpose, the poet has used these sources.

Here Ashbery articulates a notion of literary influence that eschews the "unconscious or semi-conscious assimilation of authors" in favor of a process, achieved through "stylistic detachment," by which the poet imitates and chooses from a variety of sources—literary and otherwise— "fully conscious of the direction in which he is traveling." Auden's formal and discursive diversity, and the "unified and satisfactory whole" he makes of those chosen influences, demonstrates for Ashbery a "functional" way of incorporating both the tradition and the world around him into a poetry that represents the whole vocabulary of conscious experience yet still reflects a shaping, "purposeful," self-aware intellect. This model of poetic influence and originality corresponds closely with Auden's own formulation of the relation between the tradition and the individual talent: "Originality," in modernity, says Auden in his essay "The Poet & the City," "no longer means a slight modification in the style of one's immediate predecessors; it means a capacity to find in any work of any date or place a clue to finding one's authentic voice. The burden of choice is put squarely upon the shoulders of each individual poet and it is a heavy one" [*DH*, 80]. In the pursuit of his own originality, Ashbery chooses the assimilation of Auden's example as a means of finding his own "authentic voice."

In his essay's first paragraph (quoted earlier), Ashbery had laid the groundwork for this Audenesque conception of poetic originality in his assertion that it is the new poet's rearticulation of old ideas, and his ability to make those ideas new again, that constitutes his special contribution to the tradition, not his invention of "brand-new unthought of ideas." All poets, says Ashbery, "stand acquitted on the charge of commonplace subject matter" simply because their unique selection, absorption, and expression of what they inherit from the past necessarily gives it a new spin. It is the new poet's particular sensibility, and his skill in seeing old sights with new eyes, that makes "every new poem a fresh discovery." Even as an apprentice poet, Ashbery is already demonstrating an unanxious relation to the poetic past, less worried about his belatedness and the necessity for "making it new," than cheerfully confident that his singular "way of looking at the world," his individual talent, will, in a sense, do the job for him. Much like Eliot's poet-as-shred-of-platinum, whose mind transmutes his environment into poetry without being effected by that change, the young Ashbery asserts the poet's ability to transform the world he inherits—including the poetic tradition—through the prism of his own consciousness, without having to struggle against that world.[27] Readers of Ashbery will encounter this idea again and again in his accounts, in poems and interviews: "A poem for me is very much a question of the relation between elements that are sort of given to one, or which one chooses arbitrarily when one starts to write a poem and which don't require other justification."[28]

Ashbery's approach to experience, including his experience of past poets, is a radically open, welcoming one, rather than combative, anxious, and agonistic. "I never consciously felt that I had to destroy the poets I was being influenced by," Ashbery has argued, engaging the theory of influence propounded by his friend, Harold Bloom: "When I discovered them in my work I was happy to welcome them. It was nice that they dropped by. Of course, unconsciously who knows what I may have been up to. *Harold* obviously does. . . ."[29] In this jocular corrective to Bloom's ideas about the Freudian struggle between the poet and his influences, as in his early assertion of the poet's unanxious acknowledgment of his own belatedness, Ashbery raises a crucial question about the relation of his poetry to prevailing theories of the development of poetic identity, as well as other larger questions about poetry criticism in general. Ashbery's authorial assertion of Auden's importance to his work, and Bloom's blithe dismissal of it, suggest a significant rift between Ashbery's own notion of his poetics and its critical reception. It is, of course, a truism that, as Auden himself points out in his essay "Reading," "The critical opinions of a writer should always be taken with a large grain of salt" [*DH*, 9], especially since, as "anthologists and instructors" from Brooks and Warren to Bloom have argued, questions of authorial intent are entirely ancillary—if not actively opposed—to the disinterested business of literary criticism. Yet Ashbery's protest, in the context of his own work, merits examination.[30]

Ashbery calls "The Sea and the Mirror" an "epic of self-consciousness" and it is this total exploration of consciousness that yields, he says, Auden's "finest writing to date." Taking issue with one of Auden's earliest academic critics, the "somewhat misguided" Francis Scarfe, who describes Auden's "style which is no style," Ashbery offers his reading of Auden's style:

> As Mr. Scarfe's explanation of what his term means is not helpful, may I submit that perhaps he means to refer the *consciousness* of Auden's poetry? For a style is, after all, an unnamable quality; it is only *recognized* by authors, who agree that it will develop only if left alone. Now the vast, hygenic self-consciousness of Auden, which is aware beforehand of exactly the impression a word or phrase will create, and is always darting ahead of us, clearing up new mysteries before we have arrived at them, could never be expected to have created a style which is an article, useless and decorative, to be left around to clutter up the meaning of a poem. If there were such a thing in his poetry, he would have written a poem analyzing it and pointing it out to us. What I mean is that "the style which is no style" (though I am thinking primarily of "The Sea and the Mirror," and I realize Mr. Scarfe is discussing earlier poetry) is a style in which clarity, transparency, wit, verbal decoration, and imagery are all superbly functional, so much as to be invisible. [emphasis Ashbery's]

Ashbery defines "style" as "consciousness" itself, emphasizing that while it can be "recognized" it cannot be named, much as he had defined "poetry" earlier in the essay as "a perceived relation between things; we can recognize it and point out examples of it, but can never satisfactorily describe it." Poetry for Ashbery *is* consciousness, and Auden's "vast, hygenic self-consciousness" produces, for him, a poetry whose representation of the active, "darting" mind is so complete—so "functional"—that it renders the deliberation of its own making "invisible." It is a consciousness so supremely self-aware that it achieves what Ashbery a few lines later calls the "paradox" of expressing an "unconscious quality . . . in which a small uncertainty, a not-being-sure-exactly-what-is-happening, enters." Distinguishing Auden's achievement in "The Sea and the Mirror" from his earlier poems, which "always give one an intelligent man's impressions of pity or terror, but never the deep dark emotion itself," Ashbery identifies Auden's magisterial poem—a text significantly comprised of self-conscious imitations of other poems, forms, and literary styles, from Shakespearean soliloquies and songs to villanelles to Jamesian prose—as a new kind of poetry, simultaneously familiar yet original, conscious yet apparently unpremeditated, intellectual yet emotional: "In 'The Sea and the Mirror,' by a strange twist, we are presented with such a spectacle, more moving than intuition, and yet not really planned—that of an artist seeking truth. So this poem, by its very lucidity and penetration achieves the unconscious which we find in the greatest poetry—our view of the poet himself, the unsatisfied voyager." It is a spectacle—poet as "unsatisfied voyager"—with which many of Ashbery's own readers will be familiar.

Ashbery's is a poetry deeply concerned with the representation of consciousness, and with the troubled question of authorial intent. From the daydreaming scribe of "The Instruction Manual," to "The unsatisfactoriness, the frowns and squinting, the itching and scratching as you listen without taking in what is being said to you, or only in part, so you cannot piece the argument together" [*TP*, 79] of longer, meanderingly discursive, self-descriptive poems like "The System," Ashbery's work continually construes itself as reflecting the conscious mind responding to the complex and conflicting stimuli around it. "It's a kind of mimesis of how experience comes to me," is how he has described it to more than one interviewer.[31] His poems also repeatedly address the poet's capacity to say what he wants to say, "unimportant but meant," as he puts it in "Self-Portrait in a Convex Mirror" [*SP*, 70]. His poems often begin with avowals of intention: "They are preparing to begin again" ("The Task," [*SP*, 83]); "You can't say it that way anymore" ("And *Ut Pictura Poesis* Is

Her Name," [*SP*, 235]); "And they have to get it right" ("A Love Poem," [*AWK*, 101]); "This movie deals with the epidemic of the way we live now" ("This Configuration," [*AWK*, 109]); "This poem is concerned with language on a very plain level" ("Paradoxes and Oxymorons," [*SP*, 283]); "The concept is interesting: to see, as though reflected / In streaming windowpanes, the look of others through / Their own eyes" ("Wet Casements," [*SP*, 225]). "The New Spirit" begins with the self-conscious rumination, "I thought if I could put it all down, that would be one way. And next the thought came to me that to leave all out would be another, and truer, way" [*TP*, 3], and "Self-Portrait in a Convex Mirror" takes as its ambition, as the poem's title suggests, "As Parmagianino did it, . . . to take his own portrait, looking at himself for that purpose / In a convex mirror" [*SP*, 188]. Ashbery's poet is both reacting to what he finds around him, and acting consciously upon it; trying, as he puts in it "Grand Galop," to "write poetry / Using what Wyatt and Surrey left around, / Took up and put down again / Like so much gorgeous raw material" [*SP*, 177]. Ashbery's poetics is not one of simple passive receptivity. His response to the world is active and engaged, formulating that response in particular, conscious aesthetic decisions: "There are lots of echoes in my work of not just forms but of language and conventions of the poetry of the past which I feel very close to in certain ways. I don't want simply to repeat this language but to stretch or expand it, much in the same way, I guess, as Stravinsky did in his neoclassical music where he used music by Pergolesi and Tchaikovsky, transforming it."[32]

For Ashbery, the mystery surrounding poetic intention results from the clash between "The extreme austerity of an almost empty mind / Colliding with the lush Rousseau-like foliage of the desire to communicate" [*SP*, 235]. The poet becomes for him a figure of pathos precisely because his ambitions are so often thwarted, not by the unconscious, but by his own consciousness and by the circumstances of the poem's composition, as in "Self-Portrait in a Convex Mirror":

It is the principle that makes works of art so unlike
What the artist intended. Often he finds
He has omitted the thing he started out to say
In the first place. Seduced by flowers,
Explicit pleasures, he blames himself (though

Secretly satisfied with the result), imagining
He had a say in the matter and exercised
An option of which he was hardly conscious,
Unaware that necessity circumvents such resolutions
So as to create something new
For itself, that there is no other way,
That the history of creation proceeds according to
Stringent laws, and that things
Do get done in this way, but never the things
We set out to accomplish and wanted so desperately
To see come into being. [*SP*, 201]

"Seduced by flowers, / Explicit pleasures," the poet's distractible consciousness betrays his own intentions, but it is this very betrayal that results in "something new." The poet, says Ashbery, customarily consoles and deludes himself by attributing this unexpected bounty to talents he did not even know he possessed, "imagining / He had a say in the matter and exercised / An option of which he was hardly conscious." That is, the poet typically identifies his inspiration—his muse—with the unconscious, claiming credit for his surprisingly originality through forces that are beyond his conscious control, yet unmistakably within him. But Ashbery debunks this comforting myth, asserting that it is the Audenesque notion of "necessity," not the unconscious, that calls the shots. For the American Auden that Ashbery would have been reading as an undergraduate, "necessity" is the most crucial of words and concepts. In poem after poem in the 1940s, Auden describes himself as being on a quest for "necessity" or "the necessary"—the eternally elusive condition where what we need from the world is perfectly balanced by what we owe it: what he elsewhere calls "the hidden law," "Atlantis," the Jamesian "Great Good Place," or, in other places, simply "Love."[33] Here, "necessity" is Ashbery's word for the interdependence between the poet's demand for inspirational stimuli and the world's demand for the new art it needs. Ashbery yields authorial control not to the unconscious, but to his environment, to time, to the world around him. The powers of history, the requirements of culture, the demands of the moment, one's poetic influences, these are the forces impinging on the poet's consciousness and driving him toward "something new," not some mystical but ego-satisfying trope of unknown, inner capabilities engaged in psychic agon. As he puts it in "The Ice-Cream Wars,"

> Although I mean it, and project the meaning
> As hard as I can into its brushed-metal surface,
> It cannot, in this deteriorating climate, pick up
> Where I leave off. [*SP*, 242]

For Ashbery, it is "this deteriorating climate"—the difficult but knowable world outside him, not the unknowable world within—that changes the course of the poem, resulting in "something new" but "never the things we set out to accomplish."[34]

Ashbery's poetry is also, in a literal sense, all about surfaces. "[Y]our eyes proclaim that everything is surface. The surface is what's there / And nothing can exist except what's there," as he says in "Self-Portrait in a Convex Mirror":

> And just as there is no word for the surface, that is,
> No words to say what it really is, that it is not
> Superficial but the visible core, then there is
> No way out of the problem of pathos vs. experience." [*SP*, 190]

The surface, for Ashbery, is "necessity," that liminal, evasive space where dialectic ("pathos vs. experience") gets resolved, that paradoxical point where two things truly touch, but if that point were ever to be apprehended it would vanish, as a bubble bursts or "balloon pops" at the approach of an inquisitive finger. To reach that surface—that moment of true resolution, true contact, true understanding, true love—is what the poet continually and frustratingly quests for, "emblematic / Of life and how you cannot isolate a note of it" [*SP*, 246]. But "the surface is what's there / And nothing can exist except what's there," he says: Even as we seek to inhabit that surface, to fully perceive and experience it, the pathos of our plight ("the pity of it smarts") is that we are already uncomprehendingly living in it, in the "bubble-chamber" of the instantaneous, ungraspable present. He writes in "The System,"

> These windows on the past enable us to stay on an even keel
> in the razor's edge present which is really a no-time, continual
> straying over the border into the positive past and the negative

future whose movements alone define it. Unfortunately we
have to live in it. We are appalled at this. Because its no-time,
no-space dimensions offer us no signposts, nothing to be guided
by. [*TP*, 102]

The poet's goal—through his poems' mimesis of a consciousness
trying to analyze, understand, and respond constructively to its predicament in the "no-time, no-space dimensions" of instantaneous existence—is to offer us those missing signposts, to suggest some guidance,
enabling its readers, as the young Ashbery says of Auden, "to apply it
within the realm of their experience."

So if Ashbery's poetics is manifestly *about* the "surface" of the consciousness responding to its surroundings—rather than the presumably
"deeper" unconscious, buried somewhere beneath the skin of awareness—and if "the surface isn't the surface but the visible core," perhaps it
is time his critics took the surface seriously. That is, rather than privileg-
ing Freudian concepts of sublimated conflict in defiance of his poetry's
own notion of itself and its ambition, or reading his poems as mere transcripts of what one critic calls "the aim to communicate without com-
municating anything of substance,"[35] critics should pay attention to the
activity of consciousness that the poems themselves set out to reflect: a
consciousness which is actively responsive to the world, making sense of
it by making self-aware—albeit continually frustrated—choices of order,
form, and intention. Instead of drafting Ashbery into a High Romantic
critical program that sees the solitary, contending ego as its central trope,
or reducing him to a deconstructive collagist, we can gain new insight
into Ashbery by trying to see him as he sees himself, as a self in context,
an identity questing for stability rather than dominance, a lover seeking
contact and understanding, an intellect assimilating and welcoming and
ordering the riotous world around him. As Ashbery puts it in, again,
"Self-Portrait in a Convex Mirror,"

> Each person
> Has one big theory to explain the universe
> But it doesn't tell the whole story
> And in the end it is what is outside him
> That matters, to him and especially to us
> Who have been given no help whatever

In decoding our own man-sized quotient and must rely
On second-hand knowledge. [*SP*, 81–82]

"It is what is outside" the poet, and his efforts to "decode" and pass
on to his readers what little he can—his "own man-sized quotient" of
"second-hand knowledge"—"that matters," not some grand formula—
Freudian, deconstructive, ideological, or otherwise—"to explain the
universe."

This idea of reclaiming Ashbery from the "one big theory" has,
paradoxically, a number of polemical implications. First, in its privileg-
ing of responsive dialectic over fixed cultural, conceptual, or personal
absolutes, it reasserts the importance of the post-1939 Auden's example
to Ashbery's work (and to his generation of poets in general). Second,
in its emphasis on Ashbery's constructive assimilation of experience and
his "desire to communicate" that experience, it argues for Ashbery as
a poet seeking to engage the world rather than deconstruct it. Third,
in suggesting the value of Ashbery's own articulation of his poetic process, it proposes him as an example of a new poetics that acknowledges
choice, craft, and consciousness over anxiety and agon. And fourth, in
challenging one-sided critical constructs of Ashbery's project, it figures
the relationship between criticism and the poetry it takes as its subject
as a fundamentally dialectical one. This last theme—of criticism's prob-
lematic links with its sources—is one to which Ashbery has often addressed himself, and it is with a discussion of this question, in dialogue
with Ashbery's own inaugural effort at literary criticism, that I want to
conclude.

◆ ◆ ◆

"We see us as we truly behave" is the first line of the first poem of Ashbery's first book, and we might be tempted to read it—with an assertive
emphasis on that initial "*we*"—as a proleptic authorial admonition to
his future critics. "The critics always get everything wrong," he has said,
citing one of his "favorite lines" from Nijinsky's journal: "Criticism is
death."[36] Ashbery's most sustained explicit engagement with the role of
criticism comes midway through 1979's "Litany," when one of the voices
embarks on a lengthy, and uncharacteristically prosaic, consideration of
the function of criticism at the present time:

Just one minute of contemporary existence
Has so much to offer, but who
Can evaluate it, formulate
The appropriate apothegm, show us
In a few well-chosen words of wisdom
Exactly what is taking place all about us?
Not critics, certainly, though that is precisely
What they are supposed to be doing, yet how
Often have you read any criticism
Of our society and all the people and things in it
That really makes sense, to us as human beings? [*AWK*, 32]

Ashbery, by 1979 the subject of considerable criticism himself—much of it unappreciative—in the wake of *Self-Portrait in a Convex Mirror*'s sweep of the major literary prizes three years earlier, strikes back at his critics and finds *them* wanting.[37] He continues, mocking his own impulse to sermonize in what Auden self-critically designates in his own work "the preacher's loose immodest tone" [*CP*, 204], the theatrically elevated voice of the call-and-response litanist:

It behooves
Our critics to make the poets more aware of
What they're doing, so that poets in turn
Can stand back and be enchanted by it
And in this way make room for the general public
To crowd around and be enchanted by it too,
And then, hopefully, make some sense of their lives,
Bring order back into the disorderly house
Of their drab existences. [*AWK*, 33]

The job of critics, admonishes the preacherly Ashbery, is not to impose their own theoretical structures upon the poem, but to engage it on its own terms, to participate fully in it, and, in a sense, yield themselves to it. Criticism can be constructive—in the sense of active collaboration in a shared project—but only if it enters the poetry as an attentive companion. The poem, not the critic, is the host, to reverse J. Hillis Miller's familiar—and contemporaneous—theoretical formulation.[38]

The experience of inhabiting the poem should be a didactic one, for both critic and "the general public": A true poem should teach us how to read it, and thereby teach us—if only in small "man-sized quotients"—how better to live. Only once the critic has engaged in the poem's life-affirming dialectic will he be able to offer insight of value to the poet, enabling him to write new poems that will help his readers "make some sense of their lives." The mocking, deflationary tone of the description of his readers' "drab existences"—as if he were quoting some ironic version of himself as the arrogant *artiste*, intent on enlightening the masses—serves to underscore the feeling of frustration provoking this ambition, as Ashbery acknowledged in an interview conducted around the time of the composition of "Litany": "I really don't know what to think when I read criticism, either favorable or unfavorable. In most cases, even when it's sympathetic and understanding, it's a sort of parallel adventure to the poetry. It never gives me the feeling that I'll know how to do it the next time I sit down to write, which is my principal concern. I'm not putting down critics, but they don't help the poetry to get its work done."[39] The only solution, he concludes, is to take the matter into his own hands:

> Therefore a new school of criticism must be developed.
> First of all, the new
> Criticism should take into account that it is we
> Who made it, and therefore
> Not be too eager to criticize us: we
> Could do that for ourselves, and have done so.
> Nor
> Should it take itself as a fitting subject
> For critical analysis, since it knows
> Itself only through us, and us
> Only through being part of ourselves, the bark
> Of the tree of our intellect. [*AWK*, 34–35]

Ashbery's notional school for critics recalls Auden's similarly pro-scriptive criterion for useful criticism in a 1962 essay, "Reading," in *The Dyer's Hand*:

> What is the function of a critic? So far as I am concerned, he can do me one or more of the following services:

1) Introduce me to authors or works of which I was hitherto unaware.

2) Convince me that I have undervalued an author or a work because I had not read them carefully enough.

3) Show me relations between works of different ages and cultures which I could never have seen for myself because I do not know enough and never shall.

4) Give a "reading" of a work which increases my understanding of it.

5) Throw light upon the process of artistic "Making."

6) Throw light upon the relation of art to life, to science, economics, ethics, religion, etc. [*DH*, 8–9]

For Ashbery, as for Auden, the function of criticism is to help poetry "to get its work done," and critics can do that only by joining with the poet in his project of "Making," such that new light can be shed "upon the relation of art to life." Ashbery's objection to contemporary criticism is both personal ("they shouldn't be so eager to criticize us"), reflecting perhaps a certain sense of bruised feelings, and professional ("nor should it take itself as a fitting subject for critical analysis"). Rather than being an isolated "parallel adventure" to poetry, criticism should be a dialectical partner with it, like the twin columns of "Litany," each engaging, commenting, and reflecting on the other, each driving the other forward in a shared, hopeful endeavor of describing life and "all the people and things in it" in a way "that really makes sense, to us as human beings." Again, those final three words of "Litany"—the last standing alone on its line—suggest this wished for sense of constructive collaboration, as one column calls hopefully across to the other, "Would you / Try?" As I've already suggested, the impulse to *try*—to understand, to communicate, to make contact, to love—is at the heart of Ashbery's poetics, as is the notion that he can't—or doesn't want to—do it alone.

Ashbery's critics are supposed to do what poets aim to do: "show us / In a few well-chosen words of wisdom / Exactly what is taking place all about us." That is, Ashbery's ideal critics are, in fact, not critics at all, but poets, in a Wordsworthian redefinition of "poet" suggesting the capacity for understanding that exists in, potentially, everyone. Ashbery's attack on criticism amounts to a defense of poetry as a superior form of criticism in itself. Ashbery has argued as much outside the margins of his poems: "It seems to me that poetry is already criticism and that it's criticizing something that one doesn't know about, some unknown situation. Criticism of poetry is at a further remove. The poem has already said it all in the only way that it can be said. Paraphrases merely get in the way. The poem should be read again."[40] What we know as literary criticism, the self-centered criticism of "big ideas" that has been inflicted upon his work, Ashbery agrees with Nijinsky, is "death." True criticism, on the other hand—that is, poetry—is "life itself."

As a student critic, Ashbery was already addressing the notion that poets and critics share, in Auden's words, "a common, noble and civilising task" [*DH*, 42]. He was also taking seriously the idea that poetry itself is the truest form of criticism, as demonstrated in the intimate relation between his analysis of Auden's work and his own developing poetic practice. In the first poem in "The Sea and the Mirror," the "Stage Manager" addresses "the Critics," asking "[W]ho in his own backyard / Has not opened his heart to the smiling secret he cannot quote?" [*CP*, 403]. Early on in his critique of Auden's work, Ashbery suggests a similar sense of the unsatisfactoriness of critical language for the kind of perception available only through poetry: "Clearly there is but one kind of poetry (though its subject matter be limitless) which we cannot define by any other word, and which we are continually forced to think of as a nameless ichor, a kind of perceived relation between things; we can recognize it and point out examples of it, but can never satisfactorily describe it." As critic, Ashbery attempts to describe Auden's work, but as a young poet, and throughout the rest of his career, we can see him applying the criticism that he learned from Auden's poetry to his own.

Ashbery remarks upon Auden's "overwhelming (and utterly praiseworthy) tendency to give the abstract 'a local habitation and a name'" and cites as an example a few lines from "The Sea and The Mirror": "Historic deeds, drop their hauteur and speak of shabby childhoods / When all they longed for was to join in the gang of doubts / Who so tormented them." One need only look as far as the earliest poem in *Some Trees*, "The Painter," to see Ashbery exploring this idea, and building upon it. The Painter paints "the sea's portrait," expecting "his subject / To rush up the sand, and, seizing a brush, / Plaster its own portrait on the canvas" [*ST*, 54]. Ashbery depicts the artist in his poem, as he depicts Auden in his essay, as concerned with personifying abstractions, of painting the "sea's portrait." In the poem's next canvas, however, we see Ashbery taking Auden's idea and reversing it, as the Painter chooses "his wife for a new subject, / making her vast, like ruined buildings." Here Ashbery's artist experiments with art's capacity to abstract the personal, as the wife's individuality is distilled into pure "vastness." In the poem's climax, art and artist come together in a synthesis of the personal and abstract, as the artist paints a "self-portrait," "leaving the canvas perfectly white." The Painter's audience, outraged and confused by the artist's visionary self-abstraction, responds—as Ashbery's real critics often have—with savage condemnation:[41] "They tossed him, the portrait, from the tallest of the buildings; / And the sea devoured the canvas and the brush / As if his subject had decided to remain a prayer." The artist and his portrait become one, and both plunge into the "angry and large" sea, martyred by the critical mob.

Of "The Sea and the Mirror," Ashbery observes in his essay, "the theme, announced by the title, is the venerable one of the inevitableness of life (the sea) and art (the mirror)" and calls the rebellious figure of Antonio "the personification of the sea, 'The life,' from which poetry, as long as it seeks to describe, to resolve it, will always be excluded." While Prospero surrenders his books "to the silent dissolution of the sea" [*CP*, 404], choosing his life over his art, Ashbery's artist refuses to choose one over the other—arguing, again, that art, and specifically poetry, "is life itself"—and achieves a kind of perfection in that very "dissolution." "The Painter," then, works as a triple fable for Ashbery's career. First, as an early metaphor for Ashbery's ambition to create an art in which the dialectics of poet and poem, life and art, achieve a kind of transcendent synthesis; second, as a parable of the younger artist assimilating the example of the older and then developing from it a new original perspective; and last, as the initial salvo in Ashbery's ongoing—and sometimes overtly self-defensive—war with criticism.[42]

"The concept," says Ashbery in "Wet Casements," "is interesting": to see "the look of others through their own eyes" [*SP*, 225]. This is Ashbery's vision of criticism—and, as we have seen, his own critical practice—and it is a vision that may bear some sympathetic scrutiny on the part of those whose vocation it is to read and explain his work. If poetry is in fact criticism, rather than imposing an external rubric or theory upon the work, perhaps we can derive a fruitful critical approach from within the work itself. This is not, of course, to argue for some naive conception of authorial infallibility, or even truthfulness, since as Shoptaw has convincingly shown, misrepresentativeness is one of the hallmarks of Ashbery's poetic mode.[43] Nor is it a rear-guard attempt to reduce the scope of criticism to boundaries set by the authors themselves. Rather, it is to suggest a way of reading Ashbery—and indeed of other writers, including Auden—that recognizes the poem's power to instruct, and its ambition to embrace its reader and the world. By taking the poems themselves as a model for criticism—a model that places itself in context, that welcomes contingency and influence, that emphasizes the act of consciousness, that looks outward to the consequences of its insight, that espouses collaboration over contention, that *tries*—we can gain a new, and perhaps surprising, perspective on Ashbery's work and indeed on recent literary history.

If Ashbery's work is truly "postmodern," as it is often described, it is not because it exhibits characteristics, or symptoms, that conform to the multiple "big theories" that have come to stand behind that word. What makes Ashbery postmodern is not his demonstration of various contemporary critical figurations, from ironic fragmentation, to the deaths of the metanarrative and the author, to psychoanalytic tropes of belatedness.[44] Rather, if we look at the poetry rather than the intervening theories, we find an art that is genuinely post-Modernist in its active revision of its American Modernist predecessors. Ashbery's work, in its optative, socially constructive mood, moves past the poetics of despair, isolation, solipsism, unreclaimable fragmentation, frustrated Romanticism, and cultural conservatism of Eliot, Pound, and Stevens. In its claims for poetry's didactic force, its positive dialectics, and its humane pluralism, Ashbery's poetry articulates a mode of perceiving that gives a new—and specifically poetic and literary historical—meaning to the term "postmodern." Ashbery isn't shoring fragments against his ruin, or even playing resignedly with the shards on the dump. Instead, he's trying to build a shelter out of those fragments, give to the welter of our moment—in a phrase Ashbery applies to Auden's own poetics—"a local habitation and a name," and welcome us inside. And his great teacher in this project—the "Old Master" to his "gay apprentice"—was Auden.

The Old Sources

Rich, Auden, and Making Something Happen

In her 1999 volume of poems, *Midnight Salvage*, Adrienne Rich addresses her words—as she often does—to another poet:

> Would it gladden you to think
> poetry could purely
>
> take its place beneath lightning sheets
> or fogdrip live its own life
>
> screamed at, howled down
> by a torn bowel of dripping names
>
> —composers visit Terezin, film-makers Sarajevo
> Cabrini-Green or Edenwald Houses
>
>   ineluctable
>
> if a woman as vivid as any artist
> can fling any day herself from the 14th floor

> would it relieve you to decide   *Poetry*
> *doesn't make this happen?* [*MS*, 26]

In this poem, decades into her celebrated poetic career, Rich is passing on hard-won wisdom to the poets who will follow her, as we learn
from the poem's Rilkean title, "Letters to a Young Poet." Enumerating in
shorthand some of history's more recent horrors—the death camps at
Terezin, the slaughter of Bosnia, the urban poverty of Chicago's hous-
ing projects—and observing the ways artists simultaneously use and
distance themselves from the realities they document or incorporate
into their art, Rich asks her young poet, "Would it relieve you to decide
Poetry / *doesn't make this happen?*"

For Rich, no such relief is possible: Poetry, she says, is "ineluctable,"
choosing—perhaps with irony—one of the favorite words of the proto-
typical artist as a young man, Joyce's Stephen Dedalus. Stephen, protest-
ing his plight, trapped in the nightmare of history, famously laments the
"ineluctable modality of the visible"—the separateness of the eye from the
essence of the reality it perceives, its ability only to register, not participate
in the action of the world. Addressing the young poet with a "thirst for
closure / and quick escape," Rich critiques her for choosing to believe in
the "ineluctable modality" of poetry, as if it were separate from the world
of political, economic, and sexual reality, "living its own life," content to
"take its place" amid and beneath the easily poeticized and romanticized
world of nature with its "lightning sheets / or fogdrip." The lesson Rich
wants to impart is that what is truly "ineluctable," inescapable, is the Dae-
dalian maze of history itself: "you won't get quit / of this: the worst of
the new news / history running back and forth / panic in the labyrinth"
[*MS*, 25].[1] In Rich's view, poetry is both complicit in the circumstances of
its creation, and responsible for acknowledging its role in the political and
economic system which it can't help but reflect. In short, Rich is reassert-
ing—as she often has since the late 1950s when she began contextualizing
each of her poems by including its year of composition—her belief that
poetry not only cannot stand outside history, it actually contributes to it,
for better or worse. As she puts it in a 1981 essay, "I do believe that words
can help us move or keep us paralyzed, and that our choices of language
and verbal tone have something—a great deal—to do with how we live
our lives."[2] Poetry, she has said, "makes a huge difference."[3]

But if this late poem serves as a lesson handed down from the wise and experienced older poet to the naive younger student, it also stands as the latest entry in an ongoing debate—which by 1999 had been going on for almost five decades—with one of Rich's own poetic mentors, W. H. Auden. Forty-eight years after he selected her as a Radcliffe senior for the Yale Younger Poets Prize, Rich is still arguing with, and responding to, the poet through whom she first found her voice and whose public imprimatur began her career. "Poetry makes nothing happen," Auden declared in his elegy for Yeats, and the history of Rich's career is, in some sense, the history of her ongoing response to that single line. Indeed, a recent 2006 symposium on Rich in the pages of *The Virginia Quarterly Review*, the journal that gave Rich her first major poetry publication in 1950, framed its assessment of her achievement explicitly in these terms. In the words of the editor, speaking of the panel of poets and critics invited to discuss Rich, "We have asked them to consider Rich personally and as a poet who challenges the words of W. H. Auden, that poet who discovered her work fifty years ago, who wrote that 'Poetry makes nothing happen.'"[4] From her own beginnings as a young poet deeply influenced by Auden, to her later career as a politically engaged intellectual who sees her poetry as an essential part of her work toward social change, Auden's words have continued to echo for Rich, constituting a crucial touchstone in her poetics. From her early emulation through her mature repudiation of his example, Auden's place in Rich's work and thought has persisted. As both an individual influence and as a representative of an entire range of poetic concerns which she has inherited and adapted, Auden comes to stand for poetic tradition itself—the tradition that gave her birth, and through and against which she has striven to define herself. For Rich, Auden sets the poetic terms—not always positively—out of which she constructs her own poetic identity. Like poetry itself, the figure of Auden and what he represents have been, throughout her career, ineluctable.

◆ ◆ ◆

Rich has spent much of her career arguing implicitly, and in some cases explicitly, with Auden. The terms of the debate were set early, in Auden's now-notorious foreword to Rich's first book, *A Change of World*, in which he introduced her early formalist poems as the work of a pleasantly unambitious, earnest, and polite co-ed: "Miss Rich, who is, I understand, twenty-one years old, displays a modesty not so common at that age, which disclaims any extraordinary vision, and a love for her medium, a determination to ensure that whatever she writes shall, at least, not be shoddily made" [*ACW*, 9–10].[5] The forty-four-year-old Auden closes with a characterization of Rich's poems in the same terms he uses to describe the young poet herself. "Poems are analogous to persons," Auden suggests, and for him these poems find their analogue in the clever, well-mannered girl he presumes Rich to be: "The poems a reader will encounter in this book are neatly and modestly dressed, speak quietly but do not mumble, respect their elders but are not cowed by them, and do not tell fibs."

Rich's critics have often pointed to Auden's essay as her inaugural encounter with the patronizing poetic patriarchy that she would spend much of the rest of her career rejecting.[6] That Rich felt the sting of Auden's double-edged praise and condescension appears clear from her remarks some years later in a 1966 essay called "The Tensions of Anne Bradstreet," in which she identifies the tradition of masculine critical condescension as one of the chief historical obstacles for female poetic achievement. In that essay she cites the foreword to Bradstreet's verse collection, written by Bradstreet's brother-in-law, whose tone and critique tellingly prefigure, across three centuries, Auden's dismissive response to her own work: "[The book] is the Work of a Woman, honoured, and esteemed where she lives, for her gracious demeanor, her eminent parts, her pious conversation, her courteous disposition, her exact diligence in her place, and discreet managing of her Family occasions" [*LSS*, 28].[7] Bradstreet's lament, "If what I do prove well, it won't advance. / They'll say it's stol'n, or else was by chance," finds its own echo, and revision, in Rich's own poems. As she puts it in the title poem of her third book, and the first to announce her new activist poetic stance, "Snapshots of a Daughter-in-Law," "Bemused by gallantry, we hear / our mediocrities overpraised, / indolence read as abnegation, / slattern thought styled as intuition, / every lapse forgiven, our crime / only to cast too bold a shadow / or smash the mold straight off" [*FD*, 38].

As Rich's poetics and politics continued to transform themselves—from the elegant formalism that earned Auden's approbation to the politically engaged open form of her later work—she continued to hold

Auden in mind as a contemporary example of the blinkered masculine intellectual misguidedness it was her vocation to resist. In her 1966 poem "In the Evening," she offers a public rebuke, parodying Auden's faith in the "Old Masters" of "Musée des Beaux Arts": "The old masters, the old sources / haven't a clue what we're about / shivering here in the half-dark sixties" [*FD*, 81].

In an essay entitled "Not how to write poetry, but wherefore" included in her 1993 volume, *What Is Found There*, Rich reflects from a distance of more than forty years on the significance of Auden's role as one of her early "masters," and continues her argument with him. She juxtaposes the thrill she felt when encountering the bold forthrightness of Rilke's Apollo telling her "*Du musst dein Leben ändern*, You have to change your life," with her disappointment at Auden's reactionary response in his Yeats elegy, "Poetry makes nothing happen." She cites Auden's remarks, in the foreword to her own book, on the essential conservatism of her poetic generation, condemned to be "living not at the beginning but in the middle of a historical epoch." Auden continues: "Every poet under fifty-five cherishes, I suspect, a secret grudge against Providence for not getting him [*sic*] born earlier" [Rich's emphasis]. Rich responds: "If anything, I cherished a secret grudge against Auden—not because he didn't proclaim me a genius, but because he proclaimed so diminished a scope for poetry, including mine. I had little use for his beginnings and middles. Yet he was one of the masters" [*WFT*, 191].

Rich's ironic recognition of Auden as one of her "masters" reflects the complicated ambivalence of her relation to him, even late in her career. As an "old master," one of the monolithic old men whose "mastery" suggests not only genius and skill but also gender hierarchy and sexism, he serves as an embodiment of everything the female poet must continue to struggle against in order to find her own voice, the repressive authority whose shackles she must throw off. But he is also, as she somewhat ruefully acknowledges, one of the teachers who helped her to that voice.

Despite his manifest sexism and condescension, Auden wasn't completely wrong in his assessment of Rich's early work. Rich herself writes, four years after Auden's introduction, a poem called "The Middle-aged" in terms that speak of her own grudge against being born into a past-haunted "middle age,"

> Their faces, safe as an interior
> Of Holland tiles and Oriental carpet,
> Where the fruit-bowl, always filled, stood in a light
> Of placid afternoon—their voices' measure,
> Their figures moving in the Sunday garden
> To lay the tea outdoors or trim the borders,
> Afflicted, haunted us. For to be young
> Was always to live in other people's houses
> Whose peace, if we sought it, had been made by others,
> Was ours at second-hand and not for long. [*FD*, 15]

And, as Auden points out, her poems do respect their elders. Especially in her early work, but even later in her career, when the "old masters" are supplanted for her by the mothers and sisters of a feminist poetic tradition, Rich's verse finds its authority in the voices of those who have come before. For the young Rich, those voices chiefly included the familiar canon of male metaphysical and modern poets, including Auden, as she observes in "When We Dead Awaken: Writing as Re-Vision," her landmark 1971 essay that uses the example of her own poetic evolution to call for a new vision of feminist poetry: "I know that my style was formed first by male poets: by the men I was reading as an undergraduate—Frost, Dylan Thomas, Donne, Auden, MacNeice, Stevens, Yeats. What I chiefly learned from them was craft" [*LSS*, 38].

Auden himself in his introduction identified Rich's connections to Frost and Yeats, observing that her poems "make no attempt to conceal their family tree." He neglected, however, to point out her first book's indebtedness to his own work. Indeed the first line of the first poem in the volume—"The glass had been falling all afternoon"—evokes Auden's elegiac barometric "instruments" from "In Memory of W. B. Yeats," suggesting that, a decade after his poem, the anxious cultural weather of Auden's "dark cold day" still prevails in Rich's "afternoon" of "gray unrest." Her poetic instruments agree with Auden's, as the poem, called "Storm Warnings," goes on not simply to reflect their shared cultural sensibility, but explicitly to recall Audenesque language and ideas:

> Between foreseeing and averting change
> Lies all the mastery of elements
> Which clocks and weatherglasses cannot alter.

Time in the hand is not control of time,
Nor shattered fragments of an instrument
A proof against the wind; the wind will rise,
We can only close the shutters. [*ACW*, 18]

Like the clocks of "As I Walked Out One Evening," which admonish the naive lovers, "O let not time deceive you, / You cannot conquer time," Rich's clocks and weatherglasses serve similarly to rebuke the complacent reader, confident in his use of "instruments" to "master" his condition: "Time in the hand is not control of time, / Nor shattered fragments of an instrument / A proof against the wind."[8] In Rich's poem, the instrument's shattered fragments, shored against time's ruin, stand as testament to its impotence in the face of the grim climate it aspires to reflect. This untuned instrument echoes Auden's, as in both "Storm Warnings" and the Yeats elegy the barometer serves as a figure for poetry itself and its ability to do little more than agree with the world, not alter it. Poetry, like the barometer, can "foresee change" but not avert it. The young Rich is here proclaiming—as the older Rich would later reprove Auden for doing—poetry's diminished scope. Poetry, the twenty-one-year-old poet says in tune with her "master," makes nothing happen. It can prophesy and reflect a "change of world," but it cannot bring that change about. She suggests—as she does elsewhere in her first book, in poems like "Reliquary," "For the Felling of an Elm in the Harvard Yard," "The Uncle Speaks in the Drawing Room," and "A Revivalist in Boston"—that poetry's role in the world is an essentially conservative, reactive one. Poem or no poem, the world has its madness and its weather still; the best the poet can do is "close the shutters" against the dark cold day.[9]

Auden's remarks about Rich's predicament, "living not at the beginning but in the middle of a historical epoch," suggest his own sense of the younger poet's affinities with his own poetic project and perspective. "The emotions which motivate [her poems]—the historical apprehension expressed in 'Storm Warnings,' [for instance]—are not peculiar to Miss Rich but are among the typical experiences of our time," he observes, hinting at an unspoken claim for his own priority as the author of such famously historically apprehensive poems as "Consider this and in our time," "O what is that sound," "Spain," and "The Age of Anxiety."

Both poets, as Auden recognizes, were living in the wake of the great upheavals of world war and its artistic offspring, Modernism, and looking
for an adequate response to the simultaneously static yet unsettling situation in which they found themselves. The task before them, as Auden
construes it, is to find a way to articulate the complexities of a world
that has been created—or devastated—by others, while looking ahead
to the next epoch, also presumably to be created by others. Theirs is a
mediating position and their tools are form, irony, and the low rhetorical register.[10] Auden addresses this notion at length in his introduction
to Rich's book:

> Every age has its characteristic faults, its typical temptation
> to overemphasize some virtue at the expense of others, and
> the typical danger for poets in our age is, perhaps, the desire
> to be "original." This is natural, for who in his daydreams does
> not prefer to see himself as a leader rather than a follower, an
> explorer rather than a cultivator or settler? Unfortunately, the
> possibility of realizing such a dream is limited, not only by
> talent but also by time, and even a superior gift cannot con-
> ceal historical priority; he who today climbs the Matterhorn,
> though he be the greatest climber who ever lived, must tread in
> Whymper's footsteps.
>   Radical changes and significant novelty in artistic style can
> only occur when there has been a radical change in human
> sensibility to require them. The spectacular events of the present
> time must not blind us to the fact that we are living not at the
> beginning but in the middle of a historical epoch; they are not
> novel but repetitions on a vastly enlarged scale and at a violently
> accelerated tempo of events which took place long since.
>   Every poet under fifty-five cherishes, I suspect, a secret grudge
> against Providence for not getting him born a little earlier. On
> writing down the obvious names which would occur to every-
> one as those of the great figures of "modern" poetry, novels,
> painting, and music, the innovators, the creators of the new
> style, I find myself with a list of twenty persons: of these, four
> were born in the sixties, six in the seventies, and ten in the eight-
> ies. It was these men who were driven to find a new style which

could cope with such changes in our civilization as, to mention
only four, the collapse of the liberal hope of peaceful change, of
revolution through oratory and literature; the dissolution of the
traditional community by industrial urbanization; the exposure
of the artist to the styles of every epoch and culture simultaneously; and the skepticism induced by psychology and anthropology as to the face value of any emotion or belief.

Before a similar crop of revolutionary artists can appear
again, there will have to be just such another cultural revolution replacing these attitudes with others. So long as the way in
which we regard the world and feel about our existence remains
in all essentials the same as that of our predecessors we must
follow in their tradition; it would be just as dishonest for us to
pretend that their style is inadequate to our needs as it would
have been for them to be content with the style of the Victori-
ans. [*ACW*, 9]

Auden's account of Rich's anxious cultural position is also self-
descriptive. The grudge he presumes the twenty-one-year-old Rich to
hold for being born too late to participate in the creation of Modernism's "new style" is a grudge that the forty-four-year-old poet had himself wrestled with for much of his own career. "Look shining at / New
styles of architecture, a change of heart" [*SP*, 7], he had written when he
himself was twenty-two, simultaneously prefiguring Rich's quiet gesture
toward a "change of world" in her own first book, and hinting at the
young Auden's self-consciousness that the new styles of architecture his
sonnet was praising were ones he himself had not helped build. After the
aesthetic revolution of "the great figures of 'modern' poetry," Yeats, Eliot,
and Pound, all that remains for the young, latecomer poet is to "look
shining" at their radical achievement and set about to live constructively
within it, adding ornamentation or enlarging on their original edifice.
His paradoxical task is to be original when the idea of originality itself
has become cliché.

Each of the four epochal changes he identifies are questions he himself had addressed in his own work, in each case trying to find some way
to "make it new" in the face of established cultural authority. "The dissolution of the traditional community by industrial urbanization" was

one of Auden's earliest themes, as evidenced in *The Orators*, which envisions England as a sick and dysfunctional blend of public school, cloak-and-dagger battleground, and industrial decay. The steaming engines and belching factories that had heralded the birth of the modern had, by Auden's time, become the rusting hulks and abandoned mines of his early poems. Auden's response is to idealize these emblems of industrial collapse, reclaiming the barren landscape and mechanistic imagery of the Modernist waste land for his own private romance. Similarly, Auden had responded to "the exposure of the artist to the styles of every epoch and culture simultaneously" by trying to domesticate the wide-ranging Modernist impulse through rigorously incorporating as many of these styles as possible into his own strictly disciplined work, priding himself on having attempted almost every known verse form at least once. "The skepticism induced by psychology and anthropology" was another cultural inheritance with which Auden contended, first by finding refuge in the metapsychological theories of Lane and Layard, and then, as expressed in his elegy for Freud, who "merely told / The unhappy Present to recite the Past / like a poetry lesson," seeing in psychology's didactic, revelatory power an analogue for his own art, hopeful of uncovering usable meaning amid the cultural ruins: "While as they lie in the grass of our neglect, / So many long-forgotten objects / Revealed by his undiscouraged shining / Are returned to us and made precious again" [*CP*, 275]. And Auden's ambition to maintain an "undiscouraged shining" in the face of "the collapse of the liberal hope of peaceful change, of revolution through oratory" was one of the fundamental intellectual struggles in Auden's life, leading in part to both his emigration and his new American poetics. Indeed, Auden's American career was an effort to reimagine poetry's failure to make something happen in the world as a "way of happening" in which the revolution comes within the reader, and not out in the streets.

Because Auden's disavowal of historical originality also suggests his ambivalence regarding his own inherited, mediative cultural position, his condescension toward Rich also reveals a kind of oddly sympathetic identification with her. Auden sees in Rich's adoption of his own adaptive mode a further symptom of his, and the succeeding generation's, essentially reactive response to the prevailing cultural weather, forced to wait for the "radical change in human sensibility" before a new "crop of revolutionary artists can appear." This position, while seeming to support claims of Auden's post-immigration resignation to poetry's inefficacy in the world, actually illustrates Auden's complex perspective on the relation between poetry and cultural and social change. For Auden, poetry reflects the world not by standing outside it and looking in, but by taking a fundamental, engaged place within it. Poetry is *part* of the world, and participates in the dialogue of change just as an individual in society would, as he suggests in his equation of Rich and her poems: "Poems are analogous to persons." Poems are representative of their times in exactly the same way people are, and "So long as the way in which we regard the world and feel about our existence remains in all essentials the same as that of our predecessors," the poems we write will likewise reflect that static perspective.

Auden's "instrument" metaphor is significant here. In its multiple resonance as musical instrument, tool, and climatological gauge, we see the full range of Auden's notion of poetry. It sings to give pleasure, it helps—if only incrementally—in the furtherance of a particular goal, and it measures—metrically and imaginatively—the temper of the times. In each case, it is a metaphor, not of reaction or reflection, but of active participation: The poet plays the melody, wields the tool, and, in the case of the barometer/thermometer, it is the direct effect of the environment—its interaction with the instrument's responsive material—that is registered. Unlike a mirror, which merely reflects an image, leaving the mimetic surface unchanged, the instrument's mercury is materially affected by, and engaged with, the world's heat and its pressures. The meteorological instrument feels the world around it, and communicates that feeling, providing useful, practicable information. It tells us how to act in the world, or prepares us for a change in that world.

In Auden's formulation, then, poetry serves as one of culture's most sensitive instruments, and if there is an air of perfunctoriness about his introduction of Rich it is perhaps because in her poems' studied inhabitation of the same cultural climate he himself had been articulating for decades, he sees no signs, even among the young, that change is on its way. It also reflects a rhetorical stance that is characteristic of Auden's businesslike perspective on poetry's civic role: Auden deliberately stresses a certain rhetorical perfunctoriness as a kind of praise, daring to sound bureaucratic in order to suggest that the poet has a job to do, with a definite social role, and that Rich is doing it. In this sense, Auden's anticipation of a new "cultural revolution" to replace those familiar attitudes and conventions becomes a prescription, and prediction, of future poetic achievement. The "crop of revolutionary artists" he waits for will participate in a communal "radical change in human sensibility," of which their creative work will be a crucial part. Until that happens, they—like the young Rich, in Auden's estimation—will be condemned merely to reiterate the recent past. As Auden did not know, just such a cultural revolution was just over a decade away—a revolution of political ideology, gender relations, and artistic form in which Rich herself, no longer the polite undergraduate, would play a generation-defining poetic and cultural role. It was a revolution that would leave the older Auden behind, but it was one he had prophesied and recognized as necessary for the birth of a new kind of art.

As Rich herself came to realize, for her own art to develop she would need to reject the example of those "masters" who had first helped form her identity as a poet. But, in a move that can be seen as characteristic of their embattled paradoxical poetic relationship throughout Rich's career, that rejection is itself presaged in Auden's own early estimation of her. In his introduction, even as he offers an implicit critique of her conventional beginnings, Auden suggests a vision of Rich's "radical" future. And, as Rich makes clear in her later confession of her "secret grudge against Auden" for seeing her early poetry as merely a modest product of its unrevolutionary times, she paid unhappy attention to the distinction he drew between the bold "creators of the new style" and the cultural place-holders with a "talent for versification." In the two possibilities Auden held out for her, and her dissatisfaction with the option he had apparently assigned her, Rich could see her own way more clearly. In charting her own course away from her early male mentors and—in her deep engagement with the cultural shifts of her moment—offering a new notion of poetry's role in truly achieving a "change of world," Rich would achieve, on her own terms, the "radical change and significant novelty in artistic style" that Auden had found lacking in her first book. Yet it was upon the foundation of those first poetic models, especially Auden, that she would build her new poetic persona and project. Instead of her instruments agreeing with his, she would tune hers against the pitch he had helped establish. Like the relationship between a stern parent and an independent-minded child, even in her rejection of him, the paternal influence of Auden, and of the poetic ideas he represents for her, would continue to make itself felt.[11] For Rich, Auden stands as the embodiment of a series of tensions—between influence and novelty; between parent and child; between man and woman—that lie at the heart of, and indeed generate, her poetics. By charting Rich's engagements with the "Old Master" Auden, we can chart the course of her career.

◆ ◆ ◆

The analogy of parent and child has more than metaphorical implications for Rich's poetic development. In "When We Dead Awaken," Rich traces the origins of her poetic ambitions to her early desire to please her own father:

> My own luck was being born white and middle-class into a
> house full of books, with a father who encouraged me to read
> and write. So for about twenty years I wrote for a particular
> man, who criticized and praised me and made me feel I was
> indeed "special." The obverse side of this, of course, was that I
> tried for a long time to please him, or rather, not to displease
> him. And then of course there were other men—writers,
> teachers—the Man, who was not a terror or a dream but a liter-
> ary master and a master in other ways less easy to acknowledge.
> [*LSS*, 38–39]

In her 1960 poem "Juvenilia," written a decade before this essay, Rich reconstructs this originary imaginative scene, sitting as a young girl in her father's study and absorbing the weighty atmosphere of masculine literary tradition embodied in his heavy oak desk, fountain pen, and library of leather-bound books:

> Your Ibsen volumes, violet-spined,
> each flaking its gold arabesque . . .
> Again I sit, under duress, hands washed,
> at your inkstained oaken desk,
> by the goose-neck lamp in the tropic of your books,
> stabbing the blotting-pad, doodling loop upon loop,
> peering one-eyed into the dusty reflecting mirror

of your student microscope,
craning my neck to spell above me

A DOLL'S HOUSE   LITTLE EYOLF
WHEN WE DEAD AWAKEN

Unspeakable fairy tales ebb like blood through my head
as I dip the pen and for aunts, for admiring friends,
for you above all to read,
copy my praised and sedulous lines.

Behind the two of us, thirsty spines
quiver in semi-shadow, huge leaves uncurl and thicken.
    [*FD*, 41–42]

Addressing her father, Rich recalls her initial engagements with writing as a command performance for "aunts, admiring friends, / and above all for you." Amid the theater of her father's study, fraught with patriarchal ambiance, she rehearses her "praised and sedulous lines" for her appreciative family audience. In this scene of trying to please, "or rather, not to displease," her father, Rich sketches the tensions that impelled her poetic project from its beginnings. On the one hand is the deep and exotic allure of the "violet-spined" volumes, the "inkstained oaken desk," and the "goose-neck lamp in the tropic of your books," suggesting the seductive, even sensual, appeal of tradition, form, and conventional— and conventionally masculine—aesthetic refinement and achievement. On the other is the young Rich's suppressed resentment of the standards she must conform to and the role she must play, "under duress, hands washed" and "stabbing the blotting-pad" with the nib of the dagger-like pen. We see the young poet's desire to please and be praised for her elegant accomplishments while, unknown to her smiling audience, "unspeakable fairy tales ebb like blood through [her] head."

The conflict between public performance and what remains "unspeakable" is one of Rich's constant themes, from "An Unsaid Word" in her first book, which posits a woman's capacity to "keep her peace" and leave "her man" free as "the hardest thing to learn" [*ACW*, 51], to 1975's "Cartographies of Silence," where meaningless syllables "drown the terror / beneath the unsaid word" [*FD*, 233].[12] In other poems, especially her later work, we see this same balance between the troubled, meditative, interior voice and the public declamatory one, speaking to and for others, as the formative tensions in the young Rich's poetic impulse get played out on the wider stage of her literary career. In "Juvenilia," it is the enigmatic and evocative titles of her father's Ibsen volumes that prompt in the young Rich's imagination those "unspeakable fairy tales." Onto the fanciful and inscrutable "gold arabesques" of her father's books she silently projects her own defiant and full-blooded concerns, not knowing that those texts themselves—especially *When We Dead Awaken*, which influenced Rich deeply and gave her the title for both her essay and a 1971 poem—will one day help her articulate those very concerns that as yet must remain unspoken in the face of her domineering mentor/father. "Re-vision," as Rich would later put it in that well-known essay, is "the act of looking back, of seeing with fresh eyes, of entering an old text from a new direction" [*LSS*, 35]. Rich is here presenting a "re-vision" of her own beginnings as a poet, looking back at the tensions facing her younger self between her ambition to please her father and her desire to articulate the unspeakable and seeing in those tensions her own poetic awakening.

In terms echoing Auden's critique of her "modesty" and "craftsman-ship," "Juvenilia" offers a backhanded dismissal of her own early father-pleasing work as "praised and sedulous," expressing Rich's sense of am-bivalence at the effects of this paternal influence. But the poem ends on a note of parent/child détente, as the "spines" of her father's "tropic of books" loom and grow in Rich's imagination into a tropological jungle, pages uncurling into "huge leaves" and stretching back into the "semi-shadow" of a shared past, "behind the two of us." In the shade of that remembered library, father and daughter come together in a poem whose open form has left that earlier conventionality behind but which still expresses its debt to the forbidding yet creative landscape her father provided.

Rich would not always see her father's influence from such a benign perspective, as is illustrated by her 1964 elegy for him, "After Dark." In this poem, she responds with a sorrowful bitterness to what she remem-bers as her father's oppressive presence. Reflecting on the legacy of her relationship with her now-dead father, Rich reveals buried resentments: "[O]ld man whose death I wanted / I can't stir you up now" [*FD*, 69]. Even after his death, she still hears his voice in her head, like a relentless

"phonograph needle . . . eating [her] heart to dust," repeating the patronizing refrain, "*I know you better / than you know yourself   I know /
you better than you know / yourself   I know / you.*" Yet even here, Rich
acknowledges, almost despite herself, the ongoing creative impact of her
conflicts with him: "Alive now, root to crown, I'd give // —oh,—something—not to know / our struggles now are ended."

Rich returns again and again, in both poetry and prose, to the figure
of her father and his role in her artistic and intellectual development.
Filling in the emotional background that "Juvenilia" and "After Dark"
only hint at, Rich writes in a 1982 essay of her relationship with her father in terms that recall her ambivalent response to Auden's "mastery":

> My father was an amateur musician, read poetry, adored
> encyclopedic knowledge. He prowled and pounced over my
> school papers, insisting I use "grown-up" sources; he criticized
> my poems for faulty technique and gave me books on rhyme
> and meter and form. His investment in my intellect and talent
> was egotistical, tyrannical, opinionated, and terribly wearing.
> He taught me, nevertheless, to believe in hard work, to mistrust
> easy inspiration, to write and rewrite; to feel that I *was* a person
> of the book, even though a woman; to take ideas seriously. He
> made me feel, at a very young age, the power of language and
> that I could share in it.[13]

Here, as in her critique of Auden's poetic influence, Rich admits
resentment toward her father for his stifling and egotistical authority,
but again acknowledges the crucial role he played in forming her mature identity. A year later, in a long, episodic poem called "Sources," Rich
once again traces her creative origins back to her troubled relationship
with her father:

> For years I struggled with you: your categories,
> your theories, your will, the cruelty which came inex-
> tricable from your love. For years all arguments I
> carried on in my head were with you. I saw myself,
> the eldest daughter raised as a son, taught to study but
> not to pray, taught to hold reading and writing sacred:
> the eldest daughter in a house with no son, she who

must overthrow the father, take what he taught her
and use it against him. [*S*, 15]

Here, Rich places herself in the role of the rebellious Oedipal son, needing to overthrow the father to carve out her own identity. It is a pattern that finds a suggestive parallel in her poetic response to Auden.

It is significant that, despite her rhetorical and imaginative turn from the masculine tradition personified in the father she "must overthrow," it is from his bookshelves that she must gather the tools and learn the stories that help tell her who she is and who she might become. In particular, in each of the Ibsen texts that Rich's memory retrospectively highlights in "Juvenilia," she would find themes, characters, and ideas to resonate with her own personal and intellectual project, from the bold but possibly doomed figure of female independence in *A Doll's House*, to the vexed questions of marriage convention and bourgeois sexuality in *Little Eyolf*, to the conflict in *When We Dead Awaken* between, as Rich puts it in her essay, "the use that the male artist and thinker—in the process of creating culture as we know it—has made of women, in his life and work" and "a woman's slow struggling awakening to the use to which her life has been put" [*LSS*, 34].[14] And in general, the poem makes clear that the development of a feminist poetic identity—or at least Rich's—does not preclude significant masculine, and canonical, influence. Without Ibsen, Rich would not have become the particular kind of feminist poet she did. Similarly, without the influence of her father, to both please and resist, Rich's tension-filled poetics would not have developed in the same way. She "takes what he taught her," as she puts it in "Sources," to "use against him" and the male literary tradition he represents.

As Rich makes clear in her essay, her father serves as the prototype of the "other men—writers, teachers—the Man, who was not a terror or a dream but a literary master and a master in other ways less easy to acknowledge," explicitly connecting paternal influence to literary influence and suggesting the inescapability of both. "The child's soul carries on / in the wake of home" [*FD*, 323], she writes in another poem, acknowledging influence's double edge. The grown child "carries on" with her adult independent life, but the "wake of home" ripples indelibly through her. That initial formative influence is both a burden to be borne, a curse to be endured, and, in a sense, an absence to be mourned in one's unsheltered maturity, a lost incipience for which adulthood is a continuous funereal "wake."

The link between this notion of family romance and literary influence has at least four significant implications for an analysis of Rich's poetry in general, and for a discussion of Rich's relation to Auden in particular. First, it suggests that, for Rich, even in attempts to revise or "revision" inheritance, old inheritances—even male inheritances—can still pertain. Even as she constructed a new poetic identity that repudiated the male tradition personified by her father, and embraced a new activist, revolutionary, feminist poetics, the "wake of home" still haunted her. "Blood is a sacred poison," as Rich puts it in "After Dark," and the tinct of that originary connection is indelible. While her poems look forward to an open, idealized future, the claims of history—both her own and her culture's—are always with her. "Poetry never stood a chance of standing outside history," she writes in "North American Time" [*FD*, 325], and the same is true of the poet.

Second, it complicates familiar critical assumptions about Rich's ideas on gender and the sources of poetry. Many critics, sympathetic and antagonistic, have found in Rich—bolstered by some of Rich's own well-known polemical statements against such things as "compulsory heterosexuality"[15] and in support of the creation of a new, collective, female tradition—a flag-bearer for an exclusionary brand of feminism. But an examination of Rich's own poetic practice reveals a substantially more complex, dialectical notion of the role of the old masculine-dominated tradition in building a new feminist one. Far from being reductively anti-male, Rich's poetry has continually sought to unite, rather than further divide, the antinomy of gender. In her first book, poems like "This Beast, This Angel" suggest a sense of shared male–female identity, a kind of idealized double-consciousness transcending sex, that comes from true and unconstrained human relation: "Beneath this gaze our powers are fused as one; . . . / This beast, this angel is both you and I" [*ACW*, 38]. Even in mid-career poems such as 1965's "Orion," Rich offers the stellified male warrior, the poet's "genius," "helmed lion-heart king," and "fierce half-brother," as a figure of a male tradition available for constructive assimilation by the female poet, unencumbered by the demands of gender: "As I throw back my head to take you in / an old transfusion happens again" [*FD*, 79]. In "Diving into the Wreck" from 1972, Rich

goes further, positing her relation to the tradition as that of an ambi-
gendered "mermaid"/"merman" descending into the "wreck" of the past,
looking for "the damage that was done / and the treasures that prevail"
[*FD*, 163]. Gender difference has fallen away in the poet's attempts to
salvage a collective poetic inheritance: "I am she: I am he." And even
from the perspective of her lesbian identity, Rich sees herself as uniting
both female and male identities, citing, in an essay called "A poet's education," a passage from the Chicano poet Gloria Anzaldúa to describe
her conception of lesbian artistic consciousness: "I, like other queer people, am two in one body, both male and female. I am the embodiment
of the *hieros gamos*: the coming together of opposite qualities within"
[*WFT*, 210].[16] The relationship between father and daughter, which, she
has suggested, is also both an erotic and a pedagogical one,[17] gives this
conception of female/male union a literal, biological, and biographical
precedent and analogue: The mature poet is Adrienne Rich, but she also
contains, at least in part and in more than a genetic sense, her father.

Third, in her own depiction of her relationship with her father, and
in her acknowledgment of the significance of male "masters" like Ibsen
and Auden on her intellectual, moral, and poetic development, Rich
suggests the possibility of construing inheritance by female poets of
male poets in ways that do not reinscribe notions of masculine oppres-
sion. Rich's relationship with her male precursors is not free of tension,
or even anger, but it is not an anxious one. It is complex and nuanced,
like any family relationship, but does not seek to deny their important
role in forming her identity, even while she asserts her own independence from them.

And finally, this connection between familial and poetic inheritance
reinforces the notion of Auden as a kind of literary father figure for Rich,
whose contentious poetic relationship with him mirrors her conflicted
personal relationship with her own father. As the master whose example
she first assimilates then publicly rejects; as the male authority figure
who serves as her introduction to the world of poetry, but who does
so with niggardly praise and sexist condescension; as the "middle-aged"
early influence whose knowing assessment of her and ideas about poetry's place in the world continue to trouble her throughout her career;
as the paragon of patriarchal tradition she must overthrow but whose
voice—especially his troubling claim, "Poetry makes nothing happen"—

continues to echo in her thoughts and in her work; as the mentor from whom she takes what he taught her to use against him: In all these ways, Auden stands as a kind of poetic parent, a home she is always departing from but never entirely forgets.

◆ ◆ ◆

It is an illuminating irony of Rich's career that the further she moves rhetorically and culturally from the early example Auden set for her, and the tradition he represented, the more—in some ways—she appears to resemble him. In fact, the shape of Rich's career might even be seen to parallel Auden's, a mirror image reflecting, beneath their outward differences of generation, gender, and politics, a certain familial resemblance. Auden's emigration from England, and the new American poetic identity he constructed stand as one of the twentieth-century's greatest examples of poetic self-reinvention. Unlike Yeats, whose fierce late work only revised the tone and imagery, but not the ambition or the continuous dialogue of self and soul begun in his earlier work, and unlike Robert Lowell, whose turn from stoic formalism to fiery confessionalism marked a shift in personality more than poetic purpose, Auden's renunciation of his English poetic identity amounted to a wholesale redefinition of poetry's power and place in the world. Rich, in her rejection of her early poetic self—the young Rich who saw poetry as a timeless refuge from the world, a shattered and impotent instrument in troubled times—and her re-creation of herself as a passionate political poet who believes, as she writes in 1968, "Revolution is poetry" [FD, 107], reenacts Auden's dramatic poetic self-transformation.

Rich remakes her poetic identity in interestingly similar ways to Auden, though in opposite terms. While Auden begins as a firebrand, championing leftist political causes, enlisting poetry in the struggle against fascism, and experimenting with radical poetic forms, he ends his career as a devoutly apolitical aesthetic and cultural conservative. Rich's career follows an analogous pattern, but in reverse. Rich sets out as a precocious conservator of tradition, coolly advising the would-be-iconoclast reader of her first book, "Let us only bear in mind / How these treasures handed down / From a calmer age passed on / Are in the keeping of our kind" [ACW, 45], before transforming herself into the form-breaking poetic provocateur of her later career. Rich's career demonstrates not only a shared capacity for self-"re-vision" with Auden but also suggests Auden's importance as a historical model of a notion of poetic identity that privileges personal development, cultural responsiveness, and conscious choice over conceptions of the intrinsic and immutable self. In a chiasmus that seems to turn on its head Auden's diagnosis of the young Rich as being too much like his own mid-century self, Rich begins her career as, in a sense, the late Auden, and ends it—presuming Rich has finished her poetic self-fashioning—looking more like the early one.

The connections between Auden and Rich extend beyond the complementary arcs of their careers. Each returned late in adulthood to the faiths of their fathers—Anglicanism for Auden, Judaism for Rich— bringing a new sense of spiritual depth and cultural identity to their work. Auden's embrace of America after the claustrophobia of England also finds an analogue in Rich's abandonment of the high-culture milieu of Europe and Harvard, found throughout her first two books, in favor of the open American landscape and the cultural diversity she found outside the East-Coast, white, intellectual establishment into which she had been born. Even the history of their critical receptions offers parallels, as both poets have suffered a certain lack of critical sympathy in their later years, though for opposite reasons. For Auden, his apparent retreat from the bold utterance of his English youth into the perceived domestic conservatism of his American career has prompted numerous critics to see his postwar work as a disappointing betrayal of his early promise. The question sometimes posed for Rich, in the words of fellow-poet Eavan Boland, is "What transformed the young poet Auden singled out for her good manners into one of the truly subversive poets of our time? The customary, and sometimes hostile, critical view is that [she] became feminist, activist, lesbian. That her angers cut her adrift from mainstream poetry. That America lost a gifted lyric poet and had to make do with a polemicist."[18] For both poets, it is the perceived ideology of their late careers—Auden's apparent conservatism and Rich's political activism—that has provoked critique and disappointment on the part of some enthusiasts of their earlier work.

But in both poets it is a rigorous self-scrutiny, and a fearless willingness to acknowledge—and act on—changes in their own perspective, that compel the changes in their poetic identity. For Auden, it was his recognition of his need to leave England's parochialism, a growing religious conviction, and a new belief in poetry's didactic, rather than political power, that brought about his poetic conversion. For Rich, it was the radicalizing experience of trying to write poetry as a wife and mother; an increasing awareness of the political implications of her life as a white, middle-class, female intellectual; her participation in the cultural upheavals of the late 1960s and 1970s; and a developing sense of her own lesbian identity that sparked her new poetic direction. Both poets boldly reject their earlier identities in the quest for an honest representation of their own evolving experience. "What gives us anchor but the mutable?" [*FD*, 18]. Rich early on asks in "A Walk by the Charles" from her second volume, and for both poets it is an unblinking recognition of their own mutability that stands as a shared constant in each of their careers.

For both Auden and Rich, this devotion to intellectual honesty manifests itself both in the poems themselves and in their public responses, over the course of their careers, to their own early work. For each poet, poetry serves as a site of dialectic, where opposing ideas productively conflict and contest one another. Auden's poetics of "double-focus" is a resolutely dialectical one; Rich's poetry—from the start and continuing throughout her career—maintains a similar vision and self-questioning skepticism. In an early poem like "Boundary," in her first book, she writes, "Between two opposite intents[,] / A hair would span the difference" [*ACW*, 46], rejecting the rhetoric of singularity and following Auden's observation, in "New Year Letter," on the fallacy of the egocentric and unexamined assertion of will: "The symmetry disorders reach / When both are equal each to each, / Yet in intention all are one" [*CP*, 200]. The task and the privilege of the poetic imagination, says Rich, is to be able to see both sides:

> [I]f the imagination is to transcend and transform experience it has to question, to challenge, to conceive of alternatives, perhaps to the very life you are living at the moment. You have to be free to play around with the notion that day might be night, love might be hate; nothing can be too sacred for the imagination to turn into its opposite or to call experimentally by another name. For writing is re-naming. [*LSS*, 43]

As John Ashbery credited her in a 1966 review of *Necessities of Life*, Rich "has mastered the art of tacking between alternative resolutions of the poem's tension and of leaving the reader at the right moment, just as meaning is dawning."[19] Another poet, Marilyn Hacker, makes a similar appreciative assessment, noting a connection between her tremendous popularity with readers and her dialectical mode: "Just as Adrienne Rich has, over the years, gathered a uniquely heterogeneous public for her work, so does her work draw its greatest strength from synthesis. She does not try to create a 'universal' to contain and explain all her specifics; she juxtaposes those specifics and, at her strongest, leaves, conclusion, closure, to the reader."[20] In her own poems, Rich continually revises herself and interrogates her own temptation toward insularity and dogmatism: "When my dreams showed signs / of becoming / politically correct . . . / then I began to wonder" [*FD*, 324]. Auden, too, reproves himself for his youthful naiveté, admitting "No words men write can stop the war" [*CP*, 206], and critiquing his own tendency to pontificate and "Adopt . . . what I would disown, / The preacher's loose immodest tone" [*CP*, 204].

Each poet extends this concern with truthfulness—with "not telling fibs," as Auden puts it—to the editing of their own published work. Auden notoriously eliminated from his canon some of his best-known poems, including "Sir, No Man's Enemy," "A Communist to Others," and "Spain," refusing to allow them to be reprinted on the grounds of what he later had deemed their intellectual or moral dishonesty. In the 1965 foreword to his *Collected Shorter Poems*, he explains his perspective, singling out the politically hortatory "Spain" for special censure:

> A dishonest poem is one which expresses, no matter how well, feelings or beliefs which its author never felt or entertained. For example, I once expressed a desire for "New styles of architecture"; but I have never liked modern architecture. I prefer *old* styles, and one must be honest even about one's prejudices. Again, and much more shamefully, I once wrote:
>
> > History to the defeated
> > May say alas but cannot help nor pardon.
>
> To say this is to equate goodness with success. It would have been bad enough if I had ever held this wicked doctrine, but that I should have stated it simply because it sounded to me rhetorically effective is quite inexcusable. [*CP*, xxvi]

Of his decision to repudiate "September 1, 1939," the most prominent of his canonical excisions, Auden elsewhere tells his readers,

> Rereading a poem of mine . . . after it had been published, I
> came to the line "We must love one another or die" and said to
> myself: "That's a damned lie! We must die anyway." So, in the
> next edition, I altered it to "We must love one another and die."
> This didn't seem to do either, so I cut the stanza. Still no good.
> The whole poem, I realized, was infected with an incurable
> dishonesty—and must be scrapped.[21]

While claiming to have "never, consciously at any rate, attempted
to revise my former thoughts and feelings, only the language in which
they were first expressed when, on further consideration, it seemed to
me inaccurate, lifeless, prolix, or painful to the ear" [*CP*, xxvi], Auden's
denunciation of poems that clash with his later convictions as "trash"
suggest that he viewed his oeuvre as a work-in-progress to be edited or
emended in light of new insights or truths. In his terms, the poet is an-
swerable for every poem he has written and if a poem can no longer be
defended in the face of the poet's current moral, intellectual, or aesthetic
perspective, it "must be scrapped" and the error must be acknowledged.
Once again, for Auden, "Poems are analogous to persons" and are ac-
countable for the moral stances they take.

Though Rich has never publicly repudiated any of her own work,
she has—like Auden—engaged in extensive reframing of her earlier
poems in the light of her evolving cultural, artistic, and political convictions. Her books of reprinted essays and selected poems feature sub-
stantial footnotes and explanatory remarks in which she tries to provide
some of the personal and historical context behind the texts' composition, often critiquing her earlier self for lapses of judgment, wisdom, or
social awareness. While Auden reconsiders his early more radical work
from the perspective of his later rejection of politicized poetry, in Rich's
case she re-contextualizes her early conventionalism in terms of her later
political awakening. In 1984's *The Fact of a Doorframe*, for example, she
offers a lengthy gloss in the volume's endnotes on the title poem of her
second book, which in 1955 used the work of an African "diamond cut-
ter" as a figure for a poet's labor:

Thirty years later I have trouble with the informing metaphor of this poem. I was trying, in my twenties, to write about the craft of poetry. But I was drawing, quite ignorantly, on the long tradition of domination, according to which the precious resource is yielded up into the hands of the dominator as if by a natural event. The enforced and exploited labor of actual Africans in actual diamond mines was invisible to me, and therefore invisible in the poem, which does not take responsibility for its own metaphor. I note this here because this kind of metaphor is still widely accepted, and I still have to struggle against it in my work. [*FD*, 329]

Rich's retrospective commentary on her earlier, less politically aware work illustrates her notion of the poet's continuous implication in, and responsibility to, history. Her ambition is to make the past visible, look at it afresh, and apply those lessons to future work. Rich sees the process of writing as one of self-"re-vision" and contextualization, and, like Auden, is unafraid to admit a change in perspective. In fact, her changeability, her refusal to stop moving, is also a source of a certain pride, as she boasts in 1987's "Delta": "If you think you can grasp me, think again" [*TPR*, 32].

In "The Blue Ghazals" of 1968, Rich offers another rationale for the connection between her changing politics and her changing poetics: "If I thought of my words as changing minds / hadn't my mind also to suffer changes?" [*FD*, 122]. In Rich's terms, the relationship between writer and reader, between poem and culture, between the fixity of art and the flow of history, is a reciprocal one, and it is in this conception of poetry's place in the world that we can trace her affinities with Auden most clearly. Rich sees the mutability of her own perspective as an essential part of her poetry's power to change minds. In fact, it is precisely poetry's capacity to articulate those shifts in feeling and idea that gives it illuminative power, both for her readers and for herself. As she describes the process to an audience at a 1964 poetry reading,

I know what I know through making poems. . . . [T]he poem itself engenders new sensations, new awarenesses in me as it progresses. . . . Perhaps a simple way of putting it would be to say that instead of poems *about* experiences I am getting poems that *are* experiences, that contribute to my knowledge and my emotional life even while they reflect and assimilate it.[22]

Like Auden's notion of poetry as a pedagogical process in which the experience of negotiating the dialectic of language and meaning in a poem offers the poet and the reader a productive model for addressing the conflicts and complexities of the world outside the poem, Rich sees poetry as a path to self-knowledge. Through the act of writing and reading poetry, both poet and reader engage in a process of "re-vision," of looking at themselves and their world with new eyes and learning "how we can begin to see and name—and therefore live—afresh" [*LSS*, 35].

While Rich, like many readers, has sometimes seen Auden's echoing line "Poetry makes nothing happen" as evidence of his pessimistic acceptance of the essential triviality of poetry and a proclamation of poetry's diminished scope, in her verse Rich actually demonstrates a much closer affinity to the complex sentiment behind that often misunderstood line. Auden's assertion was not simply a renunciation of poetry's power to effect change in the world. Rather, it was a redefinition of poetry's moral, intellectual, and civic value in the face of historical catastrophe and personal crisis. While poetry couldn't keep Hitler and Franco out of power, or keep bombs from destroying a city, it could in the longer term help build a "Just City" through the didactic power of its dialectic. Poetry wasn't propaganda, and didn't make specific events happen; it was, rather, a "way of happening." Rich, too, shows in her work a similar sense of poetry's nuanced role in building a progressive future. While Rich is often critically positioned as a manifesto-bearing polemicist, and she herself honors the role of committed activist, her poetic practice frequently evinces her own distrust, and sometimes despair, of poetry's function as a political weapon, to be used by one side against another in the culture wars. Some of Rich's poems, like 1972's "Cartographies of Silence," enthusiastically inhabit the more combative end of her poetic spectrum, revising Auden's "ironic points of light" into a poetic blowtorch pointed at the male "enemy":

When I dream of meeting
the enemy, this is my dream:

white acetylene
ripples from my body
effortlessly released
perfectly trained
on the true enemy

raking his body down the thread
of existence
burning away his lie
leaving him in a new
world; a changed
man [*FD*, 166–67]

Not content to "undo the folded lie" of the generalized "man-in-
the-street" of Auden's "September 1, 1939," this manifestation of Rich
wants to "burn away his lie," which is conventional masculinity itself,
torching him in the flame of self-awareness, leaving him charred but
"changed." More often, though, Rich eschews the notion of using poetry
to vanquish her "enemies." In "Implosions" from 1968, she professes her
ambition "to choose words that even you / would have to be changed
by," but closes on a note of self-doubt: "When it's finished . . ./ I'll have
done nothing / even for you?" [*FD*, 95–96]. In 1966's "Charleston in
the 1860s" she admits the inability of "imagination to forestall woe"
[*FD*, 86], and by 1975 she is confessing, "It was an old theme even for
me: / Language cannot do everything" [*FD*, 235].

For this Rich—whom I would argue is the essential poet rather than
the competing and simplifying critical personae of the early traditionalist
versus the later radical—poetry is not simply a political tool. It is a space
of contention and contradiction—of the self, of culture, of language—
and it is the effort to resolve those oppositions that brings, not specific
action, but insight that can lead to action. "A really good poem," she has
said, "opens up the possibility for others, rather than being the end of a
succession of things. Instead of wrapping something up it explodes the
possibilities."[23] Poetry, says this Rich, really does make nothing specific
happen, but—unlike the early Rich whose "shattered instrument" reflected a notion of poetry's powerlessness—that does not mean it can't
bring about change. For Rich, too, poetry is a "way of happening," an ex-

perience of the mind with real moral repercussions in the world. It isn't simply a loaded gun, but a complex pathway to change, as she declares in 1987's "Dreamwood": "She would recognize that poetry / isn't revolution but a way of knowing / why it must come" [*TPR*, 35]. In a world of conflict, division, and—in the title of another poem—"Partings," poetry offers hope: "[H]idden in all that tangle / there is a way" [*FD*, 196].

It is thus interesting, if perhaps not then so surprising, that Rich recalls turning, during one of the most difficult periods in her life, to poetry—and in particular, for all their differences, Auden's poetry—for help. In "An Atlas of a Difficult World," reflecting on the sad and troubled past of her failed marriage and her ex-husband's suicide, she remembers the two of them together in their distress: "Afternoons listening to records, reading Karl Shapiro's *Poems of a Jew* and Auden's 'In Sickness and in Health' aloud, using the poems to talk to each other" [*ADW*, 9]. Auden's unsentimental poem, which he dedicated to a troubled married couple in the hope of saving their relationship, draws a comparison between poetry and the idea of marriage. Both are human constructions whose ambitions to conquer time may be doomed, he suggests, yet, in their pushing back against the chaos and absurdity of existence they do have a life-sustaining value: "[W]ithout conscious artifice we die" [*CP*, 319].[24] It seems notable that Rich, at a moment when her marriage is falling apart and her own ambitions for her art are changing, should find some wisdom in Auden's poem's recognition of both poetry and marriage's frailty and provisionality in terms that recall, and revise, his own earlier famous assertion, "We must love one another or die." In the life she lives and the poems she writes after this pivotal moment in her career, we can see Rich embracing that wisdom: The "conscious artifice" of marriage can be productively redefined, as she enters into a happy union with the woman with whom she has spent the last four decades of her life. Poetry's artifice, too, is subject to what she calls in the title of the book she publishes at this time, *A Will to Change*. In a later poem, she will add her own revision to Auden's, telling her reader and herself, "[T]here come times—perhaps this is one of them— / when we have to take ourselves more seriously or die" [*DCL*, 74], suggesting that attending to the conscious artifice of the self is the first necessity for greater change. But through all these changes, and amid the knowledge of their imperfections and inadequacies, the worth and purpose of love, in all its human definitions, and poetry itself, remain constant. Her 1993 prose collection takes its title from William Carlos Williams's defense of poetry, "men die miserably every day / for lack / of what is found there," reminding the reader of the real power of poetry's artifice and bringing together and marshalling the resources of two of her "old masters," Williams and Auden, for her own socially constructive purposes. We can use poems—even poems by old masters—"to talk to each other" today, Rich asserts, to bridge the divides, to connect in the darkness, to love, to live. In this context, it makes sense that Rich should invoke Auden once more in her 1994 poem "Inscriptions: History." Observing again the implicatedness and ineluctability of private human love in the text of public history, she parenthetically concludes the poem with the opening lines of Auden's "Canzone," "*(When shall we learn, what should be clear as day, / We cannot choose what we are free to love?)*" [*DF*, 64]. In a different time and speaking to and for a different love, Auden's 1942 poem helps her say what she wants to say in 1994. Even this late in her career, after all the arguments and conflicts with his example and influence, she still feels free to use Auden to help tell us the truth about love.[25]

If poetry, according to both Auden and Rich, is a force for change whose influence is profound but difficult to quantify, a powerful moral and intellectual guide whose impact transcends mere cause-and-effect, the same can be said of the relationship between the two poets. As in the kinship between parent and child, and that of Rich and her own father, Auden's role in Rich's development is fundamental. Beleaguered by negation and despair in the face of his own moral and intellectual crises—including war, a collapse of political faith, and a sense of a need for a change of world—Auden's quest for his own "necessity" results in a poetic self-transformation that augurs Rich's own. Inheriting Auden's conviction in the poet's obligation to truthfulness, and sharing his belief in poetry's constructive civic power, Rich finds in Auden an enabling example of poetic independence, moral scrupulousness, and self-reinvention. As a well-known gay poet who made his sexuality a public subject for his poems, Auden also opens a way for Rich's poetic explorations of her own sexual identity.[26] His response to his own poetic and cultural situation, especially his turn to the didactic potential of poetry's dialectic, give Rich's own turn from the male poetic tradition—including Auden himself—a precedent and a process for achieving her own artistic ambitions.

Even in her rejection of him, Auden provides her, as did her father, with a useful—if often infuriating—influence and a model against which to define herself. As when a child repudiates her parents only to find with age her behavior, attitudes, and appearance echoing theirs, Rich's own mature poetic practice suggests her inheritance. Rich herself, addressing in particular this notion of the relationship between parenting and poetry, offers the most telling testament to Auden's familial influence: "If I have been a good parent to the poem," she tells her readers, in a line whose explicit echo of Auden's most famous phrase hints at her own filial debt, "something will happen to you who read it."²⁷ Rich doesn't surrender her mature agency, independence, and identity to the claims of her familial and poetic influences, but she does acknowledge them. She leaves her father's house far behind, but she does remember where she comes from. And, as Rich's estranged but ultimately sympathetic poetic parent, Auden can look to her career—and those of many of her peers— as one of the things his poetry helped make happen.

He Became His Admirers

Saying Goodbye to Auden

The first poem Auden wrote in America was an elegy. "In Memory of W. B. Yeats" proposes, in terms that resound through postwar American poetry, that "poetry makes nothing happen" yet can still be "a way of happening, a mouth." It also asserts that, in death, Yeats "became his admirers" by having only his words—all that remains of him—"modified in the guts of the living" who continue to read him. With this famously unsentimental leave-taking of the dead elder poet, Auden rewrites the rules of the modern elegy while announcing his own farewell to the poetic career he left behind in England. But even as his elegy refuses to obey the conventional expectations of praising the dead or suggesting that the world joins him in mourning the great poet's loss, it does end on a note of admiration for Yeats and his art, looking to the poems he leaves behind for continuing guidance: "With your unconstraining voice, / Still persuade us to rejoice . . . / In the prison of his days, / Teach the free man how to praise" [*CP*, 246–47]. And Auden further honors Yeats's own influence on him by writing a poem in a mode that Yeats himself had redefined. Auden credits Yeats, in a 1947 essay, with transforming the genre of "occasional poem" into a "serious reflective poem of at once personal and public interest." Citing Yeats's elegy "In Memory of Major Robert Gregory" in particular as "something new and important in the history of English poetry," Auden praises the poem for never losing "the personal note of a man speaking about his personal friends in a particular setting . . . and at the same time the occasion and the characters acquire a symbolic public significance" [*Prose*, 388]. In his elegy for Yeats, Auden builds on Yeats's advance, turning the "occasion" of Yeats's death itself into an opportunity for reflection on issues of personal and public interest, with an ironic twist: The "symbolic public significance" Yeats's death acquires in Auden's poem is that the world doesn't really care about dead poets.[1]

The lesson of Auden's homage and revision of Yeats, and his use of the occasion of the master poet's death to articulate his own poetic project, was not lost on Auden's American inheritors. The occasion of Auden's own death on September 29, 1973 prompted an enormous range of poetic responses from younger American poets, many of them following Auden's example as Auden had followed Yeats, both in using the poet's own language in their memorials for him and in turning the moment, and their readings of the meaning of Auden's life and work, toward their own individual artistic arguments and purposes. Indeed, no twentieth-century poet has spawned as many elegies, eulogies, and remembrances from as wide a range of practicing poets as Auden. And by surveying a few of these poetic farewells to Auden, from across a broad spectrum of American verse, we get a compelling testimonial to, and concluding perspective on, his impact on an entire generation—and beyond—of American poetry.

◆ ◆ ◆

One of the young poets who came to know Auden well during his years in New York was James Schuyler. Schuyler knew Auden's secretary Alan Ansen, and through Ansen met Auden's lover, Chester Kallman, with whom he became close friends. Schuyler was soon welcomed into Auden and Kallman's New York circle of intimates, eventually working as Auden's assistant and accompanying them on occasion to their summer home on Ischia. In his 1974 elegy, "Wystan Auden," Schuyler recalls—in fragmented flashes of memory—those years when he sat at the feet of, and drank at the table with, the famous poet:

I went to his fortieth birthday
party: was it really twenty-seven
years ago? I don't remember what
street he was living on, but he
was adapting *The Duchess of Malfi*
for the modern stage, in which
Canada Lee appeared in white face:
it was that long ago. It was in
that apartment I just missed
meeting Brecht and T. S. Eliot.[2]

For Schuyler, his memories of Auden conjure up an idyllic era, now
"long ago" and only partially remembered, in which young poets such as
himself and Ansen could stop by Auden's New York apartment for afternoon tea or five o'clock cocktails, to discuss poetry while one of Auden's
large collection of classical music records played in the background, and
perhaps meet the various literary luminaries who would likewise drop in
at what functioned as a kind of informal New York salon. Auden's apartment, and the parties he and Kallman threw there, not only offered his
younger poet friends the chance to meet and mingle with some of his
glamorous intellectual contemporaries, but more importantly, served as
a sort of graduate seminar in how to live and work as a publicly engaged,
professional poet. In that messy apartment, in his lively "table talk" (a
collection of which was gathered and published by Ansen), or in his poems, in New York, on Ischia, or on the many college campuses he visited
and at which he taught, Auden was continually at the center of a scene of
instruction.[3] Schuyler's elegy recounts a number of those scenes, emphasizing Auden's didacticism undercut by an ironic self-awareness, a tonal
combination familiar to any reader of Auden's poems:

On Ischia he claimed to take
St. Restituta seriously, and
sat at Maria's café in the cobbled
square saying, "Poets should
dress like businessmen," while
he wore an incredible peach-
colored nylon shirt. . . .
Once when a group

of us made an excursion from
Ischia—Capri, Sorrento, Positano,
Amalfi, Pompeii—he suddenly
said at cocktails on a pensione
terrace: "More of this sitting
around like beasts!"

During the 1940s and 1950s, this mezzogiorno scene of the rumpled
expat poet reigning over a "sun-drenched Parthenopea," as he put it in
his poem "Ischia" [*CP*, 543], sitting around the tables of Maria's café in
Forio, surrounded by other poets and friends while he handed down his
characteristically idiosyncratic artistic pronouncements, became a powerful and alluring, if slightly mythic, image for many younger American
poets, some of whom actually managed to make the pilgrimage to the
island in search of an audience. As James Merrill, one of those who visited Ischia in hopes of a meeting, remembered it, "In those years W. H.
Auden was that island's Prospero," and all of Ischia was full of "this season's gossip about the increasingly eccentric genius."[4] Among those who
also made the trip to Ischia to see Auden were Anthony Hecht and Allen
Ginsberg, whose disappointing run-in with a drunk and cranky Auden
in 1957 would prompt the young Beat poet's disgruntled declaration that
"the republic of poetry needs a full-scale revolution."

Schuyler's elegy concludes with an intimate evocation of what
Auden called—in his own elegy for Louis MacNeice—his "cave of making," the place where the didactic, sloppy, voluble man transforms into
the poet, speaking silently in graceful meters to posterity; the room
where, as Auden puts it, "Silence is turned into objects" [*CP*, 691]:

He was
industrious, writing away in
a smoky room—fug—in a
ledger or on loose sheets
poems, some of which I typed
for him (they're in *Nones*).
I don't have to burn his
letters as he asked his
friends to do: they were lost
a long time ago. So much

to remember, so little to
say: that he liked martinis
and was greedy about the wine?
I always thought he would live
to a great age. He did not.
Wystan, kind man and great poet,
goodbye.

Writing in a mode that recalls the domestic and demotic style of the later Auden, Schuyler offers a conventional—even trite-sounding— formulation of the elegist's difficulty in transforming his memories into adequate speech: "So much / to remember, so little to / say." This is the elegiac crux—turning absence into presence, memory into permanence, man into poem—and Schuyler's strategy here, as in the rest of the poem, is to let shards of inchoate recollection accrete into an incomplete but suggestive image of the absent subject. With a few spare lines he evokes Auden's character, not unlike the well-known sketch portraits by David Hockney in which a few rapidly inked penstrokes hint at the craggy and wrinkled mask of the old poet's face. Schuyler's poem makes a virtue of its limited ambition, eschewing sentiment or rhetoric for a clear-eyed Audenesque statement of loss, and further follows Auden's lead—estab- lished in Auden's own famous elegies—of asserting intimacy through measured criticism. Auden, says Schuyler, in his over-fondness for alco- hol, his occasional stinginess, and by imputation, other perhaps exasper- ating personal character flaws, was—as Auden says of Yeats—"silly like us" [CP, 248]. In the formula of the poem's penultimate line, it is "kind man," not "great poet," that comes first. When there are so many we have to mourn, the poem asserts, what distinguishes this loss is less the sub- ject's uniqueness—his status as one of the greatest poets of the century— but rather his commonness, his resemblance to ourselves. Another of Auden's younger poetic contemporaries, Richard Wilbur, sounds this same theme in his own elegy, "For W. H. Auden":

[Y]ou, who sustained the civil tongue
In a scattering time, and were poet of all our cities,
Have for all your clever difference quietly left us,
As we might have known that you would, by that common
    door.[5]

Wilbur and Schuyler frame Auden as Auden had framed Freud, who, in the end, "closed his eyes / upon that last picture common to us all" [*CP*, 273]. It is Auden's commonness, his embrace of his fortune to be "jumbled in one common box" [*CP*, 269] along with us, that transcends his "clever difference."

◆ ◆ ◆

The distinction Schuyler's poem draws between the "kind man" and the "great poet" is characteristic of many of the younger poets' responses to Auden. For these poets, Auden's presence in their lives and imaginations as a living, breathing, idiosyncratic human being was inextricably bound to his role as a specifically textual influence on their work. He was both a person they saw at parties and lectures—or from whom they sought advice, or who advanced their nascent careers through his central position in what Ginsberg calls "the republic of poetry"—and a book on their shelf, usually the crucial 1945 Random House edition of his *Collected Poems*.

John Hollander, one of the younger poets who knew Auden best while he lived in New York, recalls his early encounters with Auden at the various lectures and readings he would give around the city at Columbia, Barnard and the New School, and his eventual friendship with him, as a touchstone in his life and poetic career. Along with fellow Columbia University undergraduate poets like Ginsberg, Daniel Hoffman, Richard Howard, and Louis Simpson, Hollander came to see Auden as his "unofficial teacher, as well as the resident poet of our city."[6] In a 1974 memorial volume assembled and edited by Stephen Spender and featuring reminiscences by Auden's friends and elegies by a number of other poets including Lincoln Kirstein and Joseph Brodsky, Hollander articulates in detail what Schuyler's fragmentary and impressionistic elegy only sketches. As Hollander recounts, those encounters with Auden in his apartment or in the classrooms and streets of New York were, for him and his Columbia peers especially, more than thrilling brushes with poetic celebrity, they were a literary, and importantly, a moral, finishing school:

The New Yorker Wystan Auden—the presence in the American metropolis during the forties and fifties—was a deeply and dearly important figure for my whole generation. He was our exemplary man of letters. His public and private conscience were manifested in exemplary ways. His sallies of encounter, his refusals of the fugitive and cloistered virtue were exemplary as well, and not merely because our coming of age could find congenial what continuities we felt persisted between an unorthodox Marxism and a personal form of crisis theology. For young poets he was a living precursor, a constant teacher of poetic craft and a devoted guardian of the power of the magic of language, rather than the machinations of ideology, to yield true poetic thought.[7]

In a poem at the opposite end of the formal spectrum from Schuyler's, Hollander had offered a poem about Auden of his own two years earlier in a festschrift for Auden's sixty-fifth birthday. Taking its title in response to Auden's "Under Sirius," Hollander's poem—called "Under Aquarius" and written in the meter of the *Roman Elegies* by Auden's beloved Goethe—pays tribute to Auden's multiple roles in the poetic culture of the 1940s and 1950s. Calling the voice of the elder poet "the sound of sense" for his generation, Hollander recalls Auden's sustaining role in guiding them toward their own voices:

> Like a clever young uncle,
> Helping us over the few gurus we'd ferreted out
> Back at the end of the forties, then like a wise old aunt who
> Knew much more than the ropes, holding our hands in the
> dusk.

By the end of the poem, Auden is seen transformed from this homely, familiar, and human incarnation into one of mythic timelessness, as an old constellation given new meaning:

> And now the constellation that night has
> Dropped into water's chill, dark in this pool in a square,
> Ringed with those crystals of light and giving them back to our
> silence,
> Rises: *Der Dichter* — if not seasonal, then all the more
> Present, continuingly, and *Alpha Poetae*, the brightest
> Star, the one whose name everyone always recalls,
> Burns away knowingly, used to having been steered by, and
> glowing
> Up among us and our worlds turning in darkness around.

In Hollander's poem, Auden is both a genial personal presence and lofty poetic exemplar, the "clever young uncle" and the "*Alpha Poetae.*" He is both the nurturing water-bearer, and the "affirming flame" of "September 1, 1939," the hand-holder and the lodestar. He is a constellation, but one seen in the reflection of a "dark pool" in the middle of what Hollander calls the "Fallen City"—in contradistinction to Auden's hoped-for "Just City." He is both shining down and "glowing up among us," a luminary we can see and touch.

Hollander's poem tries to accommodate both the private and the public aspects of Auden's legacy; he was both a friend and a famous public figure and "Under Aquarius," like its Auden/Goethe models, balances an intimate tone with a public concern. The poem's figuration of Auden as a constellation, whose knowing glow illuminates, however faintly, the dark city, suggests a sense of Auden's multifarious influence, reigning like a house of the zodiac over the cultural season. Like Auden's Freud, Auden himself has become "a whole climate of opinion / under whom we conduct our different lives" [*CP*, 275]. The constellation also offers an image for the disparate functions Auden performed for those who knew or read him: friend, mentor, teacher, celebrity, public intellectual, literary critic, poet. As a collection of stars unified as a single entity, the trope of the poet-as-constellation echoes Auden's own notions of the divided and constituent self and attests that Auden's influential presence is likewise a compendium of different professional and personal moieties. Of course it also follows Auden's own elegies, which invoked artists as if they were saints, in the tradition of poetic stellification. Like Astrophel, Adonais, and the apotheosized Henry James to whom Auden prays "to make intercession / for the treason of all clerks" [*CP*, 312], Auden has become, even before his death, a literary immortal, enshrined in the poetic firmament. In the rigor of his honesty, if not always in the consistency of his convictions, he is a fixture, a model of intellectual, moral, and artistic constancy during, as Hollander puts it in the poem's prose preface, "a time of intellectual failure of nerve." His is a heroic fortitude that stands in marked and ironic contrast with the poet's younger contemporaries for whom Aquarius has a different meaning:

> Outside the door, in the street, the high millenarian voices,
> Hailing the spring's delay, solemn, unserious, rise

Over the din of their feasting. Languid and unregimental,
    Hand in hand but, alas, thereby thus somehow in step,
Young people drift in the square. . . .
Here as if light were in disrepute, now that darkness is falling,
    Some of the sadder ones huddle along the arcades,
Glaring at lamps that begin to twinkle out of our windows,
    Staring upward instead, looking for some kind of sign,
Eyes finally lighting upon the tired zodiacal emblem
    Rising, penultimate now, over the nights of our years.

The children of the Age of Aquarius—whose "high millenarian voices" may include, by polemical implication, those of the "languid" and "unserious" Beat poets like Hollander's estranged schoolfriend Ginsberg—seem to wander aimlessly and forlorn in the fading urban twilight.[8] The "din" of their revelry and their "unregimental" ethos cannot mask a sad, uninterrogated conventionality. Their iconoclasm is itself a uniform, as they march "hand in hand but, alas, thereby thus somehow in step," unlike Auden's famous "band of rivals" who clamber through "In Praise of Limestone" "Arm in arm, but never, thank God, in step" [*CP*, 541]. The "sadder ones" stare up at the sky and seize upon the "tired zodiacal emblem" of the ancient constellation as the symbol of their moment, an empty image for an empty time. Hollander offers a new Ganymede to fill that symbolic void, a new meaning for the tired emblem, and sees in the figure of Auden a redemptive ideal who can, in a dark time, be "a sesame to light" [*CP*, 220].

The poem's apotheosis of Auden, and its literalization in the image of the constellation of the older poet's famously hopeful invocation of poetry's "ironic points of light," holds him out for Hollander's peers—poetical and otherwise—as a constructive exemplum, a beacon they might have overlooked or left behind or rejected in the "glare" of revolution, but who was always there, glowing quietly and brightly and steadfastly, guiding those who knew where to look and waiting for the others to recognize his affirming presence and power. In its placement of the constellation's image on the surface of the chilled pool, the poem also suggests that guidance can be found not through gazing blankly upward and waiting for the descent of a new age, but in looking down and into the heart of where and how we live now, not through fuzzy

utopian ideology, but through reflection. Auden, whose American poetics propounded poetry's power to enlighten through dialectic, is the
poem's model for that kind of clear-eyed moral and intellectual vision:
earthbound, but aspiring; reflective, but engaged; analytical, but active.
Looking into the reflecting pool of our moment—not narcissistically
but introspectively—we see our better selves. The image of that self, in
"Under Aquarius," is Auden and his poems.

Like Ginsberg himself, who saw reflected in Auden his own need
for iconoclasm, Hollander's use of the figure of Auden enables him to articulate his own aesthetic and cultural positions. In this case, the poem's
vision of Auden as an icon of engaged liberalism serves as a polemical
entree into the poem's subordinated subject, namely the clash between
the intellectual left tradition, personified in disparate yet allied figures
like Lionel Trilling and Irving Howe, and the new left counterculture
that eschewed liberalism in favor of a radicalized future. Each side had
its poetic representatives, with Wilbur, Hollander, Howard, and Hecht
on one side, Ginsberg, Rich, and the Black Mountain School poets on
the other.[9] Hollander's poem takes aim at his opponents in the culture
wars by indicting their failure to carry on the tradition that gave them
birth, a tradition epitomized by Auden. In these terms, Auden serves the
poem as a rebuke, but he also represents a figurative olive branch offered
to misguided former allies. At its most polemical, the poem's final incarnation of Auden as a kind of intellectual demigod offers the renegades
a chance to return to the faith, but in the poem's polytropic representation of him, it also presents him as a kind of Whitmanian democratic
ideal, large enough to contain the multiple perspectives contending for
authority. Auden thus comes to stand for the American cultural landscape itself, riven with conflicts and rivalries and endlessly dialectical, yet
somehow unified and stronger for its divisions. It is a notable testament
to Auden's post-emigration transformation and to his American legacy.

◆ ◆ ◆

In Hollander's poem, Auden's is a characteristically double presence: a
private friend and a public figure, a man and myth, a career-advancer and
a co-conspirator, a moralist and an iconoclast, a divided self and a unified spirit, a climate of opinion and an ignored ideal. "Under Aquarius"
is also both a birthday poem and an elegy. There's an unmistakable tone

of mourning and farewell: Auden's elevation to a constellation is both an exaltation and an epitaph. Richard Howard's 1964 poem, "For Hephaistos, with Reference to the Deaths in a Dry Year of Cocteau, Roethke and MacNeice," the first of the three poems he would write about Auden, strikes a similar note of leave-taking of his mentor—ten years before Auden's death—even as he celebrates the depth of his indebtedness.[10] Both Hollander and Howard follow Auden in framing their memorials in terms of particular seasons. "Under Aquarius" unfolds, like Auden's Yeats elegy, in the dead of winter, while Howard's poem situates itself in a "thirsty season" of a "rainless fall" in a "dry year." Both poems evoke an atmosphere of long-shadowed twilight, presided over—explicitly, in the case of Howard's epitaphic title—by the specter of death. It is as if Auden were absent already, a shadow to be looked back on and to be haunted by. Along with Hollander and Howard, several other younger poets, including Lincoln Kirstein and James Merrill, offered elegiac remembrances of Auden several years before his actual death. Kirstein's "Siegfriedslage" presents an affectionately nostalgic account of his experiences with Auden in postwar Germany during Auden's bomb-damage assessment mission for the U.S. Army,[11] while Merrill's "Table Talk" evokes Auden's fabled dinner-conversation, construing him as a "jolly Roman priest" presiding over an imagined feast, even as it notes his absence from the contemporary festivities: "If only Wystan . . . were here."

This double sense of Auden's simultaneous absence and presence speaks to Auden's dual aspect in younger poets' lives as both man and abstraction, living colleague and timeless Old Master. It also reflects the specific historical circumstances of Auden's late career. By the late 1960s, Auden's personal involvement in the life of American poetry had begun to ebb. Critics were finding in the cultural conservatism and contented domesticity of his late books—what Randall Jarrell termed, pejoratively, their "comfiness"—evidence of Auden's increasing irrelevance, and Auden himself had begun to retreat from his position at the heart of American poetic culture. His friends observed that Auden seemed to be growing disenchanted with the city that he had so embraced three decades earlier, and he began to discuss the possibility of leaving New York. This disengagement with his American life proceeded in tandem with what his friends noticed as a general withdrawal from the world. Either as the result of his years of heavy alcohol, tobacco, and Benzedrine consumption—what Auden once cheerfully called "the chemical life"—or simply old age, Auden's health had deteriorated markedly and his social habits had become tyrannical and, to some observers, tedious. His celebrated table talk was now more like a repetitive monologue of familiar opinions and he had become a figure of sad diminishment, his famously craggy face now suggesting less a life well-lived than one almost spent. Indeed, Auden's sixty-fifth birthday itself—the occasion of the publication of the festschrift featuring Hollander's "Under Aquarius" and Merrill's "Table Talk"—was, as friends recalled, something of a funereal affair. Auden had recently announced that he would be leaving New York for good, returning to Oxford to live out his life in a little cottage on the grounds of his old college, and the assembled well-wishers couldn't help feeling that they were really saying goodbye. As one friend put it, "Nothing could overcome this deadly frost around him. He is going away (and not simply to Oxford)."[12]

In person and in print, Auden's once vital presence was in retreat even before his death, giving these premortem tributes an occasion for an early farewell. But as occasional poems intended to be read by their still-living subject, they also point to Auden's notion of the relation between poets, alive or dead, as a distinctly personal, reciprocal one. These poets are insisting on an economy of poetic exchange and intimacy, just as Auden does in "New Year Letter," in which he assembles and addresses "the quiet attentive crowd" of "influential ghosts" [*CP*, 203] whose voices have given him his own, or in "A Thanksgiving," one of his last poems, in which he offers a final acknowledgment of his many poetic tutors: "Fondly I ponder You all: / Without You I couldn't have managed / even my weakest of lines" [*CP*, 892]. These poets follow Auden's revision of Yeatsian elegies by further revising elegiac convention to eulogize not the silent absence of the distinguished dead, but a living colleague who can respond to their words. If elegy is the space where the poem takes the place of a person, these proleptic elegies posit a space where poem and person coexist, where the biographical and the textual come together, and where the influence of both can be simultaneously acknowledged.

Howard's "For Hephaistos..." starts with an epigraph from Auden himself on the relation between poetry and his own identity: "Whatever I may mean could not be equally well conveyed by gestures but can be expressed, if at all, in speech (that is why I wish to write this poem),

and wherever speech is necessary, lying and self-deception are both possible." Auden is here setting out the terms of a poetic mode in which, as
Eliot puts it, "Every poem [is] an epitaph." What Auden "may mean," he
says, can only be expressed through his poems, so every poem comes in
some way to stand for its author, and serve as a memorial to him in his
absence. In Howard's poem, the younger poet tries to account for what
Auden "may mean" to him, and in doing so composes Auden's premortem epitaph.

The poem itself begins with the speaker walking down the Audenesque "common street," amid crowds of "citizens / Whose needs and
greeds will never overlap" who are busy "buying up their brainless haul /
In a Season reasonable merchants fear / Will be too slack for a rainless
fall." The scene is conjured out of "September 1, 1939," as the figure of the
poet mingles anonymously with the "dense commuters" and the "sensual
man-in-the-street" in a blind beleaguered city. When the poet looks at
the cityscape around him, he sees it through the prism of Auden's poems: Auden's poetic New York has become Howard's real one. It is a dry,
"pining time of the year," he notes, "In a year when the poets are dying/
Of madness not murrains, not rot but rage,/ And only Great States-
men live to great age." Among those the poet has to mourn are Cocteau, termed "a forger who died trying / To lock both profiles into one
face"; Roethke, who "gave his voice / To the high wind that howled him
down"; and Auden's "Iceland playmate" MacNeice, each of whom had
died over the course of 1963. In this atmosphere of morbid aridity, the
poet stumbles into a chance encounter with Auden himself, emerging
from a bookshop:

> We're face to face. . . . I looked, and there
> Was no profession in your look back save
> A final harmlessness that made it clear
> You could not be a bum, despite your air
> Of tweedy degeneration. The stare
> Exchanged was all that passed between for proof
> I knew you, even as my onetime love.

Auden appears as a spectral blank, an almost unrecognizable shade
of his former self. He is an old man in a dry season, as if the parched atmosphere has drained his vitality and identity, granting him premature

entry into the world his late peers have recently joined. The poet and his old mentor exchange a stare, whose emptiness stands as a silent epitaph to an intimacy lost to memory and time, before the shadowy figure slips away once more into the city crowds:

> Wondering, I forgot my words and lost
> All presence of mind as you labored past.
> And yet you taught me, taught us all a way
> To speak our minds, and only now, at last
> Free of you, my old ventriloquist,
> Have I suspected what I have to say
> Without hearing you say it for me first.
> Like my old love, I have survived you best
> By leaving you, and so you're here to stay.

The encounter proves unsettling for the poet, who "forgets his words," but, like the empty stare, that void serves to remind him of Auden's once-intimate presence in his life. The words he has forgotten are the words given to him by Auden, his "old ventriloquist," who, he says, "taught me, taught us all a way / To speak our minds." Howard acknowledges in the poem what he could not do "face to face" with the older poet, namely that his own poetic identity was constructed out of the words he learned from Auden. Howard posits an idea of influence in which originality is achieved through instruction, imitation, appropriation, and the exercise of practiced craft. Howard learns to "speak [his] mind," to say what he has to say, only after "hearing [Auden] say it for [him] first." By learning to speak in the voice of Auden and other influential poets, he learns who he is. Poetic identity is constructed out of the stuff of other poets; originality derives from the assimilation and adaptation of voices of the past. The modern poet is *made*, not born, and it is an educated, self-aware exercise of professionalism that makes one. This is a conception of the poet's relation to the tradition that Auden himself propounded in theory and practice, and it is an idea of poetic identity that poets like Howard adopted under the tutelage of their old master. Auden is "Hephaistos," the originary maker whose smithy yields the tools used by all future artisans, and whose own art, as in Auden's "The Shield of Achilles" and "The Maker," is one of disenchantment and impersonality.

Both Howard and Hollander make explicit, in two later elegies, this sense of Auden as the crucible of their own poetry and of postwar American poetic practice in general. In his 1973 "Again for Hephaistos, the Last Time," Howard bids a final farewell to Auden with the encomium, "After you, because of you, / All songs are possible."[13] Hollander offers similar praise in *Reflections on Espionage*, his 1976 long poem that tropes the world of spies onto the world of poets and is written in the form of cryptic sonnet-like dispatches from the secret-agent/poet to his control/muse, codenamed "Lyrebird." In the second dispatch, Hollander (codename "Cupcake") reports the death of the agency's most distinguished operative, Auden (codename "Steampump"), and again acknowledges his debt: "He taught me, as you surely / Know, all that I know."[14] Other poets, of both older and younger generations, make the same claims about Auden's foundational role in contemporary American poetry. Karl Shapiro observes in one of his two Auden elegies, "Without him many of us would never have happened,"[15] while J. D. McClatchy's more recent "Auden's OED" figures Auden as a dictionary that continues to give younger poets the words with which they can compose, for themselves, "the language of a life."[16]

In the first "Hephaistos" poem, this acknowledgment of Auden's influence comes, paradoxically, through an assertion that the younger poet is now free of it. The two poets no longer recognize one another and the younger poet does not feel compelled to insist on his former relationship, suggesting that the earlier identity-threatening intimacy has been outgrown. It is Auden's absence—his blank gaze, his proleptic spectrality, and his departure—that signals Howard's recognition of his erstwhile presence, as if the poet needed to be assured that Auden was safely out of reach before claiming a connection.[17] The context of this evasion of acknowledgment is not simply psychic, but—crucially—social and professional. The relationship between Auden and Howard is figured not in terms of jousting intellects or battling egos, but rather in terms of two men who bump awkwardly into one another on the street. The motives for the younger poet's desire to wait for the eclipse of the older before affirming past devotion to him have little to do with literary agon and everything to do with the dynamics of human relationships and professional reputation. As a practical matter of professional—as opposed to poetic—identity, it is the question of public perception that prompts caution on the part of the younger poet. It would be dangerous to his efforts at establishing an independent reputation to be seen, as it were, in public too often in the company of the more famous artist. That is to say, any young poet who avers public allegiance early on to a particular poetic sponsor, or assumes the role of protégé, runs the risk of remaining forever in his mentor's shadow. This is not an idle concern for poets like Howard and Hecht and others, whose critical reputations have prospered or suffered in large measure in relation to their identification with an Audenesque formalism.

Howard frames questions of poetic influence as if they were questions of personal influence, as if the anxiety of establishing a poetic identity were directly analogous to that of establishing a social identity. Viewing poetic relationships through the prism of social sensibility we observe that the younger poet maintains his distance just as a "onetime love" would avoid uncomfortable contact with an old flame. The personal awkwardness of acknowledging poetic apprenticeship is troped as the embarrassment of a lover come face to face with a former paramour: "Like my old love, I have survived you best / By leaving you, and so you're here to stay." The humane civility of this notion of poetic relations reflects, in part, the highly socialized world of and out of which Howard writes. It is a characteristically urban and urbane world of manners, aesthetic refinement, and artistic friendships, a New York high-culture world whose epitome from the 1940s through the 1960s could be said to be Auden himself. As Howard recalls, for aspiring New York intellectuals of his age, "Auden was the example: this was the model, this was the style ... He represented for us a kind of conscience that was both literary and social and of course for gay people like myself, sexual as well."[18]

Auden's relationship with younger poets was a distinctively multivalent one; his presence as both person and text were inextricably intertwined. In Howard's figuration of the poetic relation as a romantic, even erotic, one, he presents a model which reflects both elements of Auden's influence and suggests a poetics that takes its theoretical principles from the world of human intercourse, in every sense. It also points to one of the most significant aspects of Auden's example for many of his inheritors: his role as a publicly gay poet. Auden's famous presence, as a gay artist whose poems—freely importing the discourse of camp—openly addressed his homosexuality, and as an uncloseted and unapologetic public intellectual, served as an enabling exemplar for younger poets like Howard, Schuyler, Ginsberg, and Frank O'Hara, along with Merrill, Ashbery, Rich, and many others. Auden's life, career, and art offered proof that their own sexual identity need not be elided in their own work and, in fact, could become an open subject for it. Auden charted a course for younger poets in general, and for younger gay poets in particular, and Howard's model of poetic influence as an erotic, and specifically gay, relation reflects this inheritance. In poems like "New Year Letter," which conjures a confraternity of dead poets by whom the living writer is willingly possessed and to whom he responds, or "At the Grave of Henry James," which, as Jahan Ramazani points out, "suggests that the relationship between master and disciple, like the relationship between poet and muse, is not entirely ascetic,"[19] Auden set forth an idea of the relation between the tradition and individual talent that some younger poets have adopted and adapted for themselves. Theirs is a humane, socialized, non-agonistic model: a construction of poetic influence in terms of friendship and social manners. It is a vision of exchange between partners; a human relation governed by civility and certain social rules, in which one's choice of association has reckonable advantages or costs; and, finally and ideally, a surrendering of self that leads to personal transformation. It is, in short, a vision of poetic influence as sex: a mutual relation governed, as Auden puts it, by a "law like love" [*CP*, 262].

◆ ◆ ◆

Younger poets' acknowledgments of Auden's central place in the postwar American poetic culture were not always without ambivalence. For some, Auden exerted *too much* influence, and represented a domineering authority whose formalism, intellectualism, and cultural conservatism threatened what they saw as the native American strain of Whitmanic song. Louis Simpson, a Columbia poet who encountered Auden while a student in New York, sounds a representative note of mixed feelings in his memoir, *A Revolution in Taste*. Upon Auden's emigration to the United States, writes Simpson,

> [He] established himself at the center of literary power, and
> exerted an influence for more than a decade. The nature of the
> influence was not clear at first, for Auden arrived in New York

with a reputation as a rebel—many even thought him a poet of
the Left. But as time passed he revealed himself to be a mainstay
of tradition. As long as Auden set the fashion—and this he
was able to do, for he was a brilliant literary journalist as well
as a poet—the stream of experiment that had begun with the
Imagist poets, especially that kind of writing of which William
Carlos Williams was the chief exponent, receded into the background. Auden ruled with wit and a knowledge of verse forms;
in comparison, the American poets who looked to Williams, or
to a poet thought to be even more rudimentary, Walt Whitman,
appeared to be fumbling provincials—certainly not worth the
attention of readers who had been trained by the New Criticism
to look for shades of irony, ambiguous meanings.[20]

Auden's dominance in the poetic establishment, as critic in places
like *The Nation*, *The New Republic*, and *The New York Review of Books*; as
prize-giver for the Yale Younger Poets Series, the Pulitzer, and the Bollingen; and as heir to Eliot as the world's most prominent poet, made
him the object of both praise and attack, of emulation and repudiation. He spawned acolytes like Howard and Hecht, and apostates like
Ginsberg and Rich. As Howard puts it, "As long as Auden was alive, I
think the poets in America organized around him like iron filings in a
magnetic field, either in repulsion or organization in a literary sense. I
think he was a very significant figure—you'd have to say he is really *the*
figure—around whom the poets of my generation, and those immediately preceding and following, could be discussed."[21]

This sense of conflict over Auden's place in postwar American poetry is reflected in a number of the poems written about him by younger
poets. Karl Shapiro's second elegy, "At Auden's Grave," exemplifies this
tension by censuring Auden even as it eulogizes him:

> Whatever commentators come to say—
> That life was not your bag—Edwardian—
> Misogynist—Greenwich Villager—
> Drifter—coward—traitorous clerk—or you,
> In your own language, genteel anti-Jew—
> I come to bless this plot where you are lain,
> Poet who made poetry whole again.[22]

Like Kipling and Claudel, whose personal failings find pardon for writing well in Auden's Yeats elegy, it is through the moral power of his own art that Auden's many flaws are forgiven. Howard, in his second elegy, also admits a shared uncertainty over Auden's apparent want of human feeling: "Cocteau, you conceded, though stagy, had the *lacrimae rerum* note, / but did *you*? The *Times*, this morning, declared you had failed to make, / or even make your way inside, 'a world of emotion'. / I wonder."[23] For Howard, the answer comes in the memory of a conversation with Auden in which he had revealed to the older poet that he was Jewish: "'My *dear*,' you broke in, and I think you were genuinely excited, / 'I never knew you were Jewish!' No, not a world of emotion— / say, for the time being, as you said, the emotion of a world." For Jewish-American poets like Howard and Shapiro, Auden's relationship with Judaism was an important aspect of his poetic legacy. Though "genteel anti-Jew," as Shapiro quotes Auden on himself, and fond, as Howard recalls, of romanticizing the Jewishness of his friends and of his own partner Chester Kallman, Auden's rejection of Modernist antisemitism—as in the Freud elegy, where Eliot's notoriously lower-cased "jew" gets its upper-case back—made him an unusual figure of tolerance and encouragement for younger Jewish poets, among them Simpson, Hollander, Hecht, Ginsberg, and Rich, who had grown up absorbing the anti-semitism of Eliot and Pound along with their poems.

Some poets use their memorial poems as occasions to argue with Auden. In "Talking Back (To W. H. Auden)," William Meredith affectionately critiques Auden's most influential dictum, asserting that poetry does, in fact, make something happen, and finding proof in Auden's own poems:

> The exact details of our plight
> in your poems, order revealed
> by the closest looking, are things
> I'm changed by and had never seen,
> might never have seen, but for them.
> Poetry makes such things happen
> sometimes, as certain people do
> at the right juncture of our lives.[24]

Meredith follows other Auden elegists in making Auden's influence as much a personal question as a textual one. For Meredith, poems behave like people and can have the same life-changing impact. Its power to reveal hidden law gives it the power to impel human transformation. Poetry, he asserts, and especially Auden's poetry, is a way of happening. Auden, of course, would agree, making Meredith's poem more of a playful misreading of Auden's ideas than an argument with them. Not all of Auden's elegists are so gentle.

Irving Feldman, taking his cue from William Empson's famous gibe at the expense of the young politically minded Auden, offers "Just Another Smack" at the older magisterial one:

> Schoolmaster Auden gave them full marks,
> "the Old Masters," for having understood
> "about suffering" its "human position."
> The view from Mt. Lectern was clear. They were,
> he noted, "*never wrong.*"[25]

Feldman takes aim at Auden's self-appointed role as "schoolmaster" to his readers and younger peers, and mocks his well-known habit—in person and on the page—of dispensing axiomatic moral and aesthetic judgments. Assailing his lofty ironic detachment in the face of human pain, illustrated in poems like "Musée des Beaux Arts," Feldman asks Auden, "Sir, respectfully, is it possible / ever to be *right* about 'suffering?'" Feldman responds to his own question, suggesting that suffering can—and should—never be generalized into some abstract academic concept, or troped with distancing literary images, but is instead always tragically solitary and inescapable:

> I mean, sir, our suffering is no
> Nativity, is never legendary
> like Innocents slaughtered, Icarus plunging.
> We lack that consolation. *Our* suffering
> is nameless (like us) and newly whelped
> and dying just to claim us for itself.

Feldman exposes what he sees as the flaw in Auden's moral vision, namely his arrogant faith in poetry's ability to simultaneously name suffering and keep it at bay. In response, he conjures a grim fantasy of the artist hoist on his own falsehood. He pictures Auden in contented old age, having "'sailed calmly on' / into Snug Harbor," secure in the knowledge that, through his poems, he has mastered the question of suffering, when, "wouldn't you know it . . . / *Suffering* just happens to happen by." The poet who took such a rarefied view of the subject is forced finally to confront it for himself as the abstracted "*Suffering*" pays a house call and "clouts enormously [his] shoulder blade, / and dispatches a knee swift to the groin." The last words the poet hears are the fell sergeant "*Suffering's*" cruel whispers in his ear: "'Listen close. It's me. Only *I* got away. / And my message is strictly for you / —Hey, old fella, you've been elected." Feldman's deeply unsympathetic vision of Auden's earthly exit is the precise reverse of Wilbur's. While Wilbur sees Auden's death as his final graceful lesson for his readers in the commonality that transcends difference, Feldman sees in Auden an hauteur deservedly surprised by the pain of its own mortality. Wilbur's Auden leaves "by that common door." Feldman's elitist is "elected" by death. Feldman's irony is heavy-handed: The Old Master is, in fact, wrong and is taught by harsh experience how little he really knows. Suffering and death are the oldest masters and *they* are never wrong.

The prospect of bringing the Old Master down a peg proved irresistible for other poets as well.[26] Theodore Weiss's elegy, "As You Like It," while not nearly as caustic as Feldman's, also uses "Musée des Beaux Arts" to take Auden to task for his generalizing approach to human life:

> An old master yourself now, Auden,
> like that much admired Cavafy and those
> older still, in this you were wrong.
>   People
> are not indifferent, let alone oblivious,
> to the momentary, great scene.[27]

Auden is wrong about human behavior in the face of epochal events. Rather than turn away in selfish disinterest, says Weiss, the natural human reaction to events larger than oneself is uncomprehending, yet constructive, attention. Weiss's example is his char-lady, Mrs. Gudgeon, who listens to great minds debating on the radio even though she doesn't understand what they are talking about. Responding to the question as to why she continues to listen, she answers:

"O I enjoy it, just the sound
of it, so musical. And anyway I take
from it whatever I like,
                    then make of it,
in my own mind, whatever I will."

For Weiss, Mrs. Gudgeon's ignorant engagement with the radio
program suggests a model for a productive response to an incomprehen-
sible world:

[L]ike Mrs. Gudgeon
                    most of us, watching
the moment, some spectacular event,
be it Icarus falling,
                    Cleopatra consorting
with the streets, or the astronauts
cavorting on the moon,
                    bear off those bits
that we can use.

Weiss's optimistic argument posits selfish attention, rather than
blinkered self-regard, as man's great gift for making sense of his confusing surroundings. Faced with the overwhelming sweep of events, we are
able to keep going only by making some small aspect of those events
relevant to ourselves. We "bear off those bits / that we can use" and build
ourselves a nest from the fragments.

While revising and critiquing Auden's notion of the indifferent human response to history, Weiss also offers up a useful metaphor for the
way Auden's inheritors respond to him. As we have seen, Auden was instrumental in the development of the poetic identities of a whole range
of younger writers. Either through appropriation or rejection, poets constructed their own careers through an interaction with his. Confronted
by the monumental and multivalent cultural presence of Auden's poems and persona, these poets found their own place by using what they
needed from him. Like Mrs. Gudgeon and the voices on the radio, they
took from Auden whatever they liked and then made of it, in their own
work, whatever they willed. Even in antipathetic elegies like Feldman's,
or revisionary ones like Weiss's, we see the poets working in Auden's

tradition. Their utilization of Auden's own poetic formulae—from fig-
uring him as an "Old Master" to their unflattering representation of
him, like Auden's Yeats and Freud, as silly and unclever—allows them
to assert their own identities while simultaneously inscribing themselves
within his.

◆ ◆ ◆

Ten years after Auden's death, Derek Walcott offered a "Eulogy for
W. H. Auden" at a memorial service at the Cathedral of St. John the
Divine in New York. Among the gallery of other poets in attendance to
pay Auden posthumous homage were Mona Van Duyn, May Swenson,
Anthony Hecht, Amy Clampitt, James Merrill, John Ashbery, Marilyn
Hacker, Alfred Corn, Richard Howard, and John Hollander. Noting the
formality of the occasion, an elaborate tribute by the American poetry
establishment in a lofty and sober setting, Walcott begins his poem by
puncturing any sense of stuffiness:

> Assuredly, that fissured face
> is wincing deeply, and must loathe
> our solemn rubbish,
> frown on our canonizing farce
> as self-enhancing, in lines both
> devout and snobbish.
>
> Yet it may spare us who convene
> against its wish in varnished pews
> this autumn evening;
> as maps remember countries, mien
> defines a man, and his appears
> at our beseeching.[28]

Reversing the humanizing formula of Auden's Yeats elegy that sees
the dead poet as "silly like us," in Walcott's poem it is the dead poet who
sees the living as ridiculous in their "canonizing farce" that aims to el-
evate him as an icon in precisely the way he refused to do for Yeats. Walcott invokes not just Auden's example, but, significantly, his face—the
famously cracked and wrinkled face of his later American life—as an
emblem of moral and social judgment, scorning the pompous frivoli-

ties of his inheritors among the Manhattan cathedral pews.[29] The iconic
force of that face, and the ancient authority it seemed to organically
express, is a recurrent theme in accounts of Auden's American cultural
presence and impact, as if the lines on his face and the lines of his verse
were reflections of each other, with the human visage of the poet becoming a text to be read along with his poems. And for Walcott, who only
met Auden in person briefly once, the sermon to be read in the photograph of Auden's face is one of ruthless honesty and disdain for poetic pretension and self-regard—what Auden termed, in his own elegy
for Henry James, "the vanity of our calling" [*CP*, 312]. In Auden's "wry
mouth bracketed with pain" and "lizard eyes," Walcott also reads another
Audenesque truth: existential loneliness and solitude. But in language
that recalls the glimpse of "salvation" afforded by "a poetic vision" to the
solitary quester of "Atlantis," as well as the melancholy assertion that "All
I have is a voice / To undo the folded lie" in "September 1, 1939," Walcott
finds his own personal power in Auden's songs of solitude:

> Tonight, as every dish deploys
> from sonar peaks its amplified
> fireside oration,
> we keep yours to ourselves, a voice
> internal, intricately wired
> as our salvation.

Amid the bombarding broadcasts of modernity, the quiet exercise
of listening to Auden humming permanently in our own heads—hard-
wired there through the force of his influence—offers us fresh news on
our own individual solitary fates. For Walcott, as for many other poets,
Auden's voice is an instrument his inheritors can tune to their own pitch,
a private machine for self-illumination and articulation.

While following other Auden elegists in framing the dead poet as
the spirit of his poetic age, Walcott's poem also reflects Auden's specific
importance in his own poetic development. As a young poet on the
Caribbean island of St. Lucia, Walcott had found in Auden's poems a
language that helped him to discover and express his own identity and
ambitions, even in a colonial world far removed from Auden's own. Recalling his "first communion" with "the English tongue" in the hymns
he heard sung in the Methodist churches of what was then still a British

colony, Walcott describes his first reading of Auden's poems as a consummation of that communion and as a double-edged act of submission and liberation: "It was such dispossession / that made possession joy, / when, strict as Psalm or Lesson, / I learnt your poetry." For the young Walcott, his poem suggests, a book of Auden's poetry was a combination of hymnal and textbook, a source of inspiration and of practical knowledge. In a 1994 interview, Walcott—who had since spent many years living and working primarily in the United States—reflects on this dual aspect of his early Auden education back on St. Lucia:

> I remember, during that period, reading Auden with a tremendous amount of elation, a lot of excitement, and discovery—everybody knows what I'm talking about. . . . The freshness of his poetry was tremendously exciting, and it induced you to model yourself on Auden. . . . What one heard reading those books—even in the Caribbean, in another climate and another culture—the distance doesn't count, really—was the vigor and wit and freshness that was there in those poems. They were really tremendous. You see, I think Auden actually dared a lot more than either Pound or Eliot. I think that his intellect was far more adventurous, far braver, far stronger, and far more reckless than either of them."[30]

In what Walcott elsewhere calls "a complete apprenticeship, a complete surrender to modeling," the young poet would diligently set himself the task of emulating Auden and other notable foreign imports like Eliot and Dylan Thomas, filling the pages of his exercise book with imitations of their different voices and styles, "almost like an overlay, down to the rhyme and the meter, but out of my own background and family and landscape, and so on."[31]

In his appropriation of the voices of Auden and others, Walcott is himself echoing Auden's own appropriative mode, literalized in poems like "New Year Letter," where the different voices of the past are consciously *used* to help the living poet articulate their own evolving poetic self. But in this narrative of his Auden-inflected poetic origins, he is also expressing one of the central theoretical concerns of his own career, the question of what he calls, in a famous 1974 essay, the supposed "mimicry" by Caribbean cultures of that of their colonizers. In "The

Caribbean: Culture or Mimicry," Walcott embraces the argument that American culture (in which, both despite and because of their vexed but intimate historical relation, he includes the Caribbean) is defined by its imitation of the models of its Old World elders. In words that explicitly prefigure his Auden eulogy, Walcott describes the differences between the colonizers and the children of colonialism. For the former, he writes, "There was no line in the sea which said, this is new, this is the frontier, the boundary of endeavor, and henceforth everything can only be mimicry. But there was such a moment for every individual American, and that moment was both surrender and claim, both possession and dispossession."[32] If Auden's poems offered excitement and instruction for the young poet, they also epitomized the complex dialectic of the subaltern, for whom the language of the colonizer represents an erasure of his own culture even as he appropriates it for his own self-definitional ends. For the American writer, says Walcott, the cultural dispossession of colonization renders every artistic effort mere mimicry, down to the very words he must use, which do not historically belong to him. But in Walcott's essay, as in his eulogy, "It was such dispossession / that made possession joy." That is, Walcott defines his appropriation—of the colonizer's language generally, and of Auden's poems specifically—as an essentially creative act. "Mimicry is an act of imagination," he declares in his essay.[33] To be dispossessed of one's culture and past brings with it the paradoxical joy of making the alien culture distinctively your own. The necessity of creating and defining yourself from a cultural void, using only the tools afforded by those who forced that necessity upon you, imposes a special imaginative burden and makes the American experience, as Walcott sees it, a fundamentally aesthetic, creative one.

There is a further Audenesque edge to Walcott's poetics of "American mimicry," as Rei Terada terms it.[34] Walcott's essay takes as a central provocation V. S. Naipaul's dismissive claim that "nothing has ever been created in the West Indies, and nothing will ever be created." To which Walcott responds, "Precisely," and then turns Naipaul's attack on its head: "Nothing will always be created in the West Indies, for quite a long time, because what will come out of there is like nothing one has ever seen before." In turning the accusation of Caribbean art as empty mimicry into a celebration of unique creativity out of nothing, Walcott himself creatively reclaims the word "nothing" while literally defining

the Caribbean artist as one who makes "nothing" happen. That the echo
of Auden is not coincidental is made clear in Walcott's own explicit association of the famous phrase from the Yeats elegy with Caribbean history and cultural identity:

> I've heard various interpretations of [the line "poetry makes
> nothing happen"], and I think that people are often too quick—
> we always quote half of the phrase—and forget that it continues
> into an image of poetry as a river which "flows south / From
> ranches of isolation." And I think if you said to a river, 'What
> do you do for the world?' the river's answer would be, 'I don't
> make anything happen.' Nature doesn't make anything hap-
> pen. . . . So Auden's comment is actually an urgent reprimand,
> and not a resignation. It says you want something to happen
> with poetry, but it doesn't make anything happen. . . . Let's
> take a parallel idea in Aimé Césaire when he talks about the
> black raising himself up, and he says 'Hooray for those who
> have not invented anything.' So if the accusation is, 'What have
> you invented?' and the answer is 'Nothing,' that's a profound
> answer. Because nothing that's ever been invented has ever cured
> a single evil. Perhaps the highest tribute that one could pay to
> one's creator would be to do 'nothing.' Maybe the beginning of
> trying to do 'something' was the cause of the fall of man—doing
> something different than simply being in Eden, you see what I
> mean? That 'do something' attitude leads to all kinds of conse-
> quences, so I think that Auden wanted to put poetry in another
> category—in the same category as well, not exactly prayer, but
> beyond that. And I think that to take his phrase as a cynical
> comment of resignation—which people often claim it to be—is
> not enough. As a matter of fact, poetry does make something
> happen because in the flow of the river which he talks about, the
> river touches many things as it passes by.[35]

In his comparison of Auden's influential aphorism with the ideas
of the Caribbean poet and anticolonialist Césaire, Walcott unites the
worlds of poetry and cultural politics and allies his ideal of appropriative
creation with political self-assertion. As Walcott sees it, Auden's endorsement of poetry's refusal to be pinned down by the ideological or practi-

cal demands placed upon it, and Césaire's celebration of the colonized Caribbean's refusal to obey his colonizer's tradition and expectation of "invention" (which has also historically included such innovations as imperialism and slavery), are "parallel." For Walcott, making "nothing" happen is, both poetically and politically, a way of happening.

This definition and defense of Auden's poetics also reflects another illuminating duality in Walcott's understanding of poetic influence itself. Walcott at once frames influence as an act of colonization whose dispossession enables a paradoxical self-possession and creative originality. And in his embrace of Auden's image of poetry as a river that "touches many things as it passes by," he also exposes the original etymological meaning of the word "influence" as an in-flow of water. And in both these ideas, and in Walcott's association of them with Auden, he suggests his own parallel metaphors for understanding Auden's influence on younger poets: Auden was both a powerful and dominating force— seen, in some quarters, as an invasive one—that gave those he influenced a new language through which they could construct their own original artistic identities, and also a sustaining source that flowed through his poetic moment like a great river, touching the lives and work of countless younger writers as it passed by.

In the ending of his poetic eulogy, which deploys the ballad form of "As I Walked Out One Evening" to depict the "slippered shadow" of Auden's ghost moving through the twilight streets of New York, Walcott invokes another metaphor of Auden's influence while creatively mimicking both his language and imagery:

> O craft, that strangely chooses
> one mouth to speak for all,
> O Light no dark refuses,
> O space impenetrable,
>
> fix, among constellations,
> the spark we honour here,
> whose planetary patience
> repeats his earthly prayer
>
> that the City may be Just,
> and humankind be kind.

Another literal meaning of "influence" since Chaucer, Auden's beloved OED tells us, is "an emanation of the stars" that "acts upon the
character and destiny of men, and affecting sublunary things generally."
And in his poem, which explicitly echoes several other Auden poems
including the Yeats elegy itself, "September 1, 1939," "At the Grave of
Henry James," Ferdinand's song in "The Sea and the Mirror," and the
final lines of "New Year Letter," Walcott both honors and bucks Auden's
own elegiac influence by elevating him from a humble, slipper-wearing,
human figure into a constellation signifying "planetary patience." Instead
of bringing the poet down to earth, as Auden did to Yeats, Walcott lifts
him up as a twinkling eternal beacon whose ironic points of light will
continue to shine as the world grows darker. But in his appropriation of
Auden's language for his own purposes, and turning Auden into a starry
embodiment of the idea of influence itself, he gives his and Auden's readers a powerful final illustration and emblem of Auden's role in his own
work and that of many poets of his, and later, generations.

◆ ◆ ◆

The 1983 memorial service at which Walcott read his poem was organized and presided over by Joseph Brodsky, Walcott's close friend and
another poet who, while a decade younger and with roots across the
planet from Walcott or any of the U.S.-born poets of his generation,
notably personifies Auden's American impact. Brodsky, who settled in
the United States after his expulsion from the Soviet Union in 1972,
is perhaps the most explicit of all Auden's poetic inheritors, crediting
Auden alone with his desire to learn to write in the language of his
new country, of which he became a citizen in 1977 and Poet Laureate in 1991. "My sole purpose," says Brodsky of his ambition to become
an English-language poet after a career as the most distinguished Russian poet of his generation, "was to find myself in closer proximity
to the man I considered the greatest mind of the twentieth century:
Wystan Hugh Auden."[36] Brodsky, born the year after Auden arrived in
America, had first encountered Auden's poetry in an old banned anthology whose editors and translators had been arrested by Stalin. He
had been powerfully struck by Auden's language in translation, but in
1964, when Brodsky himself was sentenced to an Arctic gulag for "social parasitism," it was in an untranslated English anthology that Brod-

sky discovered Auden's Yeats elegy in whose lines, "Time . . . worships language and forgives / Everyone by whom it lives," he found a guiding principle for his own poetics. After being released from the labor camp, he exchanged a few letters with Auden, who agreed to write the forward to the English translation of Brodsky's selected poems, and when Brodsky was eventually forced to leave Russia, the first stop on his journey of exile was Austria, where he made a pilgrimage to three different towns named Kirchstetten in search of the one where Auden kept a summer cottage during the last decades of his life. After finally finding the right village and address, and convincing a tired and grumpy Auden who he was and why he was there, Brodsky was invited inside where they began a warm literary friendship that would continue until Auden's death two years later. It was, in fact, through Auden's intercession that Brodsky gained his first American financial support—a $1,000 grant from the Academy of American Poets—and a teaching job at the University of Michigan that allowed him to move permanently to the United States.

In a certain sense, all of Brodsky's American work is an effort, in the words of the title of his essay on Auden, "to please a shadow," a view enthusiastically encouraged by Brodsky himself: "[W]riting in English was the best way to get near him, to work on his terms, to be judged, if not by his code of conscience, then by whatever it is in the English language that made this code of conscience possible."[37] For Brodsky, Auden is the high priest, the incarnation, the conscience of the English language itself. Speaking of Auden's encyclopedic mastery of verse forms, Brodsky asserts, "In the formal sense Auden is simply the culmination of what we consider our civilization. In essence, he is the ultimate effort to animate it."[38] And in terms that literalize the claims in the Yeats elegy that poets become their admirers, Brodsky identifies his American poetic identity wholly with Auden's: "What I think . . . of Auden is that I am he."[39] In homage to that influence and inheritance, Brodsky also wrote poems on the occasion of Auden's death. Soon after Auden's funeral he composed, in both Russian and then in English, his "Elegy for W. H. Auden," in which—like so many of his Auden-elegizing peers—he follows Auden's example in the Yeats elegy of appropriating the recently dead poet's language, modifying in his own poetic gut the words Auden left behind: .

The tree is dark, the tree is tall,
to gaze at it isn't fun.
Among the fruits of this fall
your death is the most grievous one.

The land is bare. Firm for steps,
It yields to a shovel's clink.
Among next April's stems
your cross will be the unshaken thing.

Seedless it will possess its dew
humiliating grass.
Poetry without you
equals only us.[40]

In his essay on Auden, Brodsky cites lines from "Homage to Clio"—
"To visit / The grave of a friend, to make an ugly scene, / To count the
loves one has grown out of, / Is not nice, but to chirp like a tearless
bird, / As though no one dies in particular / And gossip were never true,
unthinkable" [*CP*, 611]—as among the Auden passages he found most
personally resonant. In Brodsky's elegy, we see him recasting the scene
of "Homage to Clio," Auden's Kirchstetten garden, into the "grave of
a friend" from Auden's poem, and sublimating the "ugly scene" of the
mourner's feelings that are "not nice," onto the barren funereal landscape
that "isn't fun" to look at. The poem refuses to chirp or wail, taking from
the Yeats elegy its tone of measured observation of the place of human
loss in the broader context of nature's seasonal cycle. Unlike in the Yeats
elegy, however, in which "snow disfigures the public statues" and nature's indifference is affirmed by dispassionate "instruments," Brodsky's
Auden elegy sees the public monument to Auden's existence, the cross
on his grave, as "humiliating" nature with its "unshaken" fixity and permanence. The natural world doesn't mourn Auden's loss; rather it sees
in the unchanging figure of what Auden leaves behind—his grave, his
poems—a rebuke to its own ephemerality.

This is a central theme of Brodsky's—the poet as the vehicle for language's triumph over time—and it is a theme he identifies explicitly, and
not only in this poem, with Auden. In a second elegy for Auden, written

in 1977 and titled "York: In Memoriam W. H. Auden," Brodsky visits
the town of Auden's birth and revisits this same Audenesque theme:
"Subtracting the greater from the lesser—time from man— / you get
words, the remainder, standing out against their / white background
more clearly than the body / ever manages to while it lives."[41] And as he
puts it in his address accepting his Nobel Prize in 1987: "The poet, I wish
to repeat, is language's means for existence—or, as my beloved Auden
said, he is the one by whom it lives. I who write these lines will cease to
be; so will you who read them. But the language in which they are written and in which you read them will remain not merely because language
is more lasting than man, but because it is more capable of mutation."[42]
As Brodsky sees it, in Auden's shadow, language is permanent and "unshaken" in its eternal mutability; yet its mutability is different—as both
Auden's and Brodsky's elegies suggest—from nature's. Nature moves on
unmoved, always changing yet always indifferent, while language—and
poetry—is defined by its eternal capacity to be available to, and absorbed
and appropriated by, other human beings. Language is what determines
human meaning and, for Brodsky, it is Auden's language that gives his
own American poetry its meaning and its voice: "Poetry without you /
equals only us."

But for Brodsky, as for many others, it was not only Auden's language that mattered. The poetry and the person shared in their impact,
dual aspects of a single influence. In his Auden essay, Brodsky notes the
distinctly human gravity he felt behind Auden's most memorable poetic
lines: "You begin to feel that behind these lines there stands not a blond,
brunette, pale, swarthy, wrinkled or smooth-faced concrete author but
life itself; and *that* you would like to meet; *that* you would like to find
yourself in human proximity to. Behind this wish lies not vanity but
certain human physics that pull a small particle toward a big magnet."[43]
Brodsky fulfilled that wish in his personal friendship with Auden, who
in turn expressed his practical influence by helping Brodsky find fund-
ing, publishers, and employment in America. Of Auden's personal importance to his life and work, Brodsky summarizes, "This was a human
influence more than anything else."[44]

A significant aspect of Auden's "human influence" on postwar
American poetry was in providing an example and poetic passport to
younger poets like Brodsky and Walcott who, like him, made their own

journeys of literal and imaginative translation from worlds outside the prevailing American poetic narrative to their places firmly and importantly within it. For them, as for him, American poetry comes to be defined not by aspirations toward unified cultural heritage or idealizing claims of national identity, but by the unlimited range of languages, subjects, and influences America—Auden's "anti-country"—makes available for their unique use. And for these poets, Auden himself played a major role in enabling and encouraging that sense of availability. Evidence of Auden's continued function as an emblem of poetic reinvention for even younger poets can be found in poems like Paul Muldoon's "7, Middagh Street," which celebrates the transnational artistic community created in the Brooklyn house in which Auden lived alongside artists like Benjamin Britten, Louis MacNeice, and Carson McCullers soon after his arrival in New York. That poem, which begins with a monologue in the voice of Auden himself describing the hopes and anxieties of his new American life, served as the centerpiece of Muldoon's book, *Meeting the British*, published the year he himself moved permanently from his native Northern Ireland to the United States in 1987. But, as we have seen, Auden's influence extended just as deeply into the lives and careers of American-born poets, who likewise found in him a mentor and a model for how to write their own disparate American lives. With his unconstraining voice, he helped teach American poets in the second half of the twentieth century to sing their individual and original songs of self.

NOTES

PREFACE

1 Elizabeth Bishop, "A Brief Reminiscence and a Brief Tribute," *The Harvard Advocate*, 108.2-3 (1974), 47.

PROLOGUE
Auden in "Atlantis"

1 Auden and Isherwood's film treatment is also possibly influenced by John Dos Passos's *U.S.A.*, which tells a kaleidoscopic and thematically similar story of early twentieth-century American life, featuring a recurring first-person narrative termed "The Camera Eye." It may even be, although unlikely, an ironic rewriting of Emerson's transcendent "transparent eyeball" as an emblem of "the average American."

2 "Auden Gives Turnbull Lectures," *Johns Hopkins News-Letter*, 44.27 (February 6, 1940), 1.

3 A representative example of Auden's frequent assertion of the essential loneliness of the American character can be found in a book review he published in January, 1940: "The first feature that strikes a European about the characters in American fiction, and all the more because of its apparent contrast with the glad-handedness of American life, is their extreme

loneliness. In no other country is the separation of the intellectual from the mass wider than in America, with its vast size, its absence of strong ties between community and place, its lack of a crystallised ruling class. Not that loneliness is confined to the intellectual: during my short residence here, I have come to feel that most Americans are profoundly lonely, and that in this more than anything else lies the explanation of American violence" [*Prose*, 42]. Auden again reiterates this idea in the notes to "New Year Letter," calling the American literary tradition "a literature of lonely people" [*DM*, 152].

4 Auden's dialecticism has been much discussed by his critics, including Edward Mendelson, who argues that by 1938 Auden had learned that "by accepting division itself, he could start a dialectic between its opposing aspects," in *Early Auden* (Cambridge, MA: Harvard University Press, 1983), 359. Justin Replogle posits Auden's poetics as a balance between what he calls the "Poet" and the "Anti-Poet," in *Auden's Poetry* (Seattle: University of Washington Press, 1969). Similarly, the thesis of Herbert Greenberg's *Quest for the Necessary: W. H. Auden and the Dilemma of Divided Consciousness* (Cambridge, MA: Harvard University Press, 1968), argues that "'the doubleman' is the theme of *all* of Auden's work." John Boly's *Reading Auden: The Returns of Caliban* (Ithaca, NY: Cornell University Press, 1991) sees Auden's work in terms of a dialogism that aims to "promote an awareness of how truths are formed, and how in the process of that formation they provoke the resistance of a historical medium . . . [thereby] fulfill[ing] a cultural duty after all. By offering an opportune site for the anatomy and disruption of repressive disciplines, poetry might contribute to the society Auden never stopped hoping would one day be built," xi. Susannah Youngah Gottlieb, in "Two Versions of Voltaire: W. H. Auden and the Dialectic of Enlightenment," *PMLA 120.2* (March 2005), notes that Auden "does not prominently deploy the term *dialectical*" in a technical way, wary of its implication in a Hegelian theory of history: "Uncapitalized, however, *dialectical* in Auden's discourse comes very close to the word as it is used by Horkheimer and Adorno: [quoting Auden's 1940 Smith address] 'The term romantic I have chosen rather arbitrarily to describe all those who in one way or another reject the paradoxical, dialectical nature of freedom.' [*Prose*, 64]," 402.

5 Auden disapproved of Crane's rhetorical self-indulgence: "I cannot share Mr. [Cleanth] Brooks's admiration for Hart Crane, who seems to me the 'metaphysical' counterpart of a 'romantic' like Emma Wheeler Wilcox. A phrase like 'adagios of islands' is perfectly explicable intellectually, but corresponds to no sensory or emotional experience. Its synthesis is an act of

will" [*Prose*, 54]. In another review he called Crane a "crooked immoralist" [*Prose*, 57]. But Auden nevertheless included Crane, and selections from *The Bridge*, in his 1956 anthology of modern American poetry for Faber and Criterion.

6 For an account of the historical background behind the composition of "New Year Letter" and its pivotal role in the evolution of Auden's career, see Samuel Hynes, "The Voice in Exile: Auden in 1940," *Sewanee Review* 90.1 (Winter 1982), 31–52. For further biographical context, see Nicholas Jenkins, "Goodbye 1939," *The New Yorker* (April 1, 1996), 88–97. For a general overview of Auden's American life and poetry, including a similar and substantive valuation of the significance of "New Year Letter" in both Auden's career and twentieth-century poetry generally, see Edward Mendelson, *Later Auden* (New York: Farrar, Straus and Giroux, 1999).

7 Lucy McDiarmid, in *Auden's Apologies for Poetry* (Princeton, NJ: Princeton University Press, 1990), suggests a different reading: "Dante, Blake, and Rimbaud . . . are chosen because of the way they perceived values beyond those of literature. At some decisive moment each chose a larger, more comprehensive vision of the universe... Blake, envisioning a holy, animate universe, and Rimbaud, abandoning poetry when he had no more to say, concede literature's secondary importance," 80.

8 Auden, "The Prolific and the Devourer," *Antaeus* 42 (1981), 26. See also *DM*, 110.

9 That Auden felt this acknowledgment and deployment of influences to be a fluid, flexible, and evolving thing can be seen in his claim before a Princeton University audience in November 1940, seven months after finishing "New Year Letter," that "The three greatest influences on my own work have been, I think, Dante, Langland, and Pope" [*Prose*, 132].

10 For a discussion of Auden's own assimilation of his early poetic influences, including Hardy and Eliot, see Katherine Bucknell's introduction to W. H. Auden, *Juvenilia: Poems, 1922–1928* (Princeton, NJ: Princeton University Press, 1994), xix–lii. See also Rachel Wetzsteon, *Influential Ghosts: A Study of Auden's Sources* (New York: Routledge, 2007).

11 Humphrey Carpenter, *W. H. Auden: A Biography* (Boston: Houghton Mifflin, 1981), 333.

12 Patrick Deane has a related reading on "New Year Letter": "The raison d'etre of the poem is to accomplish some sort of mental reorientation in the reader that will have ramifications in the world beyond poetry." In Patrick Deane, "'Within a Field that Never Closes': The Reader in W. H. Auden's 'New Year Letter,'" *Contemporary Literature* 32.2 (1991), 171–93.

13 For a discussion of the relation between Auden's American citizenship and his art, see Robert L. Caserio, "Auden's New Citizenship," *Raritan* 17.2 (Fall 1997): 90–103.

14 Auden, "Influences," typewritten lecture notes, Christopher Isherwood Papers, CI-1072, Huntington Library, San Marino, CA.

15 Auden lived for a year, from October 1939 until the autumn of 1940, at 1 Montague Terrace in Brooklyn, and he loved its clear view of the East River and New York harbor, writing to a friend in November, 1939, "It is a lovely cold Sunday afternoon. Chester is reading *Measure for Measure*; the radio is playing the St. Matthew Passion, and the tugs go backwards and forwards in the bay," quoted in Carpenter, *W. H. Auden*, 279. The next year he moved a few blocks north, to a house at 7 Middagh Street, steps away from where Whitman's Brooklyn ferries would have launched.

16 Walt Whitman, "Leaves of Grass (1855)," *Poetry and Prose* (New York: Library of America, 1996), 5.

17 In the term "the Real Distinguished Thing," Auden productively conflates the title of James's story "The Real Right Thing" with his famous description, on his deathbed, of death as "the distinguished thing." For further discussion of Auden's use of James, see Adam Parkes, "Collaborations: Henry James and the Poet-Critics," *The Henry James Review* 23 (2002), 282–93.

18 Charles Miller, *Auden: An American Friendship* (New York: Paragon House, 1989), 44.

19 Henry James, *Selected Letters of Henry James*, Leon Edel, ed. (New York: Farrar Straus, and Cudahy, 1961), 20–21.

20 Miller, 32–33.

21 Piotr Gwiazda, in *James Merrill and W. H. Auden: Homosexuality and Poetic Influence* (New York: Palgrave, 2007), makes a related observation in his reading of Auden's "queer aesthetics": "We can accept it as an axiom that, notwithstanding the empowering effects of group identification, every gay male poet writing in the twentieth-century United States had to perform the process of homosexual self-interrogation *alone*," 23.

CHAPTER 1

A Way of Happening: *Auden's American Presence*

1 Randall Jarrell, "Changes of Attitude and Rhetoric in Auden's Poetry" (1941), *The Third Book of Criticism* (New York: Farrar Straus & Giroux, 1965), 115.

2 Malcolm Cowley, *The Flower and the Leaf: A Contemporary Record of American Writing Since 1941* (New York: Viking, 1985), 269.

3 Louise Bogan, *The New Yorker* 21 (April 14, 1945), 86.

4 Karl Shapiro, *Essay on Rime* (New York: Random House, 1945), 41.

5 Delmore Schwartz, "The Two Audens" (1939), *Selected Essays of Delmore Schwartz*, Donald A. Dike and David H. Zucker, eds. (Chicago: University of Chicago Press, 1970), 152.

6 Jarrell depicts himself, in the persona of the narrator of his novel, *Pictures from an Institution* (Chicago: University of Chicago Press, 1986), as "know[ing] Auden by heart, practically," 243; Bogan admired Auden as "a man of genius" and self-consciously adopted his rhetorical mode in much of her 1930s poetry, including her 1938 poem "Evening in the Sanitarium," whose original subtitle was "Imitated from Auden" (Elizabeth Frank, *Louise Bogan: A Portrait* [New York: Random House, 1985], 295–96); Shapiro recalls discovering Auden "during the Depression in a British leftist magazine" and reflects on his influence: "By writing that poetry makes nothing happen / You made a generation of makers happen / You changed the tune of poetry for our time / You left the examples / Volunteer exile, man without a country," in John Wheatcroft, *Our Other Voices: Nine Poets Speaking* (Lewisburg: Bucknell University Press, 1991), 161, 165; John Berryman sheepishly confessed "for several fumbling years I wrote in what it is convenient to call 'period style,' the Anglo-American style of the 1930s, with no voice of my own, learning chiefly from middle and later Yeats and from the brilliant young Englishman W. H. Auden," in *The Freedom of the Poet* (New York: Farrar Straus & Giroux, 1976), 324; Roethke holds out Auden, who "with a cormorant's capacity and the long memory of the elephant . . . pillages the past," as his model of poetic influence in his essay "How to Write Like Somebody Else," *On the Poet and His Craft*, Ralph J. Mills, Jr., ed. (Seattle: University of Washington Press, 1965), 67; and late in her life Bishop recalled, "All through my college years, Auden was publishing his early books, and I and my friends, a few of us, were very much interested in him. His first books made a tremendous impression on me. . . . I think I tried not to write like him then, because everybody did," quoted in George Starbuck, "'The Work!': A Conversation with Elizabeth Bishop," *Ploughshares* 3 (1977), 19. For specific critical accounts of Auden's influence on Jarrell and Bishop, see Ian Sansom, "'Flouting Papa': Randall Jarrell and W. H. Auden" in *W. H. Auden, In Solitude, for Company: W. H. Auden after 1940*, Katherine Bucknell and Nicholas Jenkins, eds. (Oxford:

Clarendon, 1996), 275–88; and Bonnie Costello, "A Whole Climate of Opinion: Auden's Influence on Bishop," *Literary Imagination* 5.1 (Winter 2003), 19–41.

7 Allen Ginsberg, "'. . . This is the Abomination,'" *The Columbia Review* (May 1946), 163. Jonah Raskin, in *American Scream: Allen Ginsberg's Howl and the Making of the Beat Generation* (Berkeley, CA: University of California Press, 2004), observes of this unreprinted, unanthologized review that it "has been ignored by scholars, though it is a key work that reflects the growth of the poet's mind and that situates the birth of the Beat Generation in the social, political, and cultural context of its time— in the atomic age. Perhaps Ginsberg did not want it to be discussed since it glorifies the savage and the primitive," 67. It is also possible that Ginsberg was interested in not complicating the antiestablishment origin myth he had cultivated for himself by reprinting an essay in praise of a poet who came to be seen, by Ginsberg as well as others, as the embodiment of that establishment.

8 Critical accounts of Auden's American influence, when offered at all, have tended to be brief digressions within larger discussions of either Auden's American career generally, or the American literary culture of the 1940s and 1950s. For a short overview of Auden's American legacy, see Claude J. Summers, "American Auden," *The Columbia History of American Poetry*, Jay Parini and Brett C. Millier, eds. (New York: Columbia University Press, 1993). See also the brief narrative of Auden's influence in Daniel Hoffman, *Harvard Guide to Contemporary American Writing* (Cambridge, MA: Harvard University Press, 1982). As Peter Firchow observed in 2002, "Though in a very few instances—and thoroughly only in the case of Randall Jarrell—critics have attempted to gauge the nature and extent of Auden's influence, what G. T. Wright wrote more than fifteen years ago nevertheless remains true: 'The influence of Auden on contemporary American poetry still has to be studied in detail.'" In Peter Firchow, *W. H. Auden: Contexts for Poetry* (Newark, DE: University of Delaware Press, 2002), 195.

9 John Hollander, "Under Aquarius," in Stephen Spender, *W. H. Auden: A Tribute* (New York: Macmillan, 1975), 201.

10 Charles Olson and Robert Creeley, *The Complete Correspondence: Vol. 1*, George F. Butterick, ed. (Santa Barbara, CA: Black Sparrow Press, 1980), 78–79.

11 T. S. Eliot, "East Coker," *Collected Poems, 1909–1962* (New York: Harcourt Brace Jovanovich, 1991), 187. It is unclear if Ginsberg's replacement of the word "mass" for Eliot's "mess" is simply one of the review's many printer's

errors, or if it is a felicitous, Auden-inflected misprision of Eliot's phrase. Further evidence of Ginsberg's sometimes ironic engagement with Eliot can be seen in his use of "Leon Bleistein," from Eliot's "Burbank with a Baedeker: Bleistein with a Cigar," as an occasional penname in his early writing (Raskin, 59).

12 Jack Kerouac, *The Town and the City* (New York: Grosset & Dunlap, 1950), 364.

13 Ezra Pound, letter to Allen Ginsberg, 5/16/1951: Allen Ginsberg Archives, Department of Special Collections, Stanford University Libraries.

14 In 1953, Neal Cassady would write to Ginsberg, inquiring after his health, his family, and his poetic relations with what Cassady sees as Ginsberg's early-1950s pantheon, including Williams, Pound, Eliot, Auden, and Dylan Thomas: "How's your brother, mother and father, W. Carlos W? Ezra P. T.S.E. W.H.A. D.T. C. Shapiro and C. Sol. and A. Gin? Did you know that flying saucers are Bees (honey, you know) from Mars." In Allen Ginsberg and Neal Cassady, *As Ever: The Collected Correspondence of Allen Ginsberg and Neal Cassady* (Berkeley, CA: Creative Arts, 1977), Barry Gifford, ed., 152.

15 Ginsberg, *The Book of Martyrdom and Artifice: First Journals and Poems, 1937–1952*, Juanita Liebermann-Plimpton and Bill Morgan, eds. (Cambridge, MA: Da Capo Press, 2006), 433.

16 Ginsberg, *Journals: Mid-Fifties 1954–1958*, Gordon Ball, ed. (New York: Harper Collins, 1995), 307.

17 "Auden had a line: 'Poetry makes nothing happen.' You know, it's not supposed to, then there's the other ivory tower view that it's just sort of like meditation—it's not supposed to make anything happen, just clarify. Clarification makes things happen maybe. Clearing your head might put you in a position to make things happen," in Allen Ginsberg, "Revolutionary Poetics: July 4, 1989" (interview with Kimi Sugioka), *Civil Disobediences: Poetics and Politics in Action*, Anne Waldman and Lisa Birman, eds. (Minneapolis: Coffee House Press, 2004), 245.

18 Ginsberg, "Remembering Auden," *Deliberate Prose: Selected Essays 1952–1995*, Bill Morgan, ed. (New York: HarperCollins, 2000), 451. Originally published, *Drummer* 282 (Feb. 12, 1974), 3. In this pointedly low-key memorial, Ginsberg observes, "I think he got a little bit silly," echoing Auden's own famously unsentimental description of Yeats in his elegy as "silly like us."

19 "Dear Mrs. Jaffe: / Thank you for your note above. I had been informed some time ago that Mr. Auden would recieve [sic] me if I wished to visit

him, and on that basis I sent the mss. I would be grateful if you would communicate to him now or when he returns that I would like him to look at several poems, and that I would like to see him. If he will be anywhere within reasonable distance from N.Y. I will be able to make it, if he is willing," in Allen Ginsberg's letter to Rhoda Jaffe, 6/2/1950: Allen Ginsberg Archives, Department of Special Collections, Stanford University Libraries.

20 Barry Miles, *Ginsberg: A Biography* (London: Viking, 1990), 230.

21 Auden's friend Charles Miller records an argument between Auden and Kallman over the merits of *Howl* in which Auden defended Ginsberg vigorously, claiming, "Of course Allen has contributed to literature. *Howl* does have much to say, and Allen may well grow to even larger achievements. Give him time," quoted in Miller, 146.

22 Miles, 230–31.

23 Allen Ginsberg and Louis Ginsberg, *Family Business: Selected Letters* (New York: St. Martins, 2001), 70.

24 Ginsberg, quoted in Miles, 453. The critic Lucy McDiarmid recalls a revealing encounter with Ginsberg's relation to Auden: "In October or November 1978, Ginsberg gave a poetry reading and workshop at Swarthmore, where I was then a faculty member in the English department. At the post-reading party, most of the faculty (who were generally conservative in their literary tastes) were in the living room talking to one another, but one other professor and I were in the kitchen talking with Ginsberg. I happened to mention to Ginsberg the photo of Auden and himself in Spender's *W. H. Auden: A Tribute*, and he said he had never seen it. He was so eager to get a look at it that I ran home and got the book, returning to the party with it. His eyes lit up when he saw the photo, and he stood there gazing at the picture and smiling for a long time. Needless to say, he was happy and pleased to see it. That was my first awareness of the depth of Ginsberg's emotional connection to Auden," in letter to the author, 8/2007.

25 Miles, 183; Michael Schumacher, *Dharma Lion: A Critical Biography of Allen Ginsberg* (New York: St. Martin's Press, 1992), 211.

26 "Who sang out of their windows in despair, who fell out of the subway window, jumped in the filthy Passaic, leaped on negroes, cried all over the street, danced on broken wineglasses barefoot smashed phonograph records of nostalgic European 1930s German jazz finished the whiskey and threw up groaning into the bloody toilet, moans in their ears and the blast of colossal steam-whistles," Allen Ginsberg, *Howl and Other Poems* (San Francisco: City Lights, 1956), 17. In a 1968 interview with Ted Ber-

rigan, Kerouac recalled Cannastra's colorful role as a point of intersection between the Beats and Auden and other literary celebrities: "He was an Italian. Italians are wild you know. He says 'Jack come with me and look down this peephole,' we saw lots of things . . . into his toilet. I said 'I'm not interested in that, Bill.' He said 'You're not interested in anything.' Auden would come the next day. Maybe with Chester Kallman. Tennessee Williams." In *Conversations with Jack Kerouac*, Kevin J. Hayes, ed. (Jackson, MS: University of Mississippi Press, 2005), 62.

27 See Alan Ansen, *Contact Highs: Selected Poems 1957–1987*, introduction by Steven Moore (Elmwood Park, IL: Dalkey Archive Press, 1989); Dorothy J. Farnan, *Auden in Love* (New York: Simon and Schuster, 1984), 165; Ansen, *The Table Talk of W. H. Auden*, Nicholas Jenkins, ed. (Boston: Faber and Faber, 1990).

28 Gregory Corso, *An Accidental Autobiography: The Selected Letters of Gregory Corso*, Bill Morgan, ed. (New York: New Directions, 2003), 106. Corso would reflect further on the significance of this visit in a letter to Isabella Gardner: "My happiest time was at Oxford (always dreamt of that place in prison, because Shelley went there) and had a dream come true when Auden, who had read my book and thought very highly of it, took me for a long walk around Magdalen Heath (it's pronounced like maudlin) and to Christ College, and his old room, when he was a student, and I asked him if he thought birds were spies, and he said 'Who would they report to?' and Allen said: 'The trees.' Anyhow, I felt as if I were walking with Shelley there; if I could only convey to you how I really dreamt so much of Oxford and Shelley as a youth; that this was very dear to my heart, that walk," 134. In another letter to Donald Allen, editor of the influential 1960 anthology *The New American Poetry*, Corso advocated his canonical cause by citing Auden's approval, while suggesting his own creative negotiations with Auden's teacherly advice: "I told Alan Ansen to send you review. He wrote me and told me Auden stayed with him for two weeks to see new Stravinsky score, and that Auden said he thought highly of my poetry but that I should not be 'discouraged' from learning more of the language. I think I know what he means, but as it is I am getting too conscious of the language, and find myself hesitating in my 'careless' 'arrogant' choice of coinage," 144. Corso would comically refract this advice in a further letter to Ginsberg: "Ansen says Auden thinks highly of my work, but feels that you shouldn't 'discourage' me from learning more of the language; whatever that means. Do you discourage me, sir? I dare say you do! I think I'll make complaints! I demand encouragement! I ain't gonna remain with

just this liddle store of language, I wanna be learned the big woids, and all their meanings," 146.

29 Gregory Corso, "'I'm Poor Simple Human Bones': An Interview with Gregory Corso" (1977), in Matt Theado, *The Beats: A Literary Reference* (New York: Carroll and Graf, 2001), 376.

30 Diana Trilling, "The Other Night at Columbia: A Report from the Academy," *Partisan Review* (Spring 1959), 223–30.

31 William S. Burroughs, interview with John Tytell, *Kerouac and the Beats*, Arthur and Kit Knight, eds. (New York: Paragon House, 1988), 247. Burroughs had his own engagement with Auden's cultural authority, inquiring anxiously of his friends, "What's this about Rexroth saying Auden says Jack is a genius but ruined by his friends? Jack wrote me that. Also Auden say I am a genius too," in Burroughs, *The Letters of William Burroughs 1945–59*, Oliver Harris, ed. (London: Picador, 1993), 247.

32 In Jay Landesman, *Rebel Without Applause* (London: Bloomsbury, 1987), Landesman recalls the founding of *Neurotica* in St. Louis in 1947:
> The next day [Richard] Rubinstein showed up with a copy of W. H. Auden's "The Age of Anxiety."
> "The poet is the first to recognize the rot, the first to celebrate the glory, and the last to be appreciated." I didn't know if it was a quote from Auden or one of Rubinstein's rationalizations.
> "Let's cure the ills of America by starting a poetry magazine."
> I broke up.
> "Your rejection slips are showing," I told him. "You'll never get laid with a poetry magazine." I knew he was serious when he didn't laugh.
> "You ought to read Auden. It's a big book. He's got his finger on the pulse of the times. The new look is going to be the anxious look." (45)

33 *Pull My Daisy*: dirs. Robert Frank and Alfred Leslie, text and narration by Jack Kerouac. G-String Enterprises, 1959.

34 Jack Kerouac, "The Roaming Beatniks" (from *Holiday* magazine, October 1959) in Fred W. McDarrah, *Kerouac and Friends: A Beat Generation Album* (New York: William Morrow and Company, 1985), 86–87.

35 Jason Shinder, *The Poem that Changed America: Howl Fifty Years Later* (New York: Farrar Straus & Giroux, 2006), xiii.

36 As Marjorie Perloff summarizes Rimbaud's influence in *The Poetics of Indeterminacy: Rimbaud to Cage* (Princeton, NJ: Princeton University Press, 1981), he points in the opposite aesthetic direction from Auden: "Rim-

baud's unsurpassed influence—on Apollinaire and Jacob, Reverdy and Char, the Dada and Surrealist poets—has long been recognized, but in Anglo-America, the Rimbaldian context becomes increasingly important. For Rimbaud was probably the first to write what I shall here call the poetry of indeterminacy. And whereas Baudelaire and Mallarme point the way to the 'High Modernism' of Yeats and Eliot and Auden, Stevens and Frost and Crane, and their Symbolist heirs like Lowell and Berryman, it is Rimbaud who strikes the first note of 'undecidability' we find in Gertrude Stein, in Pound and Williams, as well as in the short prose works of Beckett's later years, an undecidability that has become marked in the poetry of the last decades," 4.

37 Helen Vendler, *The Music of What Happens* (Cambridge, MA: Belknap, 1988), 167; Vendler, *Soul Says: On Recent Poetry* (Cambridge, MA: Harvard University Press, 1995), 92.

38 For a valuable polemical survey of many of these debates, including an engaged, if disapproving, assessment of Auden's impact on American poetry in the 1950s, see Jed Rasula, *The American Poetry Wax Museum: Reality Effects 1940–1990* (Urbana, IL: National Council of Teachers of English, 1996). Similarly, for James E. B. Breslin, in *From Modern to Contemporary: American Poetry, 1945–1960* (Chicago: University of Chicago Press, 1984), under Auden's influence the American poem of the 1950s became "a 'closed system,' a sealed enclosure that was transcendent, safe, and stultifying," 39.

39 Auden, letter to Henry Bamford Parkes, December 1931, quoted in Mendelson, *Early Auden*, 100n. Mendelson points out Auden's echoes of Rimbaud in "The Journal of an Airman" as well as comments on the significance Rimbaud plays in Auden's evolving poetics through the 1930s, 239.

40 Arthur Rimbaud, *Rimbaud Complete: Poetry and Prose*, trans. Wyatt Mason (New York: Modern Library, 2003), 220.

41 Frank O'Hara, *The Collected Poems of Frank O'Hara*, Donald Allen, ed. (Berkeley, CA: University of California Press, 1995), 17.

42 Donald Hall, *In Conversation with Ian Hamilton* (London: Between the Lines, 2000), 27. See also Brad Gooch, *Frank O'Hara: City Poet* (New York: Random House, 1993), 127. For a useful parallel account of Auden's connections to O'Hara and Ashbery, see Andrew Epstein, "Auden and the New York School Poets," *W. H. Auden Society Newsletter* 22 (November 2001), 19–28.

43 John Ashbery, interview with the author, 5/13/1997.

44 Bill Berkson, "Frank O'Hara and his Poems," *Homage to Frank O'Hara*, Bill Berkson and Joe LeSueur, eds. (Bolinas, CA: Big Sky, 1978), 163.

45 Frank O'Hara, quoted in Marjorie Perloff, *Frank O'Hara: Poet Among Painters* (New York: G. Braziller, 1977), 61.

46 Delmore Schwartz, *In Dreams Begin Responsibilities* (Norfolk, CT: New Directions, 1938).

47 O'Hara, *The Collected Poems of Frank O'Hara*, 499.

48 O'Hara, *Early Writing*, Donald Allen, ed. (Bolinas, CA: Grey Fox Press, 1977), 20–21.

49 Richard Howard, interview with the author, 4/2/1997.

50 For a definitive account of Auden's sexual poetics, see Richard R. Bozorth, *Auden's Games of Knowledge: Poetry and the Meanings of Homosexuality* (New York: Columbia University Press, 2001): "Together, his concerns with the 'I-Thou' relation in love and in lyric, and with the infidelity of poetic language to fact, suggest that by the 1950s and 60s Auden saw *all* poetry as a kind of virtual lovers' discourse. Addressed—often ambiguously—to Kallman and to others, his later love poems interpellate every reader as the beloved, seeking to honor the multiple, conflicting responsibilities of erotic experience," 14. See also David Bergman, "Choosing Our Fathers: Gender and Identity in Whitman, Ashbery, and Richard Howard," *Gaiety Transfigured: Gay Self-Representation in American Literature* (Madison, WI: Wisconsin University Press, 1991), 44–63.

51 Randall Jarrell, *Randall Jarrell on W. H. Auden*, Stephen Burt, ed. With Hannah Brooks-Motl (New York: Columbia University Press, 2005), 20–21. In a later lecture, Jarrell returns to this theme: "He is an extremely novel and original poet, but at the same time has extraordinary gifts of imitation, of mimicry, of taking and making his own. He is unusually skillful at analyzing someone else's work, taking out what he likes, and synthesizing a new style of his own that will include this," 71.

52 Ibid., 71.

53 Ibid., 21.

54 Ibid., 22.

55 For specific critical accounts of Auden's relation to "postmodernism," variously defined, see Rainer Emig, *W. H. Auden: Towards a Postmodern Poetics* (New York: St. Martin's Press, 2000) and Jerome Mazzaro, *Postmodern American Poetry* (Urbana, IL: University of Illinois Press, 1980). For more general discussions of American poetry after modernism, including the contested history of the word "postmodernism" itself in reference to postwar American poetry, see Robert von Hallberg, *American Poetry and Culture 1945–1980* (Cambridge, MA: Harvard University Press, 1985); Mutlu Konuk Blasing, *Politics and Form in Postmodern Poetry: O'Hara, Bishop,*

Ashbery, and Merrill (New York: Cambridge University Press, 1995); James Longenbach, *Modern Poetry After Modernism* (New York: Oxford University Press, 1997); and Thomas Travisano, *Bishop, Lowell, Jarrell, Berryman, and the Making of a Postmodern Aesthetic* (Charlottesville: University of Virginia Press, 1999).

56 Elizabeth Bishop, "Mechanics of Pretence: Remarks on Auden," *Edgar Allen Poe & the Juke-Box: Uncollected Poems, Drafts, and Fragments*, Alice Quinn, ed. (New York: Farrar Straus & Giroux, 2006), 183.

57 Maxine Kumin, *Always Beginning: Essays on a Life in Poetry* (Port Townsend, WA: Copper Canyon Press, 2000), 198.

58 Kumin, "Lines Written in the Library of Congress After the Cleanth Brooks Lecture," *Our Ground Time Here Will Be Brief* (New York: Viking Press, 1982), 41–42.

59 Sylvia Plath, *The Journals of Sylvia Plath* (New York: Ballantine, 1982), 76.

60 Plath, *Letters Home: Correspondence 1950–1963* (New York: Harper & Row, 1975), 107–8.

61 This poem, along with an entertaining account of a later evening spent having dinner with Auden and Kallman in Hacker's own apartment (during which the elder poets helped extinguish a kitchen fire), is included in the memoirs of Hacker's former husband, the science-fiction writer Samuel R. Delany, *The Motion of Light in Water: Sex and Science Fiction Writing in the East Village* (New York: Masquerade, 1988), 141–56.

62 Richard Howard, interview with the author, 4/2/1997.

63 Anthony Hecht, interview with the author, 12/29/1996. Richard Howard makes a similar recollection of the importance of Auden's prose criticism: "He was writing all that criticism all the time. And it was wonderful. Much underestimated, but enjoyed and we all fell upon it whenever he wrote in *The New Yorker* or in the papers. He was everywhere, in the *Times*, in the *New York Review*, and we read all those things. He was a figure of importance for us. Even, I think, for people who weren't in the least bit interested in writing that way," from interview with the author, 4/2/1997.

64 Hayden recalls the difficulties he had with the poem in an interview with Paul McCluskey: "But 'Middle Passage,' which was to be the opening poem, was nowhere near completion. In the spring of 1942 I was awarded first prize [the Hopwood Prize at the University of Michigan] for *The Black Spear*. I was studying with W. H. Auden at the time, and he was present when I received the award and came up afterwards and shook my hand— award enough," in Robert Hayden, *Collected Prose* (Ann Arbor, MI: University of Michigan Press, 1984), 169. See also Michael S. Harper, "Every

Shut Eye Aint Asleep/Every Good-bye Aint Gone," *Robert Hayden: Essays on the Poetry* (Ann Arbor, MI: University of Michigan Press, 2001), 107. Brian Conniff frames Auden's influence on Hayden in terms that recall the model of free, assimilative influence shared by so many of Auden's inheritors: "Dismissing this kind of purely literary anxiety, Auden claimed for the poet a radical freedom to reshape the canon in order to serve immediate social needs, moral imperatives, and even personal whims," in *Robert Hayden: Essays on the Poetry*, 289.

65 Hayden, quoted in Eugene B. Redmond, *Drumvoices: The Mission of Afro-American Poetry* (New York: Anchor Press, 1976), 237. Calling his time as Auden's student a "marvelous experience," Hayden remembers the impact of both Auden's pedagogy and his person: "[S]omehow or other he stimulated us to learn more about poetry in a way that we never would have been had it not been for him. . . . He came to see my daughter when she was born. Of course this was a year or so afterwards—after he had left the campus. But he did drop in to see my daughter. He was eager to see what she looked like, and so he looked down on her in her crib. I've told her, 'You must remember always W. H. Auden came to look at you.' He helped me get a job in the library. He was friends with the librarian there, Dr. Rice, who later on was the chairman of the English department, and he spoke to Dr. Rice and he got me a job in the library. He was interested in seeing that I got my poems published. He was a wonderful person. And then years later he and I read together at Columbia University," in Hayden, *Collected Prose*, 99–101.

66 William Bronk, quoted in Edward Foster, *Postmodern Poetry: The Talisman Interviews* (Hoboken, NJ: Talisman House, 1994), 8.

67 Charles Bukowski, "the poets and the foreman," *Dangling in the Tournefortia* (Santa Barbara, CA: Black Sparrow Press, 1981), 274.

68 For this and other historical details of Auden's tenure as Yale Younger Poets judge, I am indebted to George Bradley's excellent history of the series in the introduction to *The Yale Younger Poets Anthology* (New Haven, CT: Yale University Press, 1998), lviii–lxxiii.

69 Auden, quoted in Bradley, lxviii.

70 Ibid., lxix.

71 Auden, letter to W. S. Merwin, 1951, Berg Collection, New York Public Library.

72 Auden, letter to W. S. Merwin, 8/6/1951, Berg Collection, New York Public Library.

73 Auden, letter to W. S. Merwin, 8/18/1951, Berg Collection, New York Public Library.

74 Edwin Arlington Robinson, letter to Laura E. Richards, 1/20/1935, in *Selected Letters of Edwin Arlington Robinson* (New York: MacMillan, 1940), 178.

75 William Carlos Williams, letter to Babette Deutsch, 5/25/1948, in *Selected Letters of William Carlos Williams* (New York: Random House, 1954), 264.

76 Williams, "Preface to a Book of Poems by Harold Rosenberg," *Something to Say: William Carlos Williams on Younger Poets*, James E. B. Breslin, ed. (New York: New Directions, 1985), 125.

77 Ibid., 126–27.

78 Williams, "The Poem as a Field of Action," *Selected Essays of William Carlos Williams* (New York: Random House, 1954), 288. Williams's 1948 commentary echoes his earlier response to a joint public reading with Auden in 1939, where he had been chagrined at the success with the New York audience of the brash and recently arrived Auden, "with his smooth Oxford accent," in contrast to his own perceived lukewarm reception: "And they almost drowned in their slobber they were so tickled to grant him any small favor that lay to their eager hands. Their faltering hands! And he read them his verses, and very good sweet verses they were and—they raised the roof with their gracious huzzahs." For Williams, Auden's public triumph is a hollow one since it is precisely his internationalism that marks, and masks, his true poetic failure: "Listen as I would I could not find that he has traveled the world without perceiving a new measure such as I seek. What he . . . did in his best poems . . . was to give an able exposition of new materials upon the old accepted basis," quoted in Paul Mariani, *William Carlos Williams: A New World Naked* (New York: McGraw-Hill, 1981), 437.

79 William Carlos Williams, *Autobiography* (New York: Random House, 1951), 146. At one point in 1941, at the height of the Battle of Britain, Williams even seems to suggest that the possibility of British defeat by the Nazis might be predicted in the formal enervation of their modern poets, including Auden and Eliot: "If England collapses (as Athens and Rome did finally) or uniquely survives the next year or two, what is the significance of such a collapse or survival interpreted in terms of poetic form? What today remains important and what, in the form of its verse, paralleled the weakness which paved the way for a downfall? For a downfall did not occur without weakness, an inability to contend with factors which were eating away the foundations. The counterparts of these should be found in all activities of the period. That is, formal counterparts in the writing of the period—whether of Auden, Eliot, Pound or whoever it may be—cannot but be found if we will look for them, divergent tendencies which reveal wherein the collapse was accelerated or might have been written off with

foresight and energetic application of talents. These things I say—formally expressed," in Williams, *Something to Say*, 111–12.

80 Mariani, 424–26.

81 William Carlos Williams, letter to Charles Abbott 6/26/1946, in *Selected Letters of William Carlos Williams*, John C. Thirlwall, ed. (New York: McDowell, Oblensky, 1957), 245.

82 William Carlos Williams, letter to Kenneth Burke 2/4/1947, in *The Humane Particulars: The Collected Letters of William Carlos Williams and Kenneth Burke*, James H. East, ed. (Columbia, SC: University of South Carolina Press, 2003), 116.

83 Williams, letter to Robert Lowell, 3/11/1952, *Selected Letters*, 313.

84 Robert Creeley, letter to Charles Olson 5/27/1950, in Charles Olson and Robert Creeley, *The Complete Correspondence: Vol. 1*, George F. Butterick, ed. (Santa Barbara, CA: Black Sparrow Press, 1980), 54.

85 In an interview with Ginsberg in 1971, Duncan reflected on the common poetic ground he was surprised to find himself sharing with Auden: "[W]hen Auden wanted me in an anthology, [I said] yes, regardless of my own distaste for Auden's role in poetry. He *is* a poet, and it's fascinating what's in that anthology, until he came to my generation. But then he must have been right, because there I was with H. D. and Williams and people I really loved, and so did Auden, it turns out. So this must be an *entente* of some strange kind." In Allen Ginsberg and Robert Duncan, 4/7/1971, "Early Poetic Community, with Robert Duncan," Allen Ginsberg, *Allen Verbatim: Lectures on Poetry, Politics, Consciousness*, Gordon Ball, ed. (New York: McGraw-Hill, 1974), 132–33.

86 Charles Olson, letter to Irving Layton, 1954, in *Selected Letters*, Ralph Maud, ed. (Berkeley, CA: University of California Press, 2000), 220.

87 Marjorie Perloff, *Poetic License: Essays on Modernist and Postmodernist Lyric* (Evanston, IL: Northwestern University Press, 1990), 121. Christopher Beach, in *ABC of Influence: Ezra Pound and the Remaking of American Tradition* (Berkeley, CA: University of California Press, 1992), poses a similar question as he traces the diverse tradition of Pound-influenced American poetics.

88 Marjorie Perloff, *The Dance of the Intellect: Studies in the Poetry of the Pound Tradition* (New York: Cambridge University Press, 1985), 188.

89 Richard Howard, *Alone With America: Essays on the Art of Poetry in the United States Since 1950* (New York: Atheneum, 1980), frontispiece.

90 W. B. Yeats, *The Oxford Book of Modern Verse 1892–1935* (London: Oxford University Press, 1936), xxv.

91 Humphrey Carpenter, *A Serious Character: The Life of Ezra Pound* (Boston: Houghton Mifflin, 1988), 791.

92 Auden, "The Question of the Pound Award" (1949), in *A Casebook on Ezra Pound*, William Van O'Connor and Edward Stone, eds. (New York: Thomas Y. Crowell, 1959), 55. Auden had a private meeting with Eliot, Pound's publisher James Laughlin, and others in June, 1948, to discuss the possibility of getting Pound released from St. Elizabeth's. Laughlin wrote to Pound: "This Thursday a council meets on yr behalf at the request of the good parson Eliot. Cummings, Tate, Auden, Fitzgerald, Fitts, and Cornell will be there and we shall mightywise deliberate and perhaps bring forth a small mechanical mouse," in Ezra Pound and James Laughlin, *Selected Letters*, David M. Gordon, ed. (New York: W.W. Norton, 1994), 169–70. Auden, Eliot, and Tate would serve on the Library of Congress committee five months later that awarded the Bollingen Prize to Pound.

93 Auden, *A Tribute to Ezra Pound*, broadcast on December 5, 1955 by the Yale Broadcasting Company, quoted in *Ezra Pound at Seventy* (Norfolk, CT: New Directions, 1955), 1.

94 Among the notable anthologies and surveys of modern American poetry in which Auden is not mentioned: Roy Harvey Pierce, *The Continuity of American Poetry* (Middletown, CT: Wesleyan University Press, 1961); Helen Vendler, *The Harvard Book of Contemporary American Poetry* (Cambridge, MA: Harvard University Press, 1984); Hyatt Waggoner, *American Poets from the Puritans to the Present* (Baton Rouge, LA: Louisiana State University Press, 1984); Paul Hoover, *Postmodern American Poetry* (New York: Norton, 1994); Jerome Rothenberg and Pierre Joris, *Poems for the Millennium: The University of California Book of Modern & Postmodern Poetry* (Berkeley, CA: University of California Press, 1995); Jay Parini, *Columbia Anthology of American Poetry* (New York: Columbia University Press, 1995); Cary Nelson, *Anthology of American Poetry* (New York: Oxford University Press, 2000); Ron Silliman, *In the American Tree: Language Realism Poetry* (Orono, ME: National Poetry Foundation, 2002); Steven Gould Axelrod, Camille Roman, Thomas Travisano, *New Anthology of American Poetry* (Piscataway, NJ: Rutgers University Press, 2003). Three other major anthologies acknowledge Auden's significant presence in postwar American verse, but explicitly exclude him nonetheless, deeming him (in the words of the first listed, which is dedicated, "To E. P. from us all") "essentially British": Hayden Carruth, *The Voice That Is Great Within Us: American Poetry of the Twentieth Century* (New York: Bantam, 1970); Stuart Friebert and David Young, *The Longman Anthology of Contemporary*

American Poetry 1950–1980 (New York: Longman, 1983); Dana Gioia, David Mason, and Meg Schoerke, *Twentieth-Century American Poetry* (Boston: McGraw-Hill, 2004). One anthology that *does* include Auden as an American poet is that of Ashbery's teacher at Harvard, F. O. Matthiessen, *The Oxford Book of American Verse* (New York: Oxford University Press, 1950). The current edition, now called *The Oxford Book of American Poetry* (New York: Oxford University Press, 2006), edited by David Lehman, also includes Auden, though the 1976 edition under Richard Ellmann did not, Auden being deemed by Ellmann "English to the bone."

95 Harold Bloom, *Contemporary Poets* (New York: Chelsea House, 1986), 3.

96 Marjorie Perloff, *Poetic License*, 122. It is notable that of the poets Perloff suggests as having been influenced by Pound's nationalist poetics, including Donald Davie, Denise Levertov, Charles Tomlinson, Charles Wright, Thom Gunn, and Theodore Weiss, all but two resist the easy label of "American" (with at least one having no claim on Americanness whatsoever), usefully illustrating the difficulty of framing postwar poetry in the limiting terms of a specific "native tradition."

97 Nicholas Jenkins, "Auden in America," *The Cambridge Companion to W. H. Auden*, Stan Smith, ed. (Cambridge, UK: Cambridge University Press, 2004), 44.

98 I borrow this term from Jenkins, whose forthcoming book explores in depth what he calls Auden's "post-national poetics." While Jenkins focuses principally on the origins and development of Auden's post-nationalist vision in the context of his pre-American career, I'd like to extend the consideration of this question to examine Auden's transmission of this perspective into the broader narratives of postwar poetry in the United States. See Nicholas Jenkins, "Writing 'Without Roots': Auden, Eliot, and Post-National Poetry," in Steve Clark and Mark Ford, eds., *Something We Say That They Don't: British and American Poetic Relations Since 1925* (Iowa City: University of Iowa Press, 2005), 75–97.

99 Charles Olson, *Charles Olson & Ezra Pound: An Encounter at St. Elizabeth's*, Catherine Seelye, ed. (New York: Grossman, 1975), xvii.

CHAPTER 2

Father of Forms: *Merrill, Auden, and a Fable of Influence*

1 James Merrill, "Table Talk," *For W. H. Auden: February 21, 1972* (New York: Random House, 1972), 72–3. In the version of this poem published two years later in *The Yellow Pages* (Cambridge, MA: Temple Bar, 1974), 37–38, the final lines have been altered to eliminate the reference to Auden:

" I wish a doctor or at least/ A jolly Roman priest/ Were here to tell me: *Go ahead, my son, enjoy the feast!*"

2 Stevens died on August 2, 1955, and according to David Jackson, "Our Ouija experience began in Stonington on August 23, 1995"—exactly three weeks later. See David Jackson, "Lending a Hand," *James Merrill: Essays in Criticism*, David Lehman and Charles Berger, eds. (Ithaca, NY: Cornell University Press, 1983), 301.

3 See Stephen Yenser, "James Merrill: His Poetry and the Age," *The Southwest Review* 80.2-3 (1995), 186–204, for an account of Merrill's relationship to Stevens, Whitman, and the "American Romantic" poetic tradition. Harold Bloom, in *James Merrill*, (New York: Chelsea House, 1985), identifies Stevens as Merrill's "veritable precursor" over Auden, whose "example and career seem to play the same part in Merrill as in Ashbery. He is a benign presence for both, precisely because he is not the true father, but more like an amiable uncle on the mother's side, as it were," 2. Merrill himself, in a 1992 "interview" with an assortment of dead writers conducted via the Ouija board at the behest of *The Paris Review*, enthusiastically confesses to Stevens himself the early importance of his influence: "I want to say that your work has inspired me tremendously ever since I began to write my first 'grown-up' poems. Even your life seemed marvelous—that cover life as an insurance man. It proved that one didn't have to be Bohemian, that the supreme fiction didn't need cafés and brothels or gardens in Spain to flourish in," in James Merrill and David Jackson, "The Plato Club," *The Paris Review* 122 (1992), 60. Stevens makes several appearances in *Sandover*, including at the final convocation of important influences in "The Ballroom at Sandover," though in the poem he garners only the "faint praise" from the celestial hierarchy as a "DRY SCRIBE" who rates, among poets, "NEITHER TOP / NOR BOTTOM, DEEP NOR SHALLOW" but "A PERMANENCE / TAPPABLE BY LESSER TALENT" [*CLS*, 429].

4 For a discussion of *Sandover* as "an elegy writ very large, . . . a multiple elegy of epic proportions," see Peter Sacks "The Divine Translation: Elegiac Aspects of *The Changing Light at Sandover*," *James Merrill: Essays in Criticism*, 177–78. See also Gwiazda, 5.

5 For a related discussion of the continuities and divergences between Auden and Merrill, see Lynn Keller, *Re-making It New: Contemporary American Poetry and the Modernist Tradition* (Cambridge, UK: Cambridge University Press, 1987). David Lehman also provides a brief discussion of Merrill's formal debts to Auden, in "Elemental Bravery: The Unity of James Merrill's Poetry," *James Merrill: Essays in Criticism*, 49.

6 Dante, *Paradiso*, Canto I, ll. 19–21; trans. H. F. Cary.

7 Sacks also discusses the importance of the figure of Marsyas in Merrill's work but does not make mention of this poem, in *James Merrill: Essays in Criticism*, 177–78.

8 James Merrill, *A Different Person: A Memoir* (New York: HarperCollins, 1994), 226, 119–21.

9 Randall Jarrell, "Recent Poetry," *Kipling, Auden & Co.* (New York: Farrar, Straus and Giroux, 1980), 228.

10 Jarrell, "Freud to Paul: The Stages of Auden's Ideology," *The Third Book of Criticism*, 155–6.

11 For another reading of "Marsyas" that sees the figure of the elder poet as Auden, see John Shoptaw, "James Merrill and John Ashbery," *The Columbia History of American Poetry*, Jay Parini and Brett Millier, eds. (New York: Columbia University Press, 1993), 752–53.

12 Stephen Yenser, *The Consuming Myth: The Work of James Merrill* (Cambridge, MA: Harvard University Press, 1987), 62.

13 Wallace Stevens, *The Palm at the End of the Mind: Selected Poems and Plays*, Holly Stevens, ed. (New York: Vintage, 1972), 10.

14 Stevens, 97.

15 For a valuable related discussion of Merrill's assimilative model of poetic identity which, though focusing on Merrill's significant Yeatsian inheritance, also reads "Marsyas" as an emblem of poetic influence, see Mark Bauer, *This Composite Voice: The Role of W. B. Yeats in James Merrill's Poetry* (New York: Routledge, 2003), 205, 249. Bauer also interrogates Harold Bloom's model of poetic influence, pointing to the way it both helps explain the shadow-presence of Yeats in Merrill's poem but proves ultimately inadequate, in part because of its bias toward Oedipal psychodynamics, to fully account for Merrill's notion of the "composite voice."

16 William Shakespeare, *Richard II* V.ii.32.

17 Ibid., V.v.31.

18 At a public reading in 1994 in New Haven, Merrill signed the author's copy this way.

19 T. S. Eliot, "Little Gidding," *Collected Poems*, 201.

20 Robert Polito, "Afterword: Tradition and an Individual Talent," *A Reader's Guide to James Merrill's* The Changing Light at Sandover (Ann Arbor, MI: University of Michigan Press, 1994), 231–63. Also, Gwiazda, 11ff. For another discussion of Merrill's relation to Eliot, see Alan Nadel, "Replacing the Waste Land: James Merrill's Quest for Transcendent Authority," *College Literature* 20 (June 1993), 154–76.

21 T. S. Eliot, *Selected Prose of T. S. Eliot*, Frank Kermode, ed. (New York: Harcourt Brace, 1975), 38.

22 Anthony Hecht, interview with the author, 12/29/1996.

23 Eliot, *Selected Prose*, 40.

24 Willard Spiegelman also points out the echo of Auden's "New Year Letter" in *Sandover*, in *The Didactic Muse: Scenes of Instruction in Contemporary American Poetry* (Princeton, NJ: Princeton University Press, 1989), 13–21. Jeffery Donaldson draws attention to the "poetics of echo" shared by Merrill and Auden, suggesting that *Sandover* stands "as an implicit homage to Auden and the poetics of allusion that find him isolated but still attempting to make contact with a world 'out there,'" in Donaldson, "The Company Poets Keep: Allusion, Echo, and the Question of Who Is Listening in W. H. Auden and James Merrill," *Contemporary Literature* 36.1 (1995), 35–57. See also Gwiazda's book-length study of the deep connections between Auden and Merrill, emphasizing in particular their relation through shared notions of homosexual poetics.

25 Timothy Materer offers a helpful, though slightly different, account of Merrill's relation to Harold Bloom's agonistic theory, while also pointing to Auden's role in the poem in helping Merrill escape that anxiety: "*The Changing Light at Sandover* can illustrate all six of the ways poets deal with their poetic precursors that Harold Bloom identifies in *The Anxiety of Influence*; for example, Merrill's distortion of Auden's Anglo-Catholicism is the kind of misprision that Bloom calls *clinamen*, and his linking of his own poem to Yeats's occult works and Eliot's *The Waste Land* is what Bloom calls *tessera*. Moreover, Merrill's poem itself is a literal case of Bloom's '*Apophrades* or Return of the Dead.' Although Merrill's precursors return in abundance (Auden, Blake, Dante, Eliot, Hugo, Pope, Stevens, and Yeats, to name some of the major influences), there is no sense, as in Bloom, of an agonizing wrestling match with the powerful dead. Merrill's evident ambition to rival Pope's irony and descriptive powers, Auden's intellectual depth and lyricism, and Yeats's richness of imagery must weigh upon him. But he appears not to share Bloom's feeling that, 'in poems as in our lives,' the dead do not return 'without darkening the living'.... Indeed, it is Auden's schooling of Merrill in the modernist doctrine of impersonality that allays his anxieties over being a mere medium," in Materer, "The Error of His Ways: James Merrill and the Fall into Myth," *American Poetry* 7.3 (1990), 72.

26 Ovid, *Metamorphoses*, trans. Mary M. Innes (New York: Penguin, 1955), 145.

27 For another discussion of the thematic role of homosexuality in *Sandover*, see Edmund White, "The Inverted Type: Homosexuality as a Theme in

James Merrill's Prophetic Books," *Literary Visions of Homosexuality*, Stuart Kellogg, ed. (Haworth: New York, 1983), 47–52.

28 Randall Jarrell, "*The Age of Anxiety* by W. H. Auden," *Kipling, Auden & Co.*, 146.

29 For a full account of Yeats's complex influence on Merrill, see Bauer.

CHAPTER 3

The Gay Apprentice: *Ashbery, Auden, and a Portrait of the Artist as a Young Critic*

1 Peter Stitt, "The Art of Poetry XXXIII: John Ashbery," *The Paris Review* 90 (Winter 1983), 37.

2 John Ashbery, interview with the author, 3/12/1989. Ashbery repeats this assertion in his Charles Eliot Norton Lectures, noting that among the "certifiably major poets whom I feel as influences," including Stevens, Moore, Stein, Bishop, Williams, Pasternak, and Mandelstam, he considers Auden, "chronologically the first and therefore the most important influence," in Ashbery, *Other Traditions* (Cambridge, MA: Harvard University Press, 2000), 4.

3 Ashbery, interview with the author, 5/13/1997.

4 Ashbery, interview with the author, 5/13/1997.

5 Ashbery, "Recent Tendencies in Poetry" (1945). In the John Ashbery Papers, AM-6, Houghton Library, Harvard University.

6 For this information, and for his overview of Ashbery's career, I am indebted to John Shoptaw's crucial *On the Outside Looking Out: John Ashbery's Poetry* (Cambridge, MA: Harvard University Press, 1994).

7 Lynn Keller, in *Re-making It New: Contemporary American Poetry and the Modernist Tradition* (New York: Cambridge University Press, 1987), reads both "The Painter" and "Illustration" as being in dialogue with Stevens, though acknowledges "Auden's strong influence . . . in *Some Trees*," 18, 22, 271n.

8 Shoptaw, *On the Outside Looking Out*, 24. Interestingly, Marjorie Perloff places another poem from Ashbery's first book, "Two Scenes" (which includes the obviously Audenesque lines, "A fine rain anoints the canal machinery. / This is perhaps a day of general honesty / Without example in the world's history" [*ST*, 21]), within an Audenesque lineage without acknowledging that she is doing so: "In its fidelity to 'a way of happening' rather than to 'what happens,' 'Two Scenes' anticipates Ashbery's later work," in Perloff, "'Fragments of a Buried Life': John Ashbery's Dream

Songs," *Beyond Amazement: New Essays on John Ashbery*, David Lehman, ed. (Ithaca, NY: Cornell University Press, 1980), 77.

9 Ashbery, "The Poetic Medium of W. H. Auden," Senior Essay, Harvard University, 1949. In the John Ashbery Papers, AM-6, Houghton Library, Harvard University.

10 Piotr Sommer, "An Interview in Warsaw," in *Code of Signals: Recent Writings in Poetics*, Michael Palmer, ed. (Berkeley, CA: North Atlantic Books, 1983), 307–8.

11 Spiegelman offers a brief, but helpful, discussion of Ashbery's "didactic voice" and "pedagogic tone," calling him a "teacher in search of a subject," 251–54.

12 Harold Bloom, *A Map of Misreading* (New York: Oxford UP, 1975), 1.

13 Bloom, "Editor's Note," *John Ashbery* (New York: Chelsea House, 1985).

14 Mutlu Konuk Blasing, *Politics and Form in Postmodern Poetry: O'Hara, Bishop, Ashbery & Merrill* (New York: Cambridge University Press, 1995), 152. Blasing's relation of Ashbery to Fredric Jameson's notion of the integration of aesthetic production into commodity production (112), and to what she describes as the characteristically postmodern "passive stance of 'waiting'" (115), also seems apposite here. Blasing also makes a persuasive case against the way the concept of the "postmodern," in its application to poetry, has often been freighted with presumptions of an association between a poet's choice of poetic form and his or her political or cultural ideology, such that poets who employ traditional forms are frequently and inaccurately typed as conservative, reactionary, backward-looking, and non-"postmodern." For other "postmodern" constructions of Ashbery, see Perloff, *The Poetics of Indeterminacy* and Joseph M. Conte, *Unending Design: The Forms of Postmodern Poetry* (Ithaca, NY: Cornell University Press, 1991).

15 David Herd's book, *John Ashbery and American Poetry* (New York: Palgrave, 2000), makes some suggestive remarks along these lines, observing that "understanding of Ashbery has . . . been ill-served by theoretical readings of the poetry," and concluding that Ashbery "aims to make communication possible in a liberal-democratic society," 14, 19.

16 As Shoptaw, among many critics, puts it, "The emphasis in Ashbery's work is always upon the movement or rhythm between poles rather than upon the bipolar opposites themselves," *On the Outside Looking Out*, 91. For another discussion of Ashbery's "negative dialectics" as manifested in his prose poems, see Steven Monte, *Invisible Fences: Prose Poetry as a Genre*

in French and American Literature (Lincoln, NE: University of Nebraska Press, 2000), 181–226.

17 There is a connection between what I, and others, am calling Ashbery's "dialectic" (and Auden's) and Bakhtin's notion of dialogism, with its suggestion of an utterance's ambition for a listening subject. For a discussion of Bakhtin's relation to Ashbery's "desire to reach beyond the 'I,' the speaking or writing self," see Marguerite S. Murphy, "John Ashbery's *Three Poems*: Heteroglossia in the American Prose Poem," *American Poetry* 7.2 (1990), 55.

18 Shoptaw, *On the Outside Looking Out*, 21-2, 356n.

19 The illustrator and writer Edward Gorey was a college friend of Ashbery's, and Frank O'Hara's roommate (it was at one of Gorey's parties that Ashbery and O'Hara first met), and in one of his early illustrated books he depicts—in something of a non-sequitur, given the fanciful nature of the rest of the narrative—a rather chilling vignette of a writhing figure being set afire atop the statue of John Harvard by a young, torch-wielding mob, illustrating this limerick: "Some Harvard men, stalwart and hairy, / Drank up several bottles of sherry; / In the Yard around three / They were shrieking with glee: / 'Come on out, we are burning a fairy!'" See Edward Gorey, "The Listing Attic," *Amphigorey* (New York: Putnam, 1972), 25. Donald Hall, another Harvard classmate, presents a more benign view of Harvard in the late 1940s in his recollections of O'Hara: "Being gay was relatively open, even light, in the Harvard of those years. One of Frank's *givens* was that *everybody* was gay, either in or out of the closet," quoted in David Lehman, *The Last Avant-Garde: The Making of the New York School of Poets* (New York: Doubleday, 1998), 55–56.

20 Shoptaw, *On the Outside Looking Out*, 4.

21 For two readings of Ashbery that place his work specifically within a poetics of homosexuality, see John Vincent, "Reports of Looting and Insane Buggery behind Altars: John Ashbery's Queer Poetics," *Twentieth Century Literature* 44.2 (Summer 1998), 155–75, and Catherine Imbriglio, "'Our Days Put on Such Reticence': The Rhetoric of the Closet in John Ashbery's 'Some Trees,'" *Contemporary Literature* 36.2 (Summer 1995), 249–88.

22 Charles Altieri has written significantly on Ashbery as a "love poet," but does so principally within the context of generic definitions of "love lyrics" and makes little comment on the erotic basis of Ashbery's poetics. See Charles Altieri, "Ashbery as Love Poet," *The Tribe of John: Ashbery and Contemporary Poetry*, Susan M. Schultz, ed. (Tuscaloosa, AL: University of Alabama Press, 1995), 26–37. James McCorkle has also remarked on "Eros and its function of making" in Ashbery's work and relates it to Ashbery's polyvocality, arguing

"The lyric in Ashbery's poetics, becomes choral, in that the range of voices give voice(s) to the survival of the community. . . . No longer the domain of the self-sufficient self, the lyric reveals the self's reliance upon others." See James McCorkle, "Nimbus of Sensations: Eros and Reverie in the Poetry of John Ashbery and Ann Lauterbach," *The Tribe of John*, III.

23 Janet Bloom and Robert Losada, "Craft Interview with John Ashbery," *The Craft of Poetry: Interviews from the New York Quarterly*, William Packard, ed. (New York: Doubleday, 1966), 93.

24 Stitt, 35.

25 Roland Barthes, *A Lover's Discourse: Fragments*, trans. Richard Howard (New York: Noonday Press, 1978), 1. Barthes's title, and his account of his project—to present a portrait of the loving "I" that "offers the reader a discursive site: the site of someone speaking within himself, *amorously*, confronting the other (the loved object), who does not speak"—makes an admirable description of Ashbery's own poetics. Another reading of Ashbery might productively trace Barthes's various "fragments" of erotic discourse—"absence," "to understand," "body," "embrace," "identification," "unbearable," "magic," "silence," "waking," "remembrance," "truth," etc.— through their continual appearance in Ashbery's work.

26 Stitt, 50.

27 For a useful reading of Ashbery's Eliotic inheritance, and a complementary analysis of Ashbery's notion of his relation to the poetic tradition, see James Longenbach, *Modern Poetry After Modernism* (Princeton, NJ: Princeton University Press, 1997).

28 Louis Osti, "The Craft of John Ashbery," *Confrontations* 9.3 (1974), 87.

29 Ashbery, interview with the author, 5/13/1997.

30 For an account of Ashbery's ongoing response to Bloom's critical construction of his work, see Susan M. Schultz, " 'Returning to Bloom': John Ashbery's Critique of Harold Bloom," *Contemporary Literature* 37:1 (1996), 24–48. See also Peter Morris, "Harold Bloom, Parody, and the 'Other Tradition,' " *The Salt Companion to Harold Bloom* (Cambridge, UK: Salt Publishing, 2007), 425–78.

31 Sommer, 305; Osti, 87.

32 Ross Labrie, "John Ashbery: An Interview with Ross Labrie," *The American Poetry Review* 13.3 (May–June 1984), 32.

33 For a discussion of the importance of this concept to Auden's work, see Greenberg.

34 For an Ashberian fable about the ways authorial intent is overmastered by both the demands of the text and the world outside the text, see his play

"The Compromise," in which the characters of a melodrama, Pirandello-like, take over the action of the play from the smug yet indecisive figure of the "Author" who wants his play to remain unfinished in order to imitate "the very uncertainty of life, where things are seldom carried through to a conclusion, let alone a satisfactory one." At the "conclusion" of the play, all the characters walk out, leaving the Author to protest "Where are you going? Stop!... I haven't finished... You can't desert me... What are you doing to me?" The Author's folly, the audience is told by the comic stock-figure of a wise old Indian chief, is that he tried to impose his own inner vision of existence upon the intractable realities of the world outside him. As the Author falls asleep onstage, the Indian chief intones a prayer: "Now, spirit of the great raven, descend on your unhappy son. For of all of us, he suffers the most and knows the least.... Give him, for a while, the sleep you hold in your dusky sable plumes. And perhaps when he awakens the world and the people in it will be more the way he thinks they ought to be" [*TPlays*, 117].

35 Blasing, 154.
36 Sommer, 295; Sue Gangel, "John Ashbery," *American Poetry Observed: Poets on Their Work*, Joe David Bellamy, ed. (Urbana, IL: Illinois University Press, 1988), 14.
37 For a persuasive contextualization of "Litany" within the culture of deconstructive criticism in the late 1970s, see Shoptaw, *On the Outside Looking Out*, 234–35.
38 For a helpful reading of Ashbery's dialectical relation to his critics, including the argument that Ashbery's poems assimilate, engage, and preempt specific literary theoretical responses to his work, among them Miller's host/parasite paradigm, see Martin Kevorkian, "John Ashbery's *Flow Chart*: John Ashbery and The Theorists on John Ashbery against The Critics against John Ashbery," *New Literary History* 25 (1994), 459–76.
39 Gangel, 14.
40 Murphy, 24.
41 In the introduction to *Beyond Amazement*, David Lehman offers a synopsis of the history of Ashbery's negative critical reception, 21–23. Among the more notorious assaults has been Charles Molesworth's, calling Ashbery's work "a flirtation with nihilism, the fag end of an autotelic art that apotheosizes symbolism's elevation of style over content," in *The Fierce Embrace* (London: University of Missouri Press, 1979), 165.
42 This poem may also point to a particular moment in the divergence of Auden and Ashbery's poetic projects. In the Painter's heroic martyrdom to the idea that art and life are inseparable, and its implicit rejection of

Prospero's—and Auden's—decision to privilege life over art, we can perhaps see the seeds of Ashbery's disaffection with the direction Auden's later poetry would take him.

43 But the strength of Shoptaw's approach, from this polemical perspective, is that it takes its cues from the poetry itself. The poems insistently teach us to look for that thing outside the poem—the crypt word, the homosocial context, in Shoptaw's analysis—and the critic, alert to this lesson, engages the poetry on its own "misrepresentative" terms.

44 Keller's description is characteristic: Of contemporary poets, Ashbery "may well be the most thoroughly and obviously postmodern—most concerned with indeterminacy, with process, and most determined to embody his ideas about the radical uncertainties of language and experience in the diction and movement of his poems," 13–14. Perloff anticipates, and preemptively rejects, the argument for reading Ashbery as something other than a poet whose chief aim is to embody radical indeterminacy in her 1998 response to Longenbach's *Modern Poetry After Modernism* and Vernon Shetley's *After the Death of Poetry: Poet and Audience in Contemporary America* (Durham, NC: Duke University Press, 1993). These critics, says Perloff in "Normalizing John Ashbery," *Jacket 2* (January 1998), http://jacketmagazine.com, in trying to reclaim Ashbery from the "breakthrough narratives" of postmodernism, and in particular by tracing his poetic roots back to Eliot, are engaged in an effort to "normalize" Ashbery, and thereby render him insufficiently progressive and interesting.

CHAPTER 4

The Old Sources: *Rich, Auden, and Making Something Happen*

1 For a discussion of Rich's "ineluctably historical" poetics, see Roger Gilbert, "Framing Water: Historical Knowledge in Bishop and Rich," *Twentieth Century Literature* 43.2 (Summer 1997), 144–61.

2 Adrienne Rich, "Toward a More Feminist Criticism" [*BBP*, 90].

3 Matthew Rothschild, "I Happen to Think That Poetry Makes a Huge Difference," *The Progressive* 58 (January 1994), 31–36.

4 Ted Genoways, "How We Are With Each Other: A Symposium on Adrienne Rich," *The Virginia Quarterly Review* 82.2 (Spring 2006), 207.

5 Auden's own first book, *Poems*, was published when he was also twenty-one.

6 Albert Gelpi, one of Rich's most prominent and supportive critics, summarizes Auden's response to Rich as "the stereotype—prim, fussy, and schoolmarmish—that has corseted and strait-laced women poets into 'poetesses' whom men could deprecate with admiration." In Albert Gelpi, "Adrienne

Rich: The Poetics of Change," *Adrienne Rich's Poetry*, Barbara Charles-
worth Gelpi and Albert Gelpi, eds. (New York: W.W. Norton, 1975), 130.
Liz Yorke, in *Adrienne Rich: Passion, Politics and the Body* (London: Sage,
1997), characterizes Auden's remarks as "patronising faint-praise" which
"say as much about his male-centered desire for young female poets to
be subservient and respectful (to him, as to the establishment) as they do
about the cultural mores dominating the fifties" 24.

7 In the preface to the 1979 reprinting of "The Tension of Anne Bradstreet,"
in *On Lies, Secrets, and Silence*, Rich contextualizes her own response to
Bradstreet as an early manifestation of her political awakening, and points
to the number of biographical parallels she saw between herself and Bradstreet, among them: "Like her, I had known the ambiguities of patronizing
compliments from male critics" [*LSS*, 21].

8 Variations of the word "master" or "mastery" appear in three different poems in *A Change of World*, in an early reflection of a thematic concern that
will occupy much of Rich's poetry: As a young, emulative poet she begins
by seeking the "mastery" of craft and formal skill, but over time comes to
view such "mastery" as symptoms of oppressive patriarchy. In a 1993 note
on the awarding of a poetry prize to a feminist lesbian poet, Rich observes
that the judges "described the book as 'forceful' and 'masterful'—adjectives
clearly meant in praise but interesting in terms of the politics of language"
[*WFT*, 263n].

9 Other poems in *A Change of World* also clearly echo Auden, as in "At a
Bach Concert" which speaks in unmistakably Audenesque terms of "a love
that is not pity," a "union of necessity," and "suffering." Her Audenesque inheritance is also evident in her tendency to allegorize and generalize from
specific objects and characters, as in "Middle Aged," whose "how much left
unsaid" recalls both Auden's reticence and her own "Unsaid Word." Randall Jarrell, in a review of Rich's second book, *The Diamond Cutters*, memorably describes reading one of her poems as "like getting one of Auden's
old carbons for Christmas," in *Adrienne Rich's Poetry*, 128.

10 For a discussion of Auden's strategic use of plain speech as an instrument of
both irony and civic truth-telling, see David Rosen, *Power, Plain English,
and the Rise of Modern Poetry* (New Haven, CT: Yale University Press,
2006).

11 Betsy Erkkila uses Rich to propose a model of maternal influence, as opposed to Harold Bloom's Oedipal paradigm, asking, "How useful is the
Bloomian model when the poet attempts to define herself not in relation
to her poetic fathers but in relation to her poetic mothers?" Analyzing the

relationship between Rich and Dickinson, she argues, "Rather than over-throwing her parent in an attempt to give birth to herself . . . Rich projects an alternative model of relations among women poets. The influence that passes between Dickinson and Rich is double-bearing and empowering. . . . Rich sought not to misconceive but to re-conceive Dickinson, and these reconceptions led Dickinson not to reject Dickinson but to reclaim her as an influence on herself and other women writers," in Erkkila, "Dickinson and Rich: Toward a Theory of Female Poetic Influence," *American Literature* 56.4 (1984), 542, 559.

12 For Rich's discussion of the relation between the "unspeakable" and her sexual and political identity, see " 'It is the Lesbian in Us . . .'" [*LSS*, 199–202].

13 Adrienne Rich, "Split at the Root" [*BBP*, 113].

14 In her essay, Rich also cites approvingly the assessment of Ibsen's play by G. B. Shaw: "[Ibsen] shows us that no degradation ever devized or permit-ted is as disastrous as this degradation; that through it women can die into luxuries for men and yet can kill them; that men and women are becoming conscious of this; and that what remains to be seen as perhaps the most interesting of all imminent social developments is what will happen 'when we dead awaken'" [*LSS*, 34].

15 Rich, "Compulsory Heterosexuality and Lesbian Existence" [*BBP*, 23–75].

16 In fact, Rich has seen the tension of this internal dialectic as a source of her poetic power: "It is the lesbian in us who drives us to feel imaginatively, render in language, grasp the full connection between woman and woman. It is the lesbian in us who is creative, for the dutiful daughter of the fathers is only a hack" [*LSS*, 201].

17 In her essay, "Toward a Woman-Centered University," Rich analogizes a daughter's relationship with her father, including by clear biographical im-plication her own, with that of a female student and her male teacher, and does so on the grounds of erotic attraction: "The male teacher may have a genuinely 'fatherly' relation to his gifted student-daughter, and many intel-lectual women have been encouraged or trained by their gifted fathers, or gifted male teachers. . . . Like the father's favorite daughter in the patriar-chal family, the promising woman student comes to identify with her male scholar-teacher more strongly than with her sisters. . . . The eroticism of the father–daughter relationship resonates here, and romance and flirtation are invisibly present even where there is no actual seduction" [*LSS*, 139].

18 Eavan Boland, introduction to *Adrienne Rich: Selected Poems 1950–1995* (Clare, Ireland: Salmon Publishing, 1996), vi.

19 John Ashbery, "Tradition and Talent," *Reading Adrienne Rich: Reviews and Re-Visions, 1951–81,* Jane Roberta Cooper, ed. (Ann Arbor, MI: University of Michigan Press, 1984), 218. Originally published in the *New York Herald Tribune,* September 4, 1966.

20 Marilyn Hacker, "Begin to Teach" (Review of *Time's Power*), *The Nation,* October 23, 1989, 464.

21 B. C. Bloomfield, *W. H. Auden: A Bibliography* (Charlottesville, VA: University of Virginia Press, 1964), vii.

22 Rich, *Adrienne Rich's Poetry,* 89. Rich strikes a similar note about the relation between her vocation as poet and her pedagogical ambition to "change minds" in a 1972 essay about her experiences at City College in 1968, called "Teaching Language in Open Admissions": "I think of myself as a teacher of language: that is someone for whom language implied freedom, who is trying to aid others to free themselves through the written world, and above all through learning to write it for themselves" [*LSS,* 63].

23 Rich, "Three Conversations," *Adrienne Rich's Poetry,* 117.

24 For my reading of "In Sickness and in Health" and its relation to Rich, I am indebted to Susannah Young-Ah Gottlieb's discussion of the poem in "'With Conscious Artifice': Auden's Defense of Marriage," *Diacritics* 35:4 (Winter 2005), 23–41.

25 In 1994, following the success of the film *Four Weddings and a Funeral,* which prominently featured Auden's poem "Funeral Blues," Auden's poetry was marketed aggressively in American bookstores, including in a small booklet sold at cash registers for impulse purchase, containing ten Auden poems and titled *Tell Me the Truth About Love* (New York: Vintage, 1994). Rich was not alone in finding Auden's words on love resonant in the year she was writing this poem.

26 As a lesbian, Rich's relationship with Auden is further complicated. As a famously publicly gay poet, he served as a kind of father figure for more than a generation of younger homosexual poets, including Elizabeth Bishop, James Merrill, James Schuyler, Richard Howard, and many others, who saw his example as a liberating one for their own work and lives. But Rich's attitude toward male homosexuality has been a vexed one, as expressed in an essay called "The Meaning of Our Love for Women Is What We Have Constantly to Expand" in which she voices her concerns about a tradition of gay male misogyny [*LSS,* 223–30]. Once again, Auden is in the position of an authority figure with whom she feels a connection but from whom she must consciously turn away, this time in the field of sexual politics.

27 Rich, "Poetry and Experience: Statement at a Poetry Reading," *Adrienne Rich's Poetry*, 89.

EPILOGUE

He Became His Admirers: *Saying Goodbye to Auden*

1 For a sustained discussion of Auden's relation to the tradition of the elegy, see Peter Sacks's *The English Elegy: Studies in the Genre from Spenser to Yeats* (Baltimore: Johns Hopkins Press, 1985), and Jahan Ramazani's *Poetry of Mourning: The Modern Elegy from Hardy to Heaney* (Chicago: University of Chicago Press, 1994).

2 James Schuyler, "Wystan Auden," *Selected Poems* (New York: Farrar Straus and Giroux, 1993), 242–44. For another reading of this poem, and of Schuyler's relationship with Auden, see David Lehman, *The Last Avant Garde*, 249–51.

3 Spiegelman emphasizes Auden's pedagogical role in "scenes of instruction" for younger poets in *The Didactic Muse*.

4 James Merrill, *A Different Person*, 226. Another poet who visited Ischia was Anthony Hecht. For an account of his meeting with Auden, see Hecht, "Discovering Auden," *The Harvard Advocate*, 48–50.

5 Richard Wilbur, "For W. H. Auden," *New and Collected Poems* (New York: Harcourt Brace Jovanovich, 1988), 26.

6 John Hollander, "Under Aquarius," *W. H. Auden: A Tribute*, Stephen Spender, ed. (New York: Macmillan, 1975), 196. See also John Hollander, "W. H. Auden," *Yale Review* 77.4 (1988), 501–11; and "Auden at Sixty," *The Atlantic Monthly* 220.1 (1967), 84–7. Hoffman also has an elegy for Auden, "A Letter to W. H. Auden," in *Hang-Gliding from Helicon: New and Selected Poems 1948–1988* (Baton Rouge, LA: Louisiana State University Press, 1988), 214–15. Hoffman also wrote an early study of Auden's *Paul Bunyan* in his 1949 Columbia University M.A. thesis, later turned into the book *Paul Bunyan: Last of the Frontier Demigods* (Philadelphia: University of Pennsylvania Press, 1952).

7 Hollander, *W. H. Auden*, 196.

8 Hollander had published a blistering attack on *Howl and Other Poems* in the *Partisan Review* in 1957, in which he dismissed Ginsberg's book as a "dreadful little volume." See *Partisan Review* (Spring 1957), 296–97. Ginsberg and Hollander, friends and allies at Columbia, ending up staking out diametrically opposed—and sometimes bitterly contentious—positions in the poetic culture of the 1960s and 1970s.

9 For a brief account of the poetry wars of the 1960s, centered around Donald Hall's and Donald Allen's dueling anthologies, see James E. B. Breslin, *From Modern to Contemporary: American Poetry, 1945–1965* (Chicago: Chicago University Press, 1984), 53–56.

10 Richard Howard, "For Hephaistos, with Reference to the Deaths in a Dry Year of Cocteau, Roethke, and MacNeice," *Quantities/Damages: Early Poems* (Middletown, CT: Wesleyan University Press, 1984), 127–28.

11 Lincoln Kirstein, "Siegfriedslage," *For W. H. Auden: February 21, 1972*, 50–53.

12 V. S. Yanovsky, quoted in Carpenter, *W. H. Auden*, 439.

13 Howard, "Again for Hephaistos, the Last Time," *Fellow Feelings* (New York: Atheneum, 1976), 12.

14 Hollander, *Reflections on Espionage*, (New Haven, CT: Yale University Press, 2000), 3. In the introduction to a recent edition of the book, Hollander contextualizes the origins of the poem's composition in the fall of 1973: "I'd been unable to write much all that fall. One of the sources of my malaise was the death of W. H. Auden. My family and I had visited him in Austria six weeks before. His dying and the Yom Kippur war in Israel had almost coincided. Auden had meant a great deal to me—I had read his work, since my freshman year at college, and had always felt that he, preceded by George Bernard Shaw and followed by George Orwell, had been one of my moral mentors at a distance," vii.

15 Karl Shapiro, "Auden," *The Harvard Advocate*, 25.

16 J. D. McClatchy, "Auden's OED," *Ten Commandments* (New York: Knopf, 1998), 89.

17 Like Howard, Hollander's final elegy features a scene of non-recognition between the younger poet and his mentor:

> [Y]et I had to pass him
> By in the Square at evening—in the soft
> Light of the wrought-iron lamps and the rich, cheerful
> Shadows which rose up from the stones to meet it—
> Without even our eyes having touched, without
> Acknowledgment. And thereby, of course, we were
> Working together. What kind of work is this
> For which if we were to touch in the darkness
> It would be without feeling the other there.

Hollander figures the "work" of writing poetry, and his relationship with his teacher, as a silent communion. The work of the poet/spy is a "common, noble, and civilizing task," as Auden describes it in "Making, Knowing, and Judging" [*DH*, 42], but one which emerges from "ranches of isolation" [*CP*, 248].

18 Howard, interview with the author, 4/2/1997.

19 Ramazani, 201. For a useful discussion of Howard's work in the context of the theoretical relation between homosexual identity and poetic inheritance, see David Bergman.

20 Louis Simpson, *A Revolution in Taste*, (New York: MacMillan, 1978), xv–xvi.

21 Howard, interview with the author, 4/2/1997.

22 Shapiro, "At Auden's Grave," *New & Selected Poems 1940–1986* (Chicago: Chicago University Press, 1987), 102.

23 Howard, *Fellow Feelings*, 11.

24 William Meredith, "Talking Back (To W. H. Auden)," *Partial Accounts* (New York: Knopf, 1987). Meredith was a co-executor of Auden's will, so it is not surprising that his argument with Auden should be an affectionate one. Other poets have offered their own poetic variations on Auden's famous decree. Hollander's "Making Nothing Happen," *Tesserae & Other Poems* (New York: Knopf, 1993), tropes Genesis as the artistic creation of "Nothing" (6), while Mona Van Duyn, in "Minimalist Sonnet Translations of, Or Comments on, Poems by Auden, Eliot, Yeats, Frost, Hopkins, Arnold," *Firefall* (New York: Knopf, 1993), takes a reverse tack, expressing comic anxiety that poetry's power to make "nothing" happen might result in entropic apocalypse, 41.

25 Irving Feldman, "Just Another Smack," *Teach Me, Dear Sister* (New York: Viking, 1983), 34. For another reading of this poem, see Harold Schweizer, "Lyric Suffering in Auden and Feldman," *English Language Notes* 31.2 (December 1993), 66–74.

26 Randall Jarrell also has a poem, called "The Old and New Masters," that takes issue with "Musée des Beaux Arts." It begins, "About suffering, about adoration, the old masters / Disagree," in Jarrell, *The Complete Poems* (New York: Farrar, Straus & Giroux, 1969), 332–33.

27 Theodore Weiss, "As You Like It," *Selected Poems* (Evanston, IL: Northwestern University Press, 1995), 195.

28 Derek Walcott, "Eulogy for W. H. Auden," *The Arkansas Testament* (New York: Farrar, Straus and Giroux, 1987), 61.

29 There had been another memorial service ten years earlier at St. John the Divine in October 1973, soon after Auden's death, featuring readings by Robert Penn Warren, Galway Kinnell, Muriel Rukeyser, Richard Wilbur, William Meredith, Richard Howard, and Ursula Niebuhr.

30 Walcott, quoted in William Baer, *Conversations with Derek Walcott* (Jackson, MS: University of Mississippi Press, 1996), 197.

31 Walcott, quoted in Paula Burnett, *Derek Walcott: Politics and Poetics* (Gainesville, FL: University Press of Florida, 2000), 179.

32 Walcott, "The Caribbean: Culture or Mimicry," *Critical Perspectives on Derek Walcott*, Robert D. Hamner, ed. (Boulder, CO: Lynne Rienner Publishers, 1996), 54.

33 Ibid., 56.

34 Rei Terada, *Derek Walcott's Poetry: American Mimicry* (Boston: Northeastern University Press, 1992). Terada argues that "Walcott's work throws into relief the simultaneous inadequacy and resilience of the idea of 'originality': by provoking critical discussion of it; by the strength with which it presses against it; and by its tendency nevertheless to fall back on it," 44. She also relates Walcott's poetics of mimicry to American poetry generally, finding in his work—contra critics who might see his assimilation of other poets as evidence of convention-bound derivativeness—an exemplar of postmodernity.

35 Walcott, quoted in Baer, 202–3.

36 Joseph Brodsky, "To Please a Shadow," *Less Than One: Selected Essays* (New York: Farrar Straus Giroux, 1986), 357.

37 Ibid., 357–58.

38 Brodsky, quoted in Solomon Volkov, *Conversations with Joseph Brodsky: A Poet's Journey Through the Twentieth Century* (New York: Free Press, 1997), 150.

39 Brodsky, quoted in M. Sverdlov, E. Stafeva, "A Poem on the Death of a Poet: Brodsky and Auden," *Russian Studies in Literature* 42.3 (Summer 2006), 73.

40 Brodsky, "Elegy for W. H. Auden," *W. H. Auden: A Tribute*, 243.

41 Brodsky, "York: In Memoriam W. H. Auden," *A Part of Speech* (New York: Farrar, Straus and Giroux, 1977), 127. Brodsky also wrote an elegy for T. S. Eliot that models itself exactly in form, structure, and tone upon Auden's Yeats elegy.

42 Brodsky, "The Nobel Lecture," *On Grief and Reason: Essays* (New York: Farrar, Straus and Giroux, 1997), 57.

43 Brodsky, *Less Than One*, 374.

44 Brodsky, quoted in Volkov, 133.

INDEX